Transnationalizing
Viet Nam

In the series *Asian American History and Culture,*

edited by Sucheng Chan, David Palumbo-Liu, Michael Omi, K. Scott Wong, and Linda Trinh Võ

Also in this series:

Kieu-Linh Caroline Valverde

Transnationalizing
Viet Nam

Community, Culture, and Politics
in the Diaspora

TEMPLE UNIVERSITY PRESS
Philadelphia

TEMPLE UNIVERSITY PRESS
Philadelphia, Pennsylvania 19122
www.temple.edu/tempress

Copyright © 2012 by Temple University
All rights reserved
Published 2012
Paperback edition published 2013

Library of Congress Cataloging-in-Publication Data

Valverde, Kieu-Linh Caroline, 1969–
    Transnationalizing Viet Nam : community, culture, and politics in the diaspora /
Kieu-Linh
Caroline Valverde.
        p. cm. — (Asian American history and culture)
    Includes bibliographical references and index.
    ISBN 978-1-4399-0679-8 (cloth : alk. paper) — ISBN 978-1-4399-0681-1 (e-book)
    1. Vietnamese Americans—Social life and customs.   2. Vietnamese Americans—
Ethnic identity.   3. United States—Relations—Vietnam.   4. Vietnam—Relations—
United States.   5. Vietnamese diaspora.   6. Transnationalism.   I. Title.   II. Series:
Asian American history and culture.
    E184.V53V35 2012
    305.895′922073—dc23

                                                                2012008895

ISBN 978-1-4399-0680-4 (paperback : alk. paper)

091013-P

Contents

Preface

Transnationalizing Viet Nam offers an in-depth look at the dynamic and long-standing connections between Viet Nam and its diaspora in the United States. These links are especially astounding considering the many decidedly antidiasporic elements in not only the home and host countries but also the ethnic community itself. This rich transnational history—which has gone largely undetected, or at least unrecognized—is revealed through nearly two decades of careful longitudinal, multisite research, punctuated by the voices of 250 interviewees.

This study also reflects my journey as a Vietnamese American—having lost my country, the former South Viet Nam, to North Viet Nam, having participated in the historic 1975 exodus of Vietnamese to the United States, and having eventually reconnected with my "homeland." Growing up during the Cold War and now living in the age of globalization, I have been witness to some astonishing worldwide transformations in the making and the resulting adaptation to these changes on the part of the Vietnamese diasporic community. My worldview is shaped by my early international experiences, including traveling through Europe, Asia, and Africa and living in regions such as Yemen. My personal experiences as a mixed-race Asian American woman with a Vietnamese, Spanish, and French mother and a Vietnamese and English father, helped me gain insight into complex societal relations.

These personal experiences went hand in hand with my academic pursuits, which began in the late 1980s, when I worked as an undergraduate student at the Indochina Archive at the University of California, Berkeley. Before the world became an active matrix of interconnections with information transmitted to and from every corner of the globe within seconds, I had the unique opportunity of gathering and absorbing news from relatively isolated countries across the oceans, such as the reunified Socialist Republic of Viet Nam. My main duty was to read the news and laboriously archive it by hand. At the Indochina Archive I had occasion to interact with a wide range of visitors, including dignitaries from Viet Nam, independent scholars from France, and filmmakers from Hollywood. While members of my ethnic community presented a strong public stance against a communist Viet Nam and were thus perceived as traitors by the Vietnamese government, I knew this scenario to be only part of the big picture. Academia and media continued to invoke the refugee narrative claiming that Vietnamese Americans did not have the resources to maintain transnational connections with Viet Nam and that the overseas Vietnamese population could not possibly make a significant impact on the country's development. Through my work at the archive, however, I gained a nuanced understanding of the persistent and even blossoming transnational connections among individuals, families, and governments.

My interests in relations between the Vietnamese American community and Viet Nam continued during my master's-level fieldwork in Viet Nam in 1993, two years before the United States and Viet Nam formalized diplomatic relations. My research took place in extremely politically volatile times—when anticommunist right-wing groups were gunning for Vietnamese American journalists on the basis of their dissident writings and when, with no diplomatic relations between the countries, travel to Viet Nam, especially for Vietnamese Americans, was exceedingly difficult and potentially dangerous. Meetings with ethnic leaders, government officials, and people with transnational connections in both countries occurred only after many years of careful trust-building endeavors. Though I was always careful to protect the identity of my informants, everyone involved knew that sharing ideas and information could be construed as treasonous. That this study stands alone as a book-length project explicitly critical of both anticommunist red-baiting by the Vietnamese American community and human rights suppressions in Viet Nam speaks to the dangers inherent in the topic.

I observed firsthand how identity politics can intersect with and foster political scrutiny and repression in both Viet Nam and the diaspora. In 1996, while I was in Viet Nam, the security police questioned some of the people with whom I was connected about my research and personal life, and, on the basis of their findings, they compiled a file that (I would later learn) was replete with falsehoods and half-truths. I was also characterized by other fictitious personas that followed me throughout my research project, often shaping my interactions with my informants. In 2001, during the first year of my in-residence Rockefeller Fellowship in Boston to conduct research on the Vietnamese diaspora, I came under indirect fire by anticommunist groups merely because two Vietnamese nationals had also received the award that year. I met with the most vocal of the protesters, an elderly Vietnamese American and aspiring scholar who had spent years as a political prisoner in Viet Nam. Of his own accord, he had compiled his false narrative of my biography, which he proceeded to share with me at our meeting; it took some time to convince him that he was misinformed. The irony of this vignette, of course, is that although he argued against what he saw as the evils of the repressive communist state of Viet Nam, he replicated the tactics used by its government. Concerned but not deterred by these incidents, I understood the obstacles to gathering and documenting information in politically heated regions.

In the early 1990s, I entered the University of Hawaii (UH), Manoa, which boasted not only a strong Asian studies program but also (along with only one other American university) a graduate program that facilitated access to Viet Nam. With no diplomatic relations between the countries, however, there was no guarantee of entrance into Viet Nam, and preparation for fieldwork required long holdovers in Thailand, sometimes for months at a time, in the hope of receiving a long-term student research visa from the Vietnamese government. In my impatience, I made the decision to enter Viet Nam without the necessary documents. I headed straight for my sponsoring research agency, the Institute of Foreign Affairs, where the official in charge of my case expressed his understandable annoyance that I had violated protocol. Noticing my visa application on his desk, I made a case for him to push ahead with my paperwork, and, to my good fortune, he agreed.

Once I began to carry out fieldwork on relations between Cambodia and Viet Nam, I became aware of changes in Viet Nam's attitudes toward the worldwide Vietnamese expatriate community, or Việt Kiều. I had heard from young entrepreneurs and businesspeople in Ha Noi and Sai Gon that many Việt Kiều had been investing in projects in Viet Nam since its shift to a more capitalistic economy, or đổi mới. One businessman speculated that overseas Vietnamese had vested interests in about two-thirds of the business ventures he encountered. In light of the absence of diplomatic ties between Viet Nam and the United States, where most of these Việt Kiều investors lived, these financial interactions were surprising. I learned that even as the Vietnamese government welcomed Việt Kiều investors, they saw the anticommunist overseas population in the United States as a direct threat to Viet Nam's stability. These early insights, which signaled the importance of little-known, unofficial channels of influence, started me down the path to understanding how larger transnational processes shape the dynamics between Viet Nam and the diaspora.

Completely enthralled by my "peripheral" observations, I changed my master's thesis topic and completed my degree in ethnic studies at San Francisco State University (SFSU). My desire to combine Asian studies from UH and ethnic studies at SFSU in my graduate research was part of my quest to make sense of the underlying transnational processes that were taking place at the beginning of this global era. My master's thesis, "The Foundation and Future of Vietnamese American Politics in the Bay Area," looked closely at the history and development of the Vietnamese American political processes and at the political attitudes of Vietnamese Americans vis-à-vis Viet Nam's political climate.

Moving on to doctoral research at the University of California, Berkeley, I learned that three major transnational processes have affected how postwar

Viet Nam continues to affect the lives of its overseas population and how this population, in turn, has a direct hand in the development of its home country: First, remittances helped to sustain a postwar economy mismanaged by central planning. Second, advances in technology—in particular, early Internet facilities—helped to sustain connections, allowing people across the globe to discuss their common interest in developing Viet Nam. And third, even as artists and producers in Viet Nam and in the diaspora produced two distinct cultures, popular music was created across the Pacific through covert collaborations. In addition, my research revealed how changes in Vietnamese politics affected the Vietnamese American transnational immigrant identity as the choices of Vietnamese people in the United States strongly influenced Vietnamese political and economic policies.

Expanding on my dissertation research, this book offers diverse diasporic perspectives and reveals the many tensions in Viet Nam, the United States, and the Vietnamese American community that make transnational connections a challenge. During nearly two decades of active transnational interactions, I was able to document the evolution of Vietnamese diasporic connections to reveal social patterns that ranged from the institutional to the personal. I argue that Vietnamese immigrant lives are inherently transnational while I expose how generational, gender, class, and political tensions threaten to divide the ethnic community. This documentation, in turn, enabled me to elaborate on not only political changes, such as San Jose City Council Member Madison Nguyen's historic battle with her own ethnic community over the naming of the city's Vietnamese business district, but also news media and the arts, such as Chau Huynh's controversial artwork and the response to its display in the most well-known Vietnamese American newspaper, the *Nguoi Viet Daily News*.

Transnationalizing Viet Nam, in short, represents my personal and intellectual journey. Any errors or omissions are mine alone. I hope that the work I have begun here will assist others to expand the field. More research is needed in comparing the transnational connections of Vietnamese diasporas across the globe with both the homeland and one another. Vietnamese diasporic experiences in such regions as Australia, Russia, France, Germany, and Cambodia, for example, both overlap with and diverge from those in the United States. Future international projects to further unearth these transnational connections hold great promise.

Many people generously shared their experiences toward the creation of this book. I thank them all, from Viet Nam and in diaspora, for making this work possible.

Acknowledgments

I am grateful to the many people who helped this book come to life. First and foremost, I am indebted to the participants in my study, whose voices permeate every page of this text. They graciously and openly shared with me their deeply touching experiences, in the belief that alternative voices in our community should finally be heard. Three people in particular stand out in this regard—Hoanh Dinh Tran, Chau Huynh, and Madison Nguyen—the principal subjects of my research, whose experiences have enriched not only my research but the Vietnamese diaspora as well. Without their support and cooperation, my work would have been greatly impoverished. I am now privileged to count them among my friends.

Early support for my research came from Michel Laguerre, who nurtures my scholarship faithfully and has since I was a graduate student under his tutelage. Several scholars, with their intelligence, wisdom, and grace, have been wonderful role models for me: Linda Võ, Jonathan Okamura, Luis Eduardo Guarnizo, and Michael Omi. In addition to exemplifying what it is to be a scholar, they also generously read various versions of the manuscript and provided invaluable comments.

Manual Castells, Peter Zinoman, James Freeman, Aiwa Ong, and Yen Le Espiritu provided much assistance in the early stages of my research and helped move it forward with numerous recommendations and other feedback. Michael Peter Smith, Sarita See, Darrell Hamamoto, Bill Hing, Sunaina Maira, Ashley Carruthers, and Philip Taylor also diligently read the manuscript in its various stages of development. My field is rich in wonderful scholars and artists who have aided and inspired me, including Michael Chang, Sucheng Chan, Ling-Chi Wang, Ronald Takaki, Sau-ling Wong, Don Nakanishi, Viet Nguyen, Lan Duong, Mariam Beevi, Thu-Huong Nguyen-Vo, Nathalie Nguyen, Gina Masequesmay, Viet Mike Ngo, Fiona Ngo, Thuy Vo Dang, Loan Dao, Vu

Pham, Hung Thai, Angie Tran, Karin Aguilar–San Juan, Ann Marie Lesh-kowich, LiAnne Yu, Harvey Dong, Jennifer Lisa Vest, Jaideep Singh, Truong Tran, Andrew Lam, Kim Ninh, Christian Collet, and Nguyen Qui Duc. My industrious research assistants—Winnie Huynh, Christina Pham, Linda Le, Hoa Truong, Eric Keng, April Kang, Ngoc Truong, Jackie Ngo, Adam Panzer, Chantha Neung, Matt Fung, Lauria Phan, Jordan Lok, Alan Kuramoto, Mika Okamura, Jason Hsu, Justin Phan, Nancy Lê, Eddie Truong, Cathy Bui, and Cindy Huynh—helped me complete the broad range of research that grounds this book. I am certain that they are as proud to see the book come to fruition as I am to see them on their way to illustrious careers.

My research and writing endeavors were supported by the kind assistance of foundations and grants, including a Fulbright scholarship for fieldwork in Viet Nam, a Rockefeller Fellowship at the William Joiner Center for the Study of War and Social Consequences in Boston, and an Australian National University Southeast Asian Fellowship for in-residence work. I am grateful to the researchers and staffs of the following institutes for allowing me to access their archives and use their facilities and for granting me permission to work in the field: in Ha Noi the Social Science Institute–Southeast Asia, the Institute of Foreign Affairs, and the Committee on Overseas Vietnamese and in Sai Gon the Social Science Institute and the Ho Chi Minh City Committee for Overseas Vietnamese.

My editor at Temple University Press, Janet Francendese, saw potential in me while I was still a graduate student and patiently supported my progress from beginning to end. Her work demonstrates the importance of an experienced editor to the production of a solid academic text. I enjoyed learning from her about the practice of scholarly writing and cannot adequately express my gratitude for the personable and efficient way she guided me through the process. I also greatly appreciate the expert editing of Ken Worthy, who painstakingly read every paragraph of the manuscript and offered much-needed practical advice.

I am fortunate to be blessed with wonderful family and friends, who supported me by offering encouraging words and insights over the long process of research and writing. My love goes out to my mother, Eveline; my brother, Melchior; my sister, Nina; my cousins Truong and Trang; and the following friends, whom I consider family—Simmone, George, Soulwing, Elizabeth, Michael, Edward, John, Charles, Phi, Tam, Luu, and Han. I am especially thankful for Trinh, a friend I call sister, who shared enough drama from her life to keep me entertained, while always proffering the right advice and wisdom to keep my life on track. I am indebted to the Do family for their kindness and, in particular, to Hao Nhu and Thien for their enduring support during the many years of this project.

My life is enriched by my adoring partner, Brian. He lovingly takes care of our family, including our children, Toussaint and Emmanuelle. This book is dedicated to all three and to my paternal grandmother, Trần Thị Nhung, who instilled all that is good in me today.

1

Transnationalizing Viet Nam

A middle-aged Vietnamese American lawyer and self-proclaimed "low techie" composes an important e-mail from his home in Virginia. He feverishly details the reasons that overseas Vietnamese should be given citizenship in communist-controlled Viet Nam. He is aware that once he presses Send his message will reach the approximately three thousand readers of his moderated newsgroup.[1] The newsgroup's subscribers include overseas Vietnamese professionals and members of the intelligentsia as well as non-Vietnamese members interested in Viet Nam–related issues. The e-mail writer is slightly nervous, because he knows that among the subscribers is a strong contingent of Vietnamese American anticommunists who vigilantly monitor seemingly pro-Vietnamese government postings. This group is a significant segment of Vietnamese in diaspora, and they continue to be vocal about their politics. Still, this politically savvy lawyer will send the message, because he believes it can speed change in Viet Nam's development and ultimately foster positive relations with its diaspora. He is confident of this outcome because on the distribution list are government officials in Viet Nam who read every note with interest. He sends the e-mail and waits as it rapidly disseminates across the United States, Viet Nam, and the world.[2] (Field notes 2002; see also Hoanh Tran 2002)

The event described in the passage above, observed in 2002, illustrates how technology, culture, and capital move in the era of globalization (Clifford 1994; R. Cohen 1997). It also highlights the convoluted and often contentious history involving Viet Nam, the United States, and the Vietnamese diasporic community. The term *diaspora* tends to evoke a sense of positive connections to a homeland, but sometimes a country and parts of its overseas population do not have good relations; they are instead ideologically hostile to one another. Sometimes precarious relationships and negative attitudes exist between the diasporic groups and the host country, and such divisions may also form within the diasporic community itself. Such is the case with Viet Nam and its diaspora. Still, Vietnamese in Viet Nam and in diaspora maintain deep connections and lasting influence over each other as they participate in transnational acts that transgress geographic distance, restrictive nation-state legislation, international agreements, and even ethnic community pressures.

This book explores transnational connections between Viet Nam and its overseas population in the United States from 1975 to 2012 in four areas of activity: (1) exchanges and interchanges of Vietnamese and Vietnamese American popular music; (2) sociopolitical transformations in information and communication developments in Viet Nam from an influential transnational virtual community, Vietnam Forum (VNForum); (3) (re)negotiations of political and cultural identities of overseas Vietnamese communities through ethnic news media, looking at the controversial art works of Vietnamese American artist Chau Huynh as a focal point for this debate; and (4) an overseas Vietnamese battle over defining community and representation as seen through a business-district-naming controversy involving the first Vietnamese city councilwoman in the United States, the city of San Jose's vice-mayor, Madison Nguyen.

This examination reveals (1) extensive transnational connections spanning more than thirty-five years, beginning with the first departure of Vietnamese from Viet Nam after the second Indochina war (known as the Viet Nam War in the United States) in 1975 and continuing to 2012; (2) a dramatic shift during this time, in a world in which globalization is central and information, communication, and transportation technologies are the catalyst for global interdependency and connectedness; (3) a vast cross-section of people from diverse backgrounds, classes, generations, and genders participating in transnational processes; and (4) an immense influence of the native and diasporic communities on each other in politics, culture, community, generations, gender relations, technology, news media, and the arts. These transnational processes and influences have been expressed sometimes tumultuously: through the creation of transnational music even when it was illegal, the formation of transnational virtual communities with historical enemies, community control through political assassination, and multiyear protests of news media for their publication choices.

The extensive changes seen from the Cold War to the present global condition compel this work. The speed of development in Viet Nam and the creation of new diasporas abroad call for investigations into the lives of people affected by these changes. *Transnationalizing Viet Nam* is based on two decades of a longitudinal, multisite, ethnographic investigation into the lives of Vietnamese Americans in the San Francisco Bay Area and Southern California and of Vietnamese in Sai Gon (Ho Chi Minh City) and Ha Noi.[3] While twenty years is an enormous investment for a researcher, I could have not done it any other way. Events had to slowly play themselves out. Actors in the dramatic moments, particularly, needed time to grasp the situation and trust in me enough to share their experiences—all this took time. I conducted interviews with over 250 Vietnamese, overseas Vietnamese, and experts on Vietnamese and Vietnamese American issues. Having the unique opportunity to interview people at the center of important events and moments in history from both sides of the Pacific and in various political positions gave me interesting and diverse perspectives. Interviewees ranged from video store owners to high-ranking officials in Viet Nam and from leaders of anticommunist groups to ethnic newspaper editors in the United States. Their thoughts, voices, and experiences form the core of this book.[4]

Situating *Transnationalizing Viet Nam*

I situate the study of Viet Nam–Vietnamese diasporic relations in the interdisciplinary fields of Asian, or area, studies and Asian American, or ethnic, studies, two disciplines historically at odds with each other. Area studies views ethnic studies as not academically rigorous and not related to affairs in Asia, and Asian American studies, coming from grassroots origins and hence having to fight off departmental shutdowns by universities over the decades, distrusts area studies, with its governmental and university support and history of Orientalist writings (Reid 2003). But debates between the interdisciplines often concern their encroachment and survival, with little attention paid to frameworks, paradigms, or shared topics of interest that could make the union beneficial for both Vietnamese and Vietnamese American studies (Wong 1995). As transnational ties strengthen, it becomes more difficult to ignore both how Viet Nam directly and indirectly helps shape the lives of its diasporic population and how this population affects the development and identity of those in the home country. Thus, the pairing of Vietnamese and Vietnamese American studies is essential, and transnational studies helps make this connection.

In recent years Asian and Asian American studies scholars have taken notice of transnational processes of overseas Vietnamese, such as music production and consumption (Carruthers 2001; P. Taylor 2000; Valverde 2003).[5] A few Asian studies and culture studies journals have published articles about the Vietnamese diaspora or devoted a special issue to this group.[6] Asian American studies scholars, in particular, have written about the Vietnamese American connection to Viet Nam. In a special issue of *Amerasia Journal*, guest editor Linda Võ's (2003) introduction was titled "Shaping Transnationalism." Several studies of Vietnamese in diaspora in the special issue fell under this heading: Trần Ngọc Angie's comparative study on Vietnamese American electronic workers and Vietnamese garment workers, my research on transnational music production and consumption in Viet Nam and its diasporic communities, and Hung Cam Thai's discussion of international marriages between overseas Vietnamese men and Vietnamese women.

Veteran Asian American studies and sociology scholar Yen Le Espiritu made special note of this transnational studies trend in a state-of-the-field article for Vietnamese American studies, "Toward a Critical Refugee Study: The Vietnamese Refugee Subject in U.S. Scholarship," published in the premier issue of *Journal of Vietnamese Studies* (Espiritu 2006a). Espiritu bemoans that most scholarship on Vietnamese Americans portrays them as passive, pathetic victims of larger, more powerful forces. She urges scholars to take a new approach that she calls "critical refugee studies," which she believes could best be "refashioned in the fields of Vietnamese Studies, Asian American Studies, and American Studies, not around the benign narratives of American exceptionalism, immigration, or even transnationalism, but around the crucial issues of war, race, and violence" (Espiritu 2006a, 426).

I propose a restudy of Vietnamese American communities using methods and materials from both Asian and Asian American studies because, as Jonathan Okamura points out, it is important to "retain a primary concern with the community by situating it transnationally in the larger context of global economic and political forces and processes" (2003, 172). Consider, then, three related and major influences affecting and continuing to affect the lives of Vietnamese in Viet Nam and in diaspora: (1) the U.S. government and society, (2) the Vietnamese government and society, and (3) anticommunist segments within the Vietnamese American community. Central to my analysis is a consideration of how these three sources work separately or in combination to influence or dominate one another. I reveal how individuals and groups react against or cope with these forces.[7]

For this research, I consider Ling-Chi Wang's theory of "structural dual domination." Wang discusses how Chinese Americans experienced dual domination, from racial oppression and exclusion in the United States (by the U.S. state and population) and from extraterritorial nationalist forces from China (Guomindang). Using his paradigm, racial exclusion or oppression and extraterritorial domination converge and interact in the Chinese American community, establishing a permanent structure of dual domination and creating its own internal dynamics and unique institutions (Wang 1995). Certain diasporas require local, national, and international considerations before a researcher can fully comprehend their experiences.

One of the earliest writings on this concept is in Don Nakanishi's 1975 seminal work "In Search of a New Paradigm: Minorities in the Context of International Politics." Nakanishi pointed out that international politics heavily factored into movement of refugees and immigrants and eventual development of ethnic groups in the United States. Furthermore, international politics may very well affect these groups' livelihood in the United States and vice versa. He proposed that we look at minority groups in terms of not only international politics but also transnationalism and race relations (see also Valverde 1994). In a later work he explicitly explored Asian American subjects when he suggested that "by conceptualizing Asian American politics in terms of both domestic and non-domestic dimensions, our research agenda differs from what is usually undertaken under the rubric of minority politics" (Nakanishi 1985, 5). The works of Wang and Nakanishi in particular have allowed me to question the forces, from the micro to the macro level, that influenced the experiences of Vietnamese in the United States and elsewhere. I add to this work the incorporation of the personal—the inner workings of individuals and groups as they relate to each other, from the level of state structures to the extremely inward-looking personal motivations of their actions.

My transnational study stands on the shoulders of other Vietnamese American scholars. Scholars of Vietnamese Americans' experiences shortly after 1975 focused heavily on the resettlement and assimilation of refugees in the United States. Some gravitated toward the educational and economic mobility of the first and second waves of immigrants (1975–1982), with special interest in first- and second-generation youth. Beginning in the mid-1980s, these writings tended to highlight the adversity later arrivals faced and focused on juvenile crime and welfare dependency.[8] Within the first ten years of resettlement, initial research emerged on Vietnamese Americans' community-building efforts in their respective localities. Though informative, these early texts focused almost entirely on resettlement patterns using assimilationist models that did not fully reflect the complexities of the early Vietnamese American refugee population (Montero 1979; Zhou and Bankston 1998).[9] Although all these authors highlight the initial difficulties experienced by Vietnamese refugees, including a downward occupational mobility with respect to positions they had held in Viet Nam, they conclude that over time Vietnamese Americans will successfully integrate into American society (Caplan, Whitmore, and Choy 1989; Rutledge 1992).[10]

From these writings Vietnamese American scholarship expanded to include oral history and ethnographic projects offering more complex understandings of the Vietnamese American experience by focusing on community studies. Their topics included internal community strife, gender relations, economic marginalization, creation of ethnic places, political participation, and individual connections to Viet Nam (Aguilar-San Juan 2000, 2009; Chan 2006; Collet 2000; Freeman 1989, 1995; Gold 1992; Kibria 1993; Lieu 1998; Smith and Tarallo 1995; Võ 2009). Many of these scholars were actively involved with the groups they studied and developed long-term relationships with the Vietnamese American community. Using a multidisciplinary approach and knowledge of the local, national, and international forces that shape individual lives, they successfully presented a slice of the Vietnamese American experience and the subtle nuances of community life. For example, whereas mainstream opinion and earlier research suggested that Vietnamese youths were either valedictorians or gangsters, the writers in this group explained the complexities involved in social and individual choices.

The studies and scholars mentioned here have been invaluable in understanding Vietnamese diasporic history and have provided a foundation for my colleagues and me to reach across the oceans to examine connections between the diasporic community and Viet Nam. Memoirs tell of leaving Viet Nam, adjusting to the host country, and some returns to the home country (Hayslip and Wurts 1990; T.D.T. Lê 2003; Q. D. Nguyen 1994; K. Nguyen 2001; A. Pham 1999). The growing production of diverse Vietnamese and Vietnamese American art forms in the last decade allowed film and literature criticism (Beevi 1997; Duong 2005; V. T. Nguyen 2006; Pelaud 2005). Other works looked at the effect of the overseas population on Vietnamese social structures and culture productions (Carruthers 2002; Leshkowich 2003; Thai 2008; Valverde 2003).[11] These works represent an evolution leading up to ideas that I advance about the new ways the Vietnamese diaspora engages in transnational processes that shape their experiences in the United States while affecting events in Viet Nam.

Vietnamese in Diaspora

Centering diaspora as an analytic framework within Vietnamese American and Viet Nam studies scholarship is essential to an examination of the experiences of Vietnamese overseas populations and their relationships with Viet Nam and its inhabitants. As Adam McKeown states in his work with the Chinese diaspora, "A diasporic perspective would complement and expand upon nation-based perspectives by drawing attention to global connections, networks, activities, and consciousnesses that bridge these more localized anchors of reference" (1999, 307). I discuss here the formation of this diverse group, what constitutes a diaspora in the (post)modern age, and the importance of centering Vietnamese overseas experiences within a diasporic framework to incorporate a larger picture of local and international forces.

Traditionally, people in diaspora are seen as exiles scattered throughout the world and dreaming of a homeland to return to, as in the case of Jewish diasporas (R. Cohen 1997). Alternatively, some assume they will eventually assimilate into host country cultures and disappear into local cultural fabric. Diaspora is now studied with many more forms of movements and nuanced connections. Extrapolating from the ideas of diaspora scholars Robert Cohen (1997), James Clifford (1994), Paul Gilroy (1991), Wanni Anderson and Robert G. Lee (2005), Rhacel Parreñas and Lok Siu (2007), and Jana Evans Braziel and Anita Mannur (2003), I have developed a working definition of *diaspora*. Diaspora groups and individuals are displaced and living away from their homeland, have both connections to and alienation from their homeland and adopted country, experience ambivalence toward both their homeland and their adopted country, have connections with others in diaspora, and create new, shared hybrid cultures.

Since 1975 Viet Nam's overseas population has increased tremendously. Overseas Vietnamese stood at over three million in 2010; twenty-six countries have more than ten thousand Vietnamese immigrants and their immediate descendents in residence, with the majority residing in the United States. Before 1975 only several thousand Vietnamese lived in the United States, many of whom were war brides or more transient individuals such as students, soldiers in training, and diplomats. The fall of Sai Gon in 1975 and the subsequent mass movement of refugees boosted the Vietnamese population in the United States to 245,025 by 1980. This number more than doubled by 1990 to 593,213 and doubled again by 2000 to 1,122,528. Between 2000 and 2010 the population increased 38 percent, to reach 1,548,449 (U.S. Bureau of the Census 2002, 2010b; "Portrait of Vietnamese Americans" 2011).

At 581,946 in 2010, California's population of Vietnamese Americans is the largest in the United States. The city of San Jose has the most Vietnamese of any city outside Viet Nam: 112,030, or 10.6 percent of San Jose's total population. Well over 200,000 Vietnamese Americans live in a cluster of cities in Southern California. Westminster, in Southern California and home of the most visible Vietnamese ethnic enclave, Little Saigon, is often referred to as the capital of the Vietnamese diaspora (U.S. Bureau of the Census 2010b). The making of the Vietnamese diaspora spans three decades and continues to evolve.

Movement and Meaning

Though sometimes perceived as a monolithic group, Vietnamese Americans have diverse backgrounds, including socioeconomic status and time and method of arrival in the United States (Lowe 1991). Their settlement and adaptation in the United States and how they reestablish relations with one another also factor into their diasporic experiences. The physical movement of Vietnamese entering the United States really began with the fall of Sai Gon in 1975, when South Viet Nam was left in a state of chaos. The South Vietnamese had learned of the brutal, mass evacuation of Cambodians in Phnom Penh by the Khmer Rouge and anticipated similar actions in Sai Gon. Fearing the worst, people felt the urgency to leave Viet Nam (Rutledge 1992). On March 18, 1975, President Gerald Ford authorized the U.S. attorney general to use his parole power to admit 130,000 Southeast Asian refugees into the United States. He also created the Interagency Task Force with representatives from various federal agencies to oversee their resettlement (Chan 1991). Thus began the formation of the Vietnamese diaspora in many Western countries. It also meant that relations between the United States and its former ally would change, because the United States was now relating to the South Vietnamese as a refugee group entering the country.

Those without connections or resources to leave with the last of the Americans still found ways to flee Viet Nam during Sai Gon's final days. They left by many different routes and by any means necessary: U.S. military aircraft, U.S. Navy ships, small boats, and on foot (Rutledge 1992). People in this first wave left because they believed their or a family member's involvement with the U.S. government would result in persecution by the new communist government.

Leaving Viet Nam was essential to their survival, and many had preorganized departure plans.[12]

This first group of Vietnamese received little resistance from the U.S. government. At the Ninety-Fourth Congress, first session, May 5, 1975, Sen. James O. Eastland made an emotional plea for the United States to open its doors to the refugees:

> What this country should be doing now is soliciting all the funds that can be raised for Vietnam refugee relief, working to relocate these people, get them settled, try to find jobs for them, and offer them help and encouragement in every way we can. These people are largely the middle class of Vietnam. While they may have their bad citizens as well as their good, I believe that the vast majority of these people are those who voted with their feet. Hundreds of thousands of them voted that way in escaping from North Vietnam originally. They are doing it again. They are shopkeepers, doctors, lawyers, engineers, businessmen, trade unionists, journalists. They are a cross section of the same kind of people who have been making up America ever since the first immigrants came over here and met with the Indians. (Eastland 1975)

Subsequently, the Indochina Migration and Refugee Act of 1975 financed the resettlement process for these refugees.[13]

Commonly referred to as the 75ers by Vietnamese American themselves, many first-wave immigrants had a high level of education, had middle- to upper-class standing in Viet Nam, lived in urban centers, learned English or at least had a working familiarity with it, had been educated within the foreign educational system, or had been high-ranking soldiers or professionals who had worked with American personnel or companies in Viet Nam (Rutledge 1992). Many 75ers left with the belief that they could and would return to a recaptured South Viet Nam. As time passed, however, this hope diminished and the harsh reality of being nationless set in. Permanent resettlement in the United States meant 75ers set up the first ethnic enclaves and developed ethnic businesses and institutions such as news media and social, political, and cultural organizations. This population consisted of people who took leadership positions during the early years of resettlement and continued to maintain their power base as subsequent waves arrived.

Shortly after the first refugees entered the United States, a second wave began to arrive, and this wave continued until 1981. For these former South Vietnamese, the new communist government set forth punitive measures. It targeted individuals and family members of those involved with the United States, South Vietnamese military, landowners, and Chinese Vietnamese.[14] Punishment included confiscation of property or land, discrimination in the workforce and education, detainment, incarceration, and expulsion to desolate lands known as New Economic Zones. To escape persecution, hundreds of thousands of Vietnamese risked their lives at sea, hoping to settle in a country like the United States.

Boat escapes often took months to plan and meant cutting off all social ties while pulling the last resources together to pay escape fees. Many former South Vietnamese citizens chose this path even knowing capture would mean jail or worse. Once on the move, they risked getting shot by Socialist Republic of Viet Nam (SRV) guards, death by drowning, and starvation. Moreover, Thai pirate attacks severely brutalized or killed men, women, and children. Pirates who raped and kidnapped young girls and women made boat escapes all the more arduous and traumatizing. Some estimate that as many as half of the boat escapees died en route (Chan 2006; Freeman 1989; Nhat, Duong, and Vu 1981). Since most from this second wave escaped Viet Nam by sea, the images conveyed to the West were of thousands of Vietnamese refugees escaping on rickety boats: the "boat people."

Members of the second wave came from socioeconomic backgrounds much more varied than their predecessors'. Although they had lived in villages and coastal towns and were from all walks of life, the majority of the second wave were nevertheless well educated and had lived in Sai Gon (Rutledge 1992). They waited in the first asylum camps for a longer period than those in the first wave—nine months on average (Caplan, Whitmore, and Choy 1989). However, the United States still accepted Vietnamese refugees from the countries of first asylum.[15] Their adaptation was less cohesive than that of the first wave, having lost more years living under an oppressive communist regime, staying longer in refugee camps, and starting over in a less welcoming political and socioeconomic environment in the United States than their predecessors. But the business skills and informal networks of many proved invaluable in building commercial ethnic islands in resettlement areas and eventually lifting their economic status (Chan 1991; Kibria 1993). They came during a U.S. recession, but most managed to carve out a living, partly because of Vietnamese communities already in place by the time the second wave arrived. They also received refugee status with relative ease and some resettlement help along with the support of Vietnamese family and friends in the United States.

With the creation of distinctive waves, some Vietnamese Americans developed terms to distinguish the old-timers from the newcomers. Many young 75ers derogatorily referred to the second wave as FOB—"fresh off the boat." The distinction between the first-wave 75ers and the second-wave FOB newcomers led to an intraethnic class hierarchy based on time of and, in part, means of arrival. Intrinsically, this class bias relates to the impression that 75ers came from the establishment of Viet Nam before the fall and that those who immigrated later came from more modest backgrounds. It also means that earlier arrival in the United States allotted the 75ers more time to resettle in and assimilate to the new land.[16]

By 1979, when it became clear that Vietnamese continued to flee and that thousands were dying at sea during their escape, the United Nations and the

United States sought to regulate the flow of the boat people (Valverde 1992). On May 31, 1979, the United Nations High Commission for Refugees (UNHCR) and the SRV created the Orderly Departure Program (ODP) (Rutledge 1992). At the time of the ODP's inception, the UNHCR negotiated resettlement arrangements with more than twenty countries. The Vietnamese nationals who immigrated to the United States through the ODP were processed as refugees under the Refugee Act of 1980 or as holders of immigrant visas under the Immigration and Nationality Act (Kumin 1988). ODP ended September 30, 1999, twenty years after it started. During ODP operations, 467,113 Vietnamese were admitted to the United States, including over 165,718 who had gone through Viet Nam's forced reeducation programs, 89,467 through Amerasian programs, and 211,928 from other immigration programs (Daniels 2000).

This third wave, or ODP group, was even more diverse than the previous wave. Its members had also lived under the communist system and were often victims of poor central planning and a weakening economy but for an even longer time than previous waves. Some came alone; many more came with their families or were reunited with their kin in the United States. ODP encompasses programs in family reunification but also programs that processed Amerasians and then later South Vietnamese internees. With the creation of the ODP, the number of refugees escaping through dangerous channels diminished.

The ODP group brought into the United States former South Vietnamese soldiers and officials who had been imprisoned in internment camps after 1975 and who influenced the Vietnamese American political landscape. Applicants who had served in the South Vietnamese government and had been imprisoned for more than five years were eligible to immigrate to the United States. Under President George H. W. Bush, the Humanitarian Operation (HO) Program began accepting internees in 1990. In 1994 an estimated 450,000 to 550,000 internees, including family members, were living in Viet Nam. By 2000 most were resettled in the United States (Daniels 2000).[17]

Members of the HO Program are considered well educated and previously held positions of power and leadership. However, because they are older and harbor deep-rooted memories of loss from the level of family to the nation, adjusting to a foreign country and culture proved particularly difficult. Many had been important members of society in Viet Nam but now had to rely on family and friends and government assistance.[18] To make up for the lost years and possibly to regain some semblance of authority among their ethnic peers, many from these groups joined and became leaders of staunch anticommunist groups and essentially revitalized sentiments of animosity toward the SRV.[19] Yet others from this same group had no intention of perpetuating a long-standing feud with communist Viet Nam. Having endured a war, separation from family, and incarceration, they looked forward to a time of peace for themselves and their families in the United States.

Ethnic integration seemed pivotal for their adjustment in the United States. But the desire to integrate into the greater U.S. society also loomed large, especially for the younger population, who called it home. Although the U.S. government created a variety of Vietnamese refugee-immigration programs, American society has not completely accepted this new group. As the national myth goes, the United States is the land of the free and a great exponent of democracy. Its people come from all parts of the world, but once in the United States its melting pot ultimately assimilates them into American culture (Sowell 1981).[20] However, racism inherent in U.S. society surfaced for Vietnamese Americans in the form of verbal and physical racially motivated attacks. These factors contributed to the insecurity of these refugee-immigrants and their need to appear more assimilated, even at the risk of ostracizing members of their own ethnic communities. In Texas, for example, several Vietnamese-owned shrimp boats were intentionally torched in the Galveston Bay area between 1979 and 1981, most likely a result of competition for fishing grounds (Chin 2002). Violence of a different nature reached extreme heights on January 29, 1996, when former University of California, Los Angeles, honor student and Vietnamese Student Association president Thien Minh Ly was killed while rollerblading at a high school near his home. His killer became the first person Orange County sent to San Quentin State Prison's death row under California's hate-crime statute (Moxley 2008).

Besides experiencing overt racial discrimination, youths growing up in the United States were also going through difficult issues of acculturation. Many developed self-esteem and identity issues commonly experienced by people of color in the predominantly white, Eurocentric U.S. society. These conditions ultimately caused many members of the community to question their place in the United States and (re)consider their connections to the ethnic community there, while others (re)considered their connections to Viet Nam.

Some from the younger generation, beholden to their families' history of loss, continue to harbor sorrow for a perceived injustice and take on their parents' political agenda to right it. Some even internalize their parents' trauma, seeing it as their own in "postmemory," and use that history as inspiration for artistic expression and cultural production (Hirsch 2008). The proliferation of independent films, art works, and memoirs of men and women in their twenties and thirties discussing these same issues speaks to the plight of some young people and how they relate to the older generation while growing up in the United States (Timothy Bui 2001; Tony Bui 1999; T.D.T. Lê 2003; Q. D. Nguyen 1994; K. Nguyen 2001; L. Pham 2005; A. Pham 1999; H. Tran 2006).

Though characteristics vary, feelings of displacement from the home country and alienation in the adopted one are strong for all three waves and include generations that grew up or were born in the United States. To 75ers, for instance, this displacement meant losing a nation, South Viet Nam, with no hope of returning. For the boat refugees, they carry with them years of discrimination in Viet Nam, trauma from the escape and camp experience, and further struggles to make a new home in the United States. For HO members, memories of incarceration and other forms of oppression remain strong in the

United States. Younger generations experience internal struggles that can include the legacy of their parents' loss and discrimination in a racist new home. Since the sense of displacement and alienation is experienced by so many in the Vietnamese diaspora, there should not be a monopoly on pain, suffering, and loss. Yet some consider their personal or collective experience as the most real or legitimate and as best representing the Vietnamese overseas population. In particular, they continue with national rituals (such as pledging to the flag of the former South Viet Nam) while perpetuating an anticommunist political philosophy. They deem those who do not follow the practices and beliefs to be communists and, in extreme cases, they practice red-baiting.

Anticommunism within Vietnamese American Communities

Myriad immigration experiences create diverse populations. But I argue that the anticommunism embedded in the early culture production of Vietnamese living in the United States has been their overarching ideology and has most influenced their perceptions (T. N. Tran 2007; T. V. Dang 2005; Valverde 2003). The ideology includes preserving the culture that existed before 1975 and symbols that represented South Viet Nam.[21] For them, all individuals, groups, and institutions either have a strong anticommunist stance or they are communist. But because no legitimate unifying leader exists and there is no unitary law enacted, monitoring the behavior of overseas Vietnamese for communist tendencies is an uncontrolled and unregulated act, with punitive measures against the "communists" varying greatly in style and intensity. Dozens of organizations have arisen for the sole purpose of advancing anticommunist ideology and have come to dominate overseas Vietnamese communities. Expressions of anticommunist sentiments from these groups and individuals have resulted in assassinations, protests, and social exclusion.

In many ways, however, it is unclear what anticommunism means for these individuals and groups. It may entail a rejection of Hồ Chí Minh–style communism born from colonial influences and nationalist revolutionary ideals or disdain for a series of communist endeavors to equalize classes through draconian methods of land reforms and purges. Perhaps it means disliking Hồ Chí Minh's imperialist intentions of creating an Indochinese communist state incorporating Laos and Cambodia. Or the word *communist* has taken the place of "North Viet Nam," the victors who defeated South Viet Nam. There seem to be many wildly different permutations of these ideas among members of anticommunist groups. By *staunch anticommunists*, I mean the people who actively and aggressively push an agenda centered on nationalist loyalties to the former South Viet Nam and completely reject a reunified Viet Nam.

Shortly after resettlement, exiled Vietnamese refugees organized with the hope of taking back Viet Nam by force. A prime example is the National United Front for the Liberation of Vietnam (NUFLVN), the largest of the anticommunist resistance movements. Formed by Hoang Co Minh, former vice admiral of the Sai Gon Navy, and Pham Van Lieu, former chief of the Sai Gon National Police Force, this group supposedly trained fighters on the border of Thailand with the intention of taking back Viet Nam by force. However, by 1984, internal strife divided the group when Lieu accused Minh of using contributions to the Front to open a chain of Vietnamese restaurants and buy a fishing boat (McLaughlin 1990). Even with these early problems, over time, groups like NUFLVN evolve to keep up with political fluctuations. Such was the case in 2004 when the group changed its name to Việt Nam Canh Tân Cách Mạng Đảng (Việt Tân for short), or the Vietnam Reform Party. Seeing the futility of military action against Viet Nam, this new group instead "holds that the Vietnamese people must solve the problems of Vietnam. Democratic change must come through the power of the people in the way of grassroots, peaceful means" (Viet Tan 2009). A longtime member of the group, Dan The Hoang (2009), notes that the "struggle to change Viet Nam is by getting to the hearts and minds of the people so they can stand up and speak up for human rights and freedom and multi-party system."

With this new focus, Viet Tan has adopted a two-pronged approach to establish change in Viet Nam: (1) spread democratic ideas and a multiparty system and (2) lobby for U.S. policy for human rights in Viet Nam.[22] Viet Tan continues to defend its actions abroad and in Viet Nam. It spreads its viewpoints through the Internet and a daily radio broadcast inside the home country: New Horizon Radio. As of 2012, the group is an active anticommunist force.

Groups like NUFLVN remain popular primarily because they speak to a people who have collectively experienced an immense amount of loss. Because of strong sentiments about their lost nation, anticommunist groups believe that working toward shaping Viet Nam's future in line with their values is well worth a continued fight. Of course, the manner of this fight varies greatly, from silent protest to more active engagement in political change. Extreme measures to influence and control usually get the most attention and incite the most fear in the general Vietnamese American population.

Anticommunist groups and individuals have strengthened their influence on diasporic communities even through physical attacks on suspected dissidents. On July 21, 1981, in San Francisco, Duong Trong Lam was the first Vietnamese assassination victim. An antiwar activist and community organizer, he had been in the United States since 1971, originally as a student. A group calling itself the Anti-Communist Viets Organization (ACVO) took responsibility for the killing. They claimed that Duong was assassinated because he was a communist agent who edited *Cai Dinh Lang (Village Temple)* newspaper to "bolster the image of the hated Vietnamese communist regime" (Coburn 1983, 19). This act effectively signaled the beginning of terrorism in the community. Lam's assassination, along with the slaying of four other journalists by purported death squads in the United States since 1981, remains unsolved (Brody 1994; Kleinknecht 1999).

In another violent incident that took place in 1989, an unknown assailant shot and wounded Doan Van Toai near his Fresno, California, home. Toai coauthored *The Vietnamese Gulag* and headed a political group called Institute for Democracy in Vietnam (Doan and Chanoff 1986). Sources in the Vietnamese American community claimed he met with Ha Noi officials and advocated United States–Viet Nam dialogue. He admittedly wanted better ties between the two countries, though he also often sharply criticized the Ha Noi government. He was even arrested and jailed in Viet Nam after 1975. Nonetheless, some members of the Vietnamese community thought he was a communist agent and wanted him dead (Associated Press 1989). Protests against suspected communist sympathizers continue today even though the most severe forms of violence, like assassination, have ended.

Culturally motivated protests have had the same intent as political ones: to advance the anticommunist ideological perspective and control the mind-set of members of the diaspora. For example, anticommunist Vietnamese Americans accused Thanh Lan, a famous Vietnamese singer who in 1994 was in the United States on a ninety-day culture visa to perform throughout the country, of being an agent of communist Viet Nam and boycotted her show in San Jose. She denied being a communist or even cooperating with communists, and then she went into hiding. Shortly thereafter, she requested asylum in the United States. Thanh Lan was shocked by the protests and the ferocity of the demonstration against her, including death threats (Jung 1994).

Even though the extreme anticommunist hard line has lightened over the years, a vocal minority still reminds Vietnamese American community members that any person having relations with Viet Nam will be labeled a communist and a traitor to South Viet Nam's legacy. "Relations" may be as personal and benign as sending remittances to or visiting family in Viet Nam. The term may have a more serious meaning, such as participating in cultural and business dealings in Viet Nam. Those who risk such links know they can fall victim to threats, protests, and even arson.

These pressures have created incentives to dissociate from individuals labeled communists within the Vietnamese American community. Even in 2012 the most effective way to silence an opponent is to label him or her a communist. Members of the Vietnamese American community know explicitly and implicitly the importance of overtly maintaining a strong stance against communism in Viet Nam, even if privately they bridge connections to Viet Nam and its citizens. But there is much dissent in the diverse Vietnamese American community. Many Vietnamese visit their families in Viet Nam, work on humanitarian projects operating there, have business dealings there, or consume cultural products from there, such as music. Such strong connections to the home country are common knowledge and practice in the community but are seldom acknowledged publicly. Historical precedent of threats and fear of such threats help explain this self-censorship. But transnational connections show how, even with these anticommunist pressures, Vietnamese Americans can and do cross political divides and national borders to create their own diasporic experiences in the age of globalization.

Globalization as Context

According to the Hansen effect, it takes three generations for an immigrant group to reconnect with its homeland. Arthur Hansen made several related claims based on a study of Japanese Americans: first-generation Asian American immigrants retain their homeland culture, the second generation adapts to the new culture of the host country, and the third generation returns to the homeland culture for identity validation (Hansen 1983).[23] However, Vietnamese Americans seemingly have experienced all three stages in a far shorter period. Technological developments have made communications and transportation far easier, cheaper, and more rapid in recent decades than in the past, when many Japanese Americans first came to the United States. Accounting for the current global conditions is fundamental to understanding the recent history of the Vietnamese diaspora and its connection to Viet Nam.

Following David Harvey (1990) and Arjun Appadurai (1991), I define *globalization* by using today's condition, which is characterized by increasing connectedness of countries and regions, creating new governance; the spread of capitalism, creating new migration patterns; a worldwide interconnectedness, by way of financial networks and dominant-culture productions and distribution; and new technologies in travel and communications.

Beyond the need to escape for safety reasons, Vietnamese left because of perceived lack of opportunities at home and hope for a more prosperous future in a place like the United States. Nina Glick Schiller, Linda Basch, and Cristina Szanton Blanc articulate the importance of global capitalism as push-pull factors in transnational migration. They argue that currently in the world there is "a global restructuring of capital based on changing forms of capital accumulation [that] has led to deteriorating social and economic conditions in both labor sending and labor receiving countries with no location of a secure terrain of settlement" (1995, 158).

By the late 1980s, global forces like technological advances in travel and communication facilitated rapid movements of people, cultures, and currency across borders and shaped new immigrant relations and experiences (Appadurai 1991; Castells 1996; Harvey 1990).[24] These new conditions contributed to dramatic changes in both Viet Nam and its overseas population. Most striking are the ways the people from both sides of the ocean remain connected. This process of connecting and reconnecting defines many overseas Vietnamese while affecting development in Viet Nam. It also allows us to think differently about how diasporas are formed and their impact on the host and home countries even as they transcend traditional nation-state borders to maintain linkages in multiple sites.

Financial Forces

Most journalists and many scholars explain globalization in terms of worldwide capital penetration. However, Robert Cohen reminds us that global processes also include the "institutional and social mechanisms that manage and structure the marketplace and the agents who engage in the market transactions" (R. Cohen 1997, 158).[25] For example, since the commencement of diplomatic relations between Viet Nam and the United States on July 11, 1995, the two nations have been in intensive negotiations for normalized bilateral trade relations. The United States pushed for Viet Nam to liberalize its markets, essentially hoping to have some stake in its economic development. Although Viet Nam wanted to join the international market, its World Trade Organization (WTO) membership was impeded by a number of issues, including historical angst between the former enemies. Also, like other developing countries wanting to increase trade without putting themselves at a disadvantage, Viet Nam feared that regulated tariffs, quotas, and controlled subsidies would do just that. After eleven years of preparation, including eight years of negotiations and fourteen major meetings from July 1998 through October 2006, Viet Nam finally received full WTO membership on November 7, 2006 (WTO 2006). By 2009, the United States had become the largest foreign investor in Viet Nam (Vietnam Business News 2010). Globalization, in this instance, advances liberalism and creates détente between the former enemies even while memories of the war are quite fresh for many people in the United States, in Viet Nam, and in diaspora.

Viet Nam faced the contradiction of not wanting to deal with former enemies but welcoming them when it meant economic gain. This contradiction applied to Vietnamese Americans as well since many of them, though averse to communist philosophy, nevertheless saw financial opportunities in Viet Nam. From shortly after the war to the present (2012), remittances remain a crucial component of the Vietnamese economy. Remittances to Viet Nam increased from $1.2 billion in 1999 to $7.2 billion in 2008. In 2010 they exceeded $8 billion, a rise of 25.6 percent from 2009 (VNS 2011). As scholar Dang Phong revealed and as my research confirmed, remittances took several forms, starting in the initial years after resettlement with items valuable for resale on the black market. Over time they shifted to monetary gifts and eventually investment in property and land in Viet Nam (Phong 2000).

During the early years following the war, service centers and small shops were the obvious choices for sending remittances. However, with the rising number of *Viet Kieu* (Vietnamese expatriates or overseas Vietnamese returning to Viet Nam for any length of time), hand-carried remittances became more popular. As more consumer goods became readily available in Viet Nam, monetary remittances became far more popular than gift packages.[26] Nguyễn Việt Thuận, vice-director of Ho Chi Minh's Committee for Vietnamese Residing Abroad, believes that, whatever the official number of remittances sent through legal means, the same amount is most likely sent illegally (Thuận 2002).

In 1999 approximately 5 percent of the Vietnamese population received remittances from overseas. On average, remittances paid for 38 percent of all expenditures of recipient households. Over a billion dollars in remittances is approximately 5 percent of the country's gross domestic product and 20 percent of the state's budget (Haughton 1999).[27] Unrecorded remittances fuel the black market for foreign exchange, making it easier for smugglers to finance clandestine imports. Remittances from abroad also aid in maintaining the value of the đồng and finance a part of the national government's sizable deficit (Haughton 1999). They thus initially helped Viet Nam stabilize its postwar economy, and the flows of currency later aided Viet Nam's adjustment from a communist to a more market-driven state.

Because of economic and political interests, Viet Nam extended unprecedented offers to improve relations with its overseas population. For example, Viet Nam hosted a conference for Viet Kieu in Sai Gon in February 1993. Of the one hundred Viet Kieu who attended, ten came from the United States. Võ Văn Kiệt, Viet Nam's prime minister, opened the conference by saying that he wanted to forget the past and now be friends with the Viet Kieu. He added that he was willing to let everyone talk freely. An American Viet Kieu later said that the conference focused on economics, but he hoped that future conferences would have more discussion on politics and more diversified attendees (McLaughlin 1993). Aside from conferences to spark Viet Kieu interest in investing, Viet Nam has given Viet Kieu tax incentives and liberalized rules on business participation (Tan 1994).

Overseas Vietnamese also benefited from global financial restructuring. With the eventual thawing of relations between Viet Nam and the United States in the mid-1990s, Viet Kieu visits to Viet Nam became more frequent. Different forms of Viet Kieu investment took place, from large industry projects to smaller ghost investments in family property. Thousands returned to Viet Nam to work, and some even opted to stay, remitting their own labor to advance their careers while helping Viet Nam move toward a market economy (Carruthers 2002; Long 2004). Viet Nam welcomed this multilingual, multicultural group equipped with a Western education. These Viet Kieu aided Viet Nam in its move toward a market economy and better understanding of globalization. Similarly, Viet Nam offered the Viet Kieu population job opportunities, which were especially appealing during U.S. economic downturns. Global financial forces compounded with personal sentiments regarding the home country, and host countries helped create these transnational crossings.

Cultural Forces from the Home Country

Viet Nam and its diaspora have enormous cultural influence over one another, each keeping a constant watch over the progress of the other. The lure of the homeland for Vietnamese Americans and interest in the diaspora from Viet Nam seem all the more surprising when considering the political tensions between the two. The home country has many levels of appeal for Vietnamese Americans. For some it offers economic opportunities. For others, the home country is the object of more personal longings based on cultural needs, which extend to maintaining family ties and expressing filial piety through transnational practices. For others, especially a new generation of Vietnamese Americans who grew up in the United States, Viet Nam serves almost as a cultural haven. A sense of alienation and nonacceptance in their host country is additional motivation for seeking transnational connections with a perceived open and welcoming home country (Schiller, Basch, and Szanton Blanc 1995; Takaki 1989). During the difficult process of acculturation in the United States, some looked to Viet Nam as the cultural center of their ethnic identity. Getting to the point of relatively open exchange in 2012, however, took decades to achieve. Viet Nam's lack of relations with the United States and, consequently, Vietnamese Americans was a major obstacle.

Following the fall of Sai Gon in 1975, relations between the communist government and the United States were chilly. For example, in 1977, concerning the Nixon Doctrine, which was first implemented in 1969 during the Cold War and essentially requires nations to bear the brunt of their own national security but states that the United States would provide military aid per treaty agreements, the Vietnamese government asserted:

> The Nixon-Kissinger doctrine met with shameful defeat and was dealt a decisive blow in Vietnam with the general offensive and uprising in the spring of 1975. The completely victorious resistance of our people ended both the neocolonialist war of aggression and the so-called Nixon doctrine. ("A Lesson for Carter" 1977)

The attitude in the Vietnamese government at the time was that Viet Nam had defeated the most powerful country in the world and was owed certain concessions such as reparations.

Even though the Vietnamese government had a direct hand in making conditions economically and politically unbearable for segments of its population, causing them to choose emigration or escape, the SRV viewed those who fled Viet Nam as traitors (Human Rights Watch 1992). Having lost South Viet Nam to the communists and having fled to resettle overseas, emigrants were initially not welcomed back to the reunified nation-state. Overseas Vietnamese became over time more welcome because of economic necessity, but the SRV has no intention of sharing political power with citizens of the former South Viet Nam.

Mindful of the hostile anticommunist elements of its overseas population, shortly after the war, on July 9, 1977, Viet Nam adopted a superficial policy praising the Viet Kieu and welcoming them home. But this policy, known as 127-CP, is based on a disingenuous piece of legislation that was never properly implemented. Instead, a policy that preceded it by a few months more faithfully reveals the nation's intent toward the Viet Kieu. Conceived on May 25, 1977, 122-CP regulated the movements and welfare of Viet Kieu in Viet Nam, making their lives unbearable if they ever chose to live in their home country (Phong 2000; Valverde 2002).

As decades passed without viable threat from overseas Vietnamese, the Vietnamese government slowly changed its perception. For example, it took great pains to rename its overseas population. Vietnamese who left after 1975 were once labeled *Mỹ ngụy* (American puppets); now they are referred to by names like *Kiều Bào* (people coming from the same womb). Indicative of how semantics can reflect politics, this change in terms signified the government's more open attitude toward overseas Vietnamese and, I argue, directly coincides with Viet Nam's need for economic investment and its desire to join the global market. The government sees the Viet Kieu as a possible bridge for making this arduous crossing. Also, a growing number of Vietnamese performers, students, workers, and even tourists enter the United States annually. Some older anticommunist Vietnamese Americans, for whom memories of the war are still vivid, fear that the rapid movement of people, culture, and finance back and forth has created closer relations with Viet Nam and eased previously strong anticommunist points of view.

Such fears have a basis in reality. The Vietnamese government has indeed been proactive in incorporating overseas Vietnamese in Viet Nam's national development project. The most notable action in this vein was Resolution 36-NQ/TW of 2004. One of its many provisions is the following:

> The overseas Vietnamese community is an integral part and resource of the Vietnamese nation, acting as an important factor to strengthen Viet Nam's friendship and cooperation with other countries. The State is responsible for negotiating with countries to set up legal frameworks for overseas Vietnamese to settle down and have their legitimate rights protected in accordance with the residing countries' laws and international conventions and practices as well. ("Resolution no. 36-NQ/TW" 2005)

This wording suggests that Viet Nam wants overseas Vietnamese to feel a close relationship and possess an identity tied to Viet Nam. Conversations I had with Vietnamese party officials and with leaders within Vietnamese American communities revealed that rapprochement at a limited informal level has existed between the two groups since the mid-1990s.[28] More formal overtures have been made, in the form of open and public awards given to individuals overseas who the government believes have contributed to Viet Nam. These informal and formal steps seem to be a logical way for the Vietnamese government, many of whose officials are well over sixty years old, to approach their counterparts in diaspora. The idea is that the officials are more open to dialogue with their former enemies. Some leaders of the older generation of Vietnamese Americans accept that Viet Nam is a strong sovereign nation and that it is best to have some influence versus none. These developments add to the ultimate fear of staunch Vietnamese American anticommunists: having lost their country of South Viet Nam, they now could lose the allegiance of the diaspora as well.

The forces of globalization have linked even former enemies economically and culturally. These connections mark globalization's importance in creating new diasporic experience, but globalization alone does not define transnational practices among actors in Viet Nam and in diaspora. Rather, the practices of diasporic populations are made more interesting by globalization. This is ever a reality of Vietnamese Americans and their connections to Viet Nam.

The Nation and Transnationalism

The Vietnamese diasporic community's transnational connections evolved largely from community members' strong desire to connect with people in their homeland. Also, diasporic communities stir the imaginations of people at home and subsequently transform peoples' views of their nation and the world. *Transnationalism* can thus be defined as "the process by which immigrants forge and sustain simultaneous multi-stranded social relations that *link* together their societies of origin and settlement" (Schiller, Basch, and Szanton Blanc 1995, 48 [emphasis added]). These processes are seen as going above (having power that influences governing bodies), below (generally by illegal means and non-state-sanctioned activities), and through (with knowledge and acceptance by governments, but often with ramifications beyond their vision and control) traditional nation-states (Smith and Guarnizo 1999).[29] The term *transnationalism* needs further clarification to accurately frame a study of Vietnamese and Vietnamese American issues.

Debates about the role of nation-states once fell solely within the realm of political science. Struggles between international powers dominated the discourse. When transnationalism surfaced as a study, it was (and is) often conflated with international relations studies. Although the nation-state remained the central theoretical framework for their research, political scientists still called this approach transnationalism. Inversely, transnational scholars discuss transnational practices without fully investigating the role of the nation-state governing bodies and their relationships to world powers and local identities. These are highly problematic issues.

Because the term *transnational* implies moving across nation-state boundaries, pundits have often jumped to the conclusion that nation-states are weakening, but that is a false assumption. Michael Peter Smith and Luis Eduardo Guarnizo offer four reasons that transnationalism has not weakened the state: (1) historically, states seeking nationhood have kept close relations with their overseas populations, (2) nationalist identity projects and competing identity projects continue to be important, (3) state projects include reincorporating their often large emigrant populations into the government system, and (4) receiving countries retain the legitimate means of coercive power within their borders (1999, 7–10).

The nation-state plays a major role in the lives of Vietnamese Americans because their history links them to international policies based on nation-states. Furthermore, their sense of home relies on nationalist sentiments for Viet Nam. As individuals in the postmodern flux, Vietnamese Americans find the lure of certain nation-state benefits appealing. In the case of Viet Nam, these benefits include identity affirmation or political, economic, and social linkage.[30] The complicated relationship between the Vietnamese and U.S. governments that shapes Vietnamese American ethnic angst is worth exploring.

Viet Nam's contemporary history of conflict started in the mid-nineteenth century. It began with the successful Vietnamese anticolonial campaign against the French in the first Indochina war, December 19, 1946, to August 1, 1954, which resulted in the division of Viet Nam at the seventeenth parallel. It was during this period that the United States worked closely with the nationalists, led by Hồ Chí Minh, to fight off the occupying Japanese during World War II. The United States remained connected to Viet Nam when it funded France's unsuccessful campaign to recolonize the country (Duiker 2000; Karnow 1983).[31] The second Indochina war, lasting from the late 1950s to 1975, known in the United States as the Viet Nam War and in Viet Nam as the American War, was essentially a civil war. This conflict was mainly fought between the communist Democratic Republic of Viet Nam in North Viet Nam and the democratic Republic of Viet Nam in South Viet Nam, but it quickly spilled over to neighboring countries. Taking place in the midst of the Cold War, foreign intervention was inevitable; the People's Republic of China (PRC) and the former Soviet Union (USSR) backed North Viet Nam and the United States supported South Viet Nam. Besides Cold War ideology, the United States employed a number of other philosophies to justify foreign intervention. For example, liberalism, which called for creating or preserving liberal-democratic societies, was explicitly used as justification for U.S. involvement in the Viet Nam War. Furthermore, realpolitik advanced the idea that ethically dubious tactics can be deployed for the overall stability of a region. This approach resulted in repeated negotiations among the superpowers, as in President Nixon's 1972 visit to China to manipulate the outcome of the Viet Nam War (Kubek 1992).

During the Cold War, U.S. scholars and politicians perceived the globe in geopolitical terminology such as *core/periphery, first world/third world, north/south,* and *communist/anticommunist.* These binaries projected a "good us" versus "bad them" image to many in the U.S. government and contributed to the initial U.S. acceptance of Vietnamese refugees in 1975. The thinking in the United States was that, as a democratic country, it should accept and shelter people fleeing an oppressive communist regime.[32] In the midst of coping with its refugee-immigrant issue, the United States had other Viet Nam–related concerns. During the postwar years, the American government and general public experienced what President Ronald Reagan termed the Vietnam Syndrome, caused by events during the war that divided the country, including the antiwar movement, and by the Watergate scandal. U.S. aggression was considered ill conceived, and the public was especially resistant to further military offensives. After the first Gulf War victory in 1991, President George H. W. Bush prematurely announced that the United States had "kicked the Vietnam syndrome once and for all" (Boot 2009). Subsequent military action, such as the second Gulf War and U.S. presence in Afghanistan through 2012, further calls into question the "success" of such military endeavors. Still, the United States managed to deploy various methods of revisionist history to cast a positive light on the U.S. mythology, especially during and shortly after the Viet Nam War. Yen Le Espiritu astutely points this out in her examination of American mainstream news coverage of the twenty-fifth anniversary of the fall of Sai Gon. "The U.S. War in Viet Nam is re-narrated as a noble and moral mission in defense of freedom and democracy, rather than as an attempt to secure U.S. geopolitical hegemony in Southeast Asia, and by extension, in Asia" (Espiritu 2006b, 337). Essential to this retelling of history were the United States' "rescue fantasies" of saving the supposed hapless Vietnamese refugee victims who fled an oppressive and poor Vietnamese nation for a much more prosperous and democratic United States (341). This reimagining of the United States as a "winner" rather than a "loser" of the war may have been the psychological boost the United States needed to approach Viet Nam more vigorously. Since communist Viet Nam and the United States established formal diplomatic relations in 1995, economic interests have trumped political ones. Indeed, the United States may have lost the conventional war, but with neoliberalist justifications in place, it is looking to win the economic one. These improved relations are primarily the result of increased trade, which surpassed $18.5 million in 2010 (U.S. Bureau of the Census 2010a).

The current situation is starkly different from that of the Cold War period, when being a good American citizen meant shunning communist states such as Viet Nam. On a political level, this approach proved acceptable for the initial Vietnamese refugees and immigrants, who had essentially lost South Viet Nam to the communist North. The Vietnamese American community and the U.S. government are supposed to be based on democracy and a multiparty system. They were allies during the Viet Nam War, and the former South Vietnamese benefited from generous immigration policies for decades after the war. Keeping Viet Nam isolated was a joint goal. Travel, communications, and even sending remittances from the United States to Viet Nam were forbidden. Though these forced divisions were politically acceptable, they proved personally difficult for many Vietnamese Americans to endure after the war, since they still had family living in Viet Nam. Furthermore, knowing that their loved ones were suffering economically compounded their already heightened sense of "survivor's guilt" (Freeman 1995). U.S. society also subjected Vietnamese Americans to a nation-building ideology that included the assimilation myth with all the sociocultural barriers to becoming an American that it carries. Vietnamese Americans recognized the inherent contradiction of assimilation with the racism and xenophobia they were exposed to in the United States.

Transnational links between people in Viet Nam and in diaspora take place in the context of strong conflict between Viet Nam and the United States. Added pressure then comes from anticommunist groups in the United States that keep the idea of a South Viet Nam nation alive. Yet political ideology eventually took a back seat to family connections and responsibilities. Once communication was established between people who had left and those who remained, the top priority for most overseas Vietnamese was the welfare of family back home and how to get resources to them to ensure their survival. The Cold War climate made it difficult for Vietnamese in Viet Nam to communicate with Vietnamese in the United States, but these groups used mutually friendly nations as conduits for communication. The speed of these transnational connections relies heavily on globalization. Along with overarching nation-state obstacles, these factors are the context that makes the Vietnamese diaspora a unique subject of inquiry. The case studies that I investigate further demonstrate these people's dynamic transnational experiences as a new diaspora.

Case Studies

Case studies were selected to represent in the aggregate the breadth and depth of transnational linkages between Viet Nam and its diaspora over a period of thirty-five years. Each study sheds light on the social, political, economic, sexual, and cultural transformations experienced by people from diverse backgrounds when transnational linkages occur. Far from being isolated case studies, they intersect in time, people, and modes of transnational connection created. Collectively, they show how people in Viet Nam and in diaspora interact with and react to the sources of influence previously outlined here.

Chapter 2 discusses how conditions in Viet Nam and abroad influenced the production, dissemination, and consumption of contemporary popular Vietnamese music. Vietnamese music history since 1975 is documented by highlighting voices of musicians, producers, and consumers in the United States and Viet Nam. Focusing on three well-known music-production companies, Paris by Night (PBN; a division of Thúy Nga Productions), Trung Tâm Asia, and Kim Loi, together with one network of independent overseas Vietnamese musicians, Bflat, Chapter 2 illustrates the transnational culture flows and forms of collaboration and influence between Vietnamese Americans and Vietnamese music makers. Since the arrival of the largest exodus of Vietnamese to the United States in 1975, diasporic popular music production has evolved in interesting ways. Led by enthusiastic artists and producers and catapulted by technological advances, members of the overseas Vietnamese population created a truly global music industry. Heavily influenced by exiled sentiments and anticommunist ideologies, overseas Vietnamese music exhibits a special blend of nostalgia that appeals to not only members of the diasporic community but also residents of Viet Nam. A Vietnamese music invasion, in which highly skilled performers captured the imaginations of Vietnamese living in diaspora, began in the mid-1990s. Conversely, some overseas Vietnamese singers have braved being labeled communist by the overseas community to return to adoring fans in Viet Nam. The transnational development of Vietnamese popular music in recent decades serves as a good example of the deeply entrenched transnational processes that take place with or without public knowledge.

Not waiting for states to decide when it was acceptable, individuals in Viet Nam and in diaspora created their own timeline for informal relations, avenues for cooperation, and venues for political discussion. Chapter 3 discusses the role of Internet virtual communities in advancing these kinds of changes. Through the work of American expatriates and overseas Vietnamese introducing and promoting information communication technology (ICT) in Viet Nam, thousands of Vietnamese worldwide are now able to express themselves and promote sociopolitical change. They include people from unique transnational virtual communities, particularly the influential newsgroup VNForum. Members of VNForum played a major role in facilitating transpacific exchanges from inside and outside Viet Nam and fostered areas of communication where none had existed. A primary goal of subscribers was to beget change in Viet Nam through civil discourse and the propagation of information as the Internet grew.

Chapter 3 examines the development of the VNForum virtual community in spawning political movements, furthering technological advances, and fostering additional Internet communities—most notably, the labor rights campaign No-Nike. This historical moment of collaboration between Viet Nam and overseas Vietnamese in the United States speaks to the issue of the continued political divide between the two groups even while connections are made in relative obscurity. Dealing with the former enemy while attempting to connect to the home country continues to be an arduous task for overseas Vietnamese. Differing political philosophies have always been the reason for limited transnational linkages between the two groups. In addition to fostering social movements, VNForum served as a starting point for unprecedented Internet dialogue and organization by those living in the authoritarian communist state of Viet Nam. VNBiz, an offshoot of VNForum, boasts an administration of mostly female Vietnamese nationals who lead discussions about crucial policy issues in Viet Nam. Their audience includes international members and Vietnamese in diaspora. Finally, even as Viet Nam cracks down on its population's nascent attempts at free speech through blogs, members of the former VNForum have created a blog, *Đọt Chuối Non* (http://dotchuoinon.com), to bring controversial topics to Vietnamese readers that is seemingly apolitical enough to avoid state censors. Rapid changes in these relations between Viet Nam and overseas Vietnamese are a result of Viet Nam entering the global market and the new forms of transnational exchange that are a direct product of globalization.

Chapter 4 analyzes the diverse cultural and political streams struggling for political representation and dominance within contemporary Vietnamese American communities. This struggle arises in the context of several facets of life within these communities: continued relations with the home country, adjustment to the host country, and the need to mediate divergent ideas within ethnic communities. Artwork by Chau Huynh, the publication and validation of her works in the *Nguoi Viet Daily*, and the resulting protests against their perceived symbolic interpretations serve as my primary starting points for exploring emerging forms of Vietnamese diasporic culture and political ideology previously deemed unacceptable. I examine the ways Vietnamese Americans with differing ideas and identities react to such forces.

I argue that it is precisely the many local, national, and international obstacles and tensions arising from these sites of contention that create complex diasporic subjects able to maneuver through difficulties and carve out their own cultural and political identities. Examining Chau Huynh's 2006 art exhibit reveals how art, and venues for art like ethnic news media, can shift the limits of acceptable cultural production. Conversations defining the range of acceptable cultural production create a forum for shaping the political, cultural, and social landscape for recent immigrant groups like Vietnamese Americans. In addition to offering a new approach to understanding cultural struggles, I analyze the reasons these struggles come to exist and explore what they imply about the future of identity formation for Vietnamese Americans.

An example of how Vietnamese Americans interact with the United States, Viet Nam, and anticommunists elements as they struggle to define the cultural and political identity of their community is presented in Chapter 5. Many Vietnamese Americans wanted to name their city's Vietnamese commercial area Little Saigon, but a young city council member, Madison Nguyen, won the support of a majority of her fellow council members to name the area the Saigon Business District instead. Proponents of the name Little Saigon asserted that it was the only name that represented overseas Vietnamese and their experiences as refugees fleeing communist-controlled Viet Nam. They declared Nguyen a communist and launched an unsuccessful campaign to recall her from the city council. These events call into question the demarcation of an ethnic community. They also represent a visible political shift away from staunch anticommunist thought and action and the public vocalization of these changes. Observing these developments grounds an understanding of the psychological, sexual, and cultural-political motivations that the actors involved have when they create, lead, and protest.

Methods

My unique personal history and experiences helped shape the methods used in this study. Born in Viet Nam to Eurasian parents, I came to the United States just before the fall of Sai Gon in 1975. As an immigrant growing up in cities with large Vietnamese American populations, I, my peers, and our families experienced firsthand the sorrow of losing our nation and the difficulties of adjusting to our new home in the United States. However, rather than a hindrance, this background and these early experiences of having to negotiate my own place in the Vietnamese American community and, more broadly, American society and international communities, helped me develop valuable coping mechanisms to interact with people from different backgrounds possessing varying biases. Additionally, I contend that my status as a 1.5-generation (born in Viet Nam but raised in the United States), mixed race, bilingual woman made me neither fully the outsider nor insider and therefore more difficult to label and dismiss. Being seen as nonthreatening allowed me access to the otherwise distrusting political groups and their leaders both in Viet Nam and in diaspora.

The San Francisco Bay Area of Northern California is my home and where I have been a member of the Vietnamese community for more than thirty-five years. Here I have taught at and run youth programs; organized cultural events, including an exhibit on the *áo dài* (Vietnamese national costume) that I also curated; and consulted for leaders of various political and cultural groups. As an adult, I lived in Viet Nam off and on for nearly five years doing research, starting even before the United States lifted the economic embargo there in 1994.[33] The connections and networks built in these social and professional circles over time helped me gather crucial and sensitive information from my informants. These groups were also instrumental in providing introductions to potential participants in my study and gaining their trust.

Beyond Internet correspondence and virtual community organizing and participation, I carried out ethnographic fieldwork in Ha Noi in 1993 and 1996 and in Ho Chi Minh City (formerly Sai Gon) in 1999, 2002, 2004, 2006, and 2008. In California, my fieldwork took place from 1992 to 2012 and centered on San Jose, San Francisco, Oakland, Westminster, Garden Grove, Santa Ana, and Anaheim—all cities with a large proportion of Vietnamese Americans. In Viet Nam and the United States, I used ethnographic methods, particularly informal interviews with carefully chosen persons. Participant observation helped me better understand the culture and transnational practices of my subjects. Primary and secondary resources, including documents, archival materials, and journal articles, provided theoretical perspective, historical context, and confirmation of facts.

My interview subjects for this work included over 150 adults in Viet Nam and over 100 in the United States, whom I interviewed from 1993 to 2012. My informants for Chapter 2 included composers, singers, and producers of Vietnamese pop music in Viet Nam and the United States; for Chapter 3 they were Vietnamese directly involved in the development of the Internet in Viet Nam and founders of VNForum; for Chapter 4 they were the artist Chau Huynh and individuals leading protests against her work as well as ethnic leaders and journalists who supported her work; and for Chapter 5 they were Vice-Mayor Madison Nguyen and leaders and organizers of the Little Saigon advocacy groups and recall movement.

All interviews were carried out one on one with adults of eighteen years or older, though on rare occasions interviews included two or more subjects together. Interviews were conducted in English or Vietnamese according to informants' preferences. All translations from interviews and primary and secondary sources are my own.

For sociolinguistic integrity, I spell Vietnamese geographic locations using monosyllabic separations, such as Viet Nam and Ha Noi. I refer to some Vietnamese and overseas Vietnamese by their first name, which is customary in Vietnamese culture when addressing individuals. Doing so helps identify my subjects since most Vietnamese have one of just a few family names, such as Nguyen, Le, Tran, Pham, Bui, Vu, and Do. To maintain a distinction and to respect the way individuals spell their names, I use diacritic marks for the names of Vietnamese nationals, and I omit them for overseas Vietnamese. Ethnographic methods and interviews brought me closer to understanding the truly complex and convoluted experiences individuals have had and their perceived and real struggles. These techniques also humanized every aspect of this work because it is the people who create, destroy, and rebuild every facet of their transnational lives.

Conclusion

The great physical distance between the United States and Viet Nam, alienation in an adopted society, and assimilationist forces on one end and draconian forms of control over the population on the other might be expected to inhibit relationships of Vietnamese Americans with their home country and its inhabitants, but dissolution of relationships has not generally occurred. Transnational practices among diasporic groups disprove the notion that new immigrant populations will eventually conform to the dominant culture of the adopted country. As James Clifford notes, "Transnational connections break the binary relation of *minority* communities with *majority* societies—a dependency that structures projects of both assimilation and resistance" (Clifford 1994, 255). Connections between Viet Nam and its diaspora have persisted through technological advances in travel and communications and growing interconnections in finance and culture—characteristics of globalization.

These tenacious connections beg us to reconsider the conditions and practices that form a contemporary diaspora and remake a nation. Cold War politics and the immense changes experienced during globalization have created unique interconnections among Viet Nam, the Vietnamese diaspora, and the United States. From these groups people who wish to (re)connect with one another have had to contend with state and local sources of influence that shape their (in)actions. These sources include two national governments, those of Viet Nam and the United States, plus staunch anticommunist groups in the diaspora. Yet despite ethnic pressures to hold anticommunist sentiments against the Vietnamese state and state-imposed obstacles in both countries, including restrictions on travel and communication aimed at inhibiting reconnections across the Pacific, overseas Vietnamese have managed to establish and maintain connections with Viet Nam.

These transnational connections take place through political, technological, and cultural means and affirm the overseas Vietnamese community as a diaspora living and acting transnationally. This book documents and theorizes the transnational practices of peoples of Viet Nam and its diaspora. Using an interdisciplinary approach and observations of relations among the United States, the overseas Vietnamese community, and Viet Nam, this study illuminates the complex nature of emerging transnational subjects on both sides of the ocean. In doing so, it lays to rest the notion of Vietnamese Americans and Vietnamese nationals as nation bound and without the resources, will, or imagination to connect with each other.

2

Popular Music

Sounds of Home Resistance and Change

In 1992, Be, a young Vietnamese American woman from California, visits her eldest sister, Lisa, and youngest sister, Nina, in Atlanta, Georgia. Excitedly, the host brings out the latest installment of the Paris by Night (PBN) video series. PBN produces videos of Vietnamese diasporic variety shows. These cabarets feature celebrity masters of ceremonies, popular overseas Vietnamese singers with elaborately choreographed performances, and even actors in comedy skits. Lisa relates how a friend had recently purchased the video from a store in Houston, Texas, copied it, and sent it to her in time for Be's visit. While watching the video, Lisa gossips about which body parts of which singers had been augmented. Be comments that their cousin was a good friend of the Madonna-like pop singer Lynda Trang Dai and that she and her friends often saw her perform in the late 1980s at the famous San Jose nightclub catering to Vietnamese Americans, the Lido. Lisa then adds that the mistress of ceremonies, Nguyen Cao Ky Duyen, the daughter of the former vice president of South Viet Nam, Nguyen Cao Ky, was then engaged to a Euro-American lawyer. At that point, Nina, who had never purchased or voluntarily seen a PBN video before, corrected her sisters by proclaiming that the MC was dating a doctor, not a lawyer. (Field notes 1992)

In 1996, while Be is staying with family in Sai Gon, her aunt, Hạnh, and the aunt's boyfriend, Tuấn, bring home popular music videos produced by

Portions of this chapter were originally published as Kieu Linh Caroline Valverde, "Making Vietnamese Music Transnational: Sounds of Home, Resistance and Change," *Amerasia Journal* 29, no. 1 (2003): 29–50, and reprinted as Kieu Linh Caroline Valverde, "Making Transnational Vietnamese Music: Sounds of Home and Resistance," in *East Main Street: Asian American Popular Culture*, ed. Shilpa Davé, LeiLani Nishime, and Tasha G. Oren, 32–54 (New York: New York University Press, 2005).

Vietnamese Americans. Tuấn proudly proclaims that his video store was one of the first to have that particular edition and boasts of how quickly he can get pirated copies. Hạnh says one of the featured male singers was a professional dancer in Sai Gon and had begun his singing career at a small nightclub that she frequented before he immigrated to the United States. She notes how Americanized some of the women in the videos look and how living abroad seems to have lightened their skin. In a now-familiar ritual, they gossip about plastic surgery and whom the masters of ceremonies had married. (Field notes 1996a)

The events described in the two passages above are not unique to this family; they are fairly common among working- and middle-class Vietnamese adults in both Viet Nam and the United States. Beyond a frivolous fixation with popular music, entertainers, and performers, the videos represent a peculiar, quotidian (re)construction of shared culture across borders. Complex and variegated dimensions inform these multilayered discussions, including aesthetic and artistic concerns, social gossip, copyright infringement, government restrictions, and technological advances. Vietnamese American popular music and music cassettes, videos, CDs, DVDs, and Internet downloads have found their way into nearly every overseas Vietnamese home and have reached millions of people living in Viet Nam. This global reach is remarkable in light of the considerable political obstacles both in Viet Nam and abroad, such as censorship and restrictions from the Vietnamese government, pressures from fanatical anticommunists in the Vietnamese American community, and even issues of racism and assimilation in the United States. These sources of influence control the production and consumption of popular music according to their respective political ideologies. However, professionals in the popular music industry and fans alike have found clever ways, including using the black market, to collaborate transnationally from "below" in the areas of production, distribution, and consumption of the music they choose (Smith and Guarnizo 1999).

This creativity has wielded a rich transnationally produced body of music consumed by millions on both sides of the ocean. Collaborations between artists, producers, and promoters in Viet Nam and in diaspora have gone unnoticed by the Vietnamese government and anticommunist groups. This chapter highlights the voices of these people and the many who listen to their music. Through their enlightening stories we get a larger picture of the issues that people in Viet Nam and abroad face when producing hybrid culture. These stories expose accepted notions of what constitutes culture and the belief that consumption can be controlled.

Overseas Vietnamese popular music production began with the large-scale arrival of Vietnamese in the United States in 1975. Heavily influenced by exile and displacement, overseas Vietnamese popular music incorporates a special blend of nostalgia that appeals to members of diasporic communities and residents of Viet Nam. Overseas Vietnamese popular music has many fans in the homeland even though the Vietnamese government has since unification in 1975 restricted the types of popular music that may be heard publicly, especially those from overseas. As government restrictions on popular music production loosened, most notably since the mid-1990s, Vietnamese artists, whether state sponsored or independent, emerged to make Viet Nam a new popular music center. The popular music from there has reached Vietnamese living outside Viet Nam in what some observers in the United States have called "Viet Nam's music invasion" (Marosi 2000, A1, A16). The first phase of this so-called invasion took place in the mid-1990s and consisted exclusively of popular music recorded in Viet Nam. The second phase began in the early 2000s, when pop singers from the homeland began to perform in the United States. Similarly, after decades of listening to music and video recordings from the diaspora, by the mid-1990s people in Viet Nam were finally able to see their favorite singers perform live. This development may be dubbed an overseas Vietnamese invasion, which was a considerable feat considering that Vietnamese singers were not even allowed to sing in Viet Nam until the mid-1990s and songs from the pre-reunification period that came from the South were banned until the late 1990s.

The ethnomusicological journey in this chapter uncovers the psychological motivations and sociological processes of those who produce and consume the music and how the music affects the lives of people in Viet Nam and in the diaspora (Titon 1984). As Stephen Blum and colleagues suggest, this type of ethnomusicological investigation "shed[s] new light on human creativity [and] on the fundamental importance of musical skills in human adaptive responses" (Blum, Bohlman, and Neuman 1991, 1). Music clearly constitutes an important transnational product that binds a people and their diasporic community: "Music [and other arts] do[] not simply 'reflect.' Rather, they provide the means by which the hierarchies of place are negotiated and transformed" (Stokes 1994, 4). In the overseas Vietnamese and Vietnamese popular music industries, however, popular music's role is transnational, because dominating forces include the Vietnamese state and Vietnamese American anticommunist groups.

Popular Music in South Viet Nam before 1975

Tân nhạc, or modern popular music, began with the French presence in the early nineteenth century. Popular traditional forms of music in Viet Nam, which represent only a small sample of the richness and diversity of the country's musical forms, continued into the twentieth century. Vietnamese traditional music borrowed from multiple cultures, including Western music when it entered Viet Nam sometime before 1940 (Gibbs 2004). Western music from France initially came through the church and then the military shortly after France occupied Ha Noi in 1873. The new injections of French popular songs were made even more popular by French talking movies (often musicals) and ballroom dancing. Elite, urban youth in particular found the new Western style of music exciting and appealing (Gibbs 1998).

In the mid-1930s, Vietnamese people began to write songs in their native language using French melodies. The monosyllabic, tonal character of the Vietnamese language made such adaptations challenging. The lyrics often differed greatly from the original French; nevertheless, the new combination became the rage among people in cities. Even folk theater, *cải lương*, incorporated French songs and melodies into productions (Gibbs 2004). Vietnamese began writing their own compositions following this model. The modern Vietnamese song may have originated from one of these early composers, Nguyễn Văn Tuyến. A native of the city of Hue and the lone Vietnamese student at the Philharmonic Society of Sai Gon, Tuyến first performed his songs there in 1937. By 1938 he was touring in Ha Noi and other cities to rave reviews (Gibbs 1997).

Inspired by these external influences, a number of Vietnamese composers and singers began to follow the new Western styles. From that period, *nhạc tiền chiến* (pre–Indochina war music) was developed (Thương Lê 1970). According to the Vietnamese journalist and cultural critic Nguyễn Thanh Đức (2001), this style represented the folk music of Viet Nam that is still widely listened to today. This genre included marching songs, love songs, and songs about resistance and independence from France. Though widely popular with urban, educated youth, it was largely ignored by the poor, rural population and the feudalistic intellectuals.[1] *Nhạc tiền chiến* supposedly ended about 1947, though some songs written as late as 1954 are considered part of this genre (Gibbs 1998). This music is still sometimes heard on stages across Viet Nam and in the United States.[2]

As noted previously, French chansons strongly influenced the popular musical style of Viet Nam before and after 1975.[3] Vietnamese composers continued to establish their own special brand of popular music by incorporating a variety of foreign and domestic influences. The famous composer Văn Cao, for example, combined elements of Vietnamese folk music, legends, popular sayings, and French chanson styles. Other legendary composers such as Pham Duy looked to the United States for inspiration and ideas. Pham Duy turned Vietnamese poetry into lyrics and translated Western ballads into Vietnamese songs (Gerke 1999). Pham Duy lived through and actively participated in Viet Nam's quest for modernity, its fight for independence from the French, and its civil war. He was exiled but eventually returned to the homeland. Journalist Nguyen Ngoc Bich writes that "one cannot write the history of modern Vietnamese music in the last half century or so without using Pham Duy as the axis for that history" (N. B. Nguyen 2010; see also Henry 2005). Nguyen Ngoc Bich adds:

> Without Pham Duy, especially in the period 1946–1950, there would be no revolutionary music to speak of. Put differently, he was the soul of Vietnamese revolutionary music during the anti-French War of Resistance (1946–54). Of course, there were other composers during this period, but none as productive or leaving a lasting impact as he. (N. B. Nguyen 2010)

Equally famous was the composer Trịnh Công Sơn, who gained fame during the Viet Nam War period. Thien Chi Do, an overseas Vietnamese musician and critic, explained:

> More than being a musical conscience for his nation, Sơn was a prolific observer of the human condition, a romantic poet who loved and wrote about love in a war-torn land, and a voice that spoke of the despair shared by countless others. (T. C. Do 2001)

Like the composers of contemporary Vietnamese popular music, singers of this period attracted legions of fans in predominantly urban centers of Viet Nam. Such singers include Khánh Ly, most known for her renditions of Trịnh Công Sơn's songs.[4] As did popular contemporary composers, these singers continued to have a following even when both they and their fans lived outside Viet Nam. Elvis Phuong, Tuan Ngoc, and Duc Huy initially sang and performed Vietnamese, French, and American songs with their rock bands in Viet Nam, and they continued to have successful careers performing abroad after leaving the country in 1975 (Gerke 1999).

In addition to Vietnamese popular music, Vietnamese listened to Western favorites of the time. In the 1960s and 1970s, these included the French singer Christophe and rock icons such as Elvis Presley, the Beatles, and the Rolling Stones (Gerke 1999).[5] American popular music had the biggest cultural impact in the former South Viet Nam. During the war, popular musical creativity was influenced by rock and roll and pop (James 1989). Radio stations played the American popular music that the youth of Sai Gon liked to hear. Furthermore, city streets were lined with bars that frequently played popular music from the United States (T. D. Nguyễn 2001). To Van Lai, founder of the Paris by Night series, described the variety of musical influences in contemporary Viet Nam:

> In Viet Nam, they love American music. [Now] they like to imitate singers like Whitney Houston. Before, Vietnamese musicians imitated French music because of the nearly hundred years of French domination. So, the melody of Viet Nam came from the French. That is the sound of my generation. The melody of the new generation is from America and China. When the singers sing [nowadays], they go up real high. The French melody was a lot more straightforward. (Lai 2000)

Thanh Thủy, owner of Music Fans Company in Ho Chi Minh City, remembered the pre-1975 music of her youth:

> Before 1975, music was used for official purposes. In Sai Gon there was a different kind of music scene. I was eighteen at the time, already had some contact with the local music scene. The Saigonese music scene at the

time was very abundant. There were Khánh Ly and Thái Thanh among the *sang* singers, and for the *bình dân* or *sến* listeners, there were people such as Thanh Tuyền and Chế Linh. Sai Gon residents listened to only this kind of music at that time because they had little interest in and access to the music produced in the North of Viet Nam.[6] (Thanh 2001)

Thanh Thủy recalled her surprise when she heard that people in Ha Noi were listening to the same music that she and her peers were listening to in Sai Gon:

People in the North were also listening to this kind of music. In fact, shortly after Liberation [the April 30, 1975, communist victory], I went to the North for an official trip and realized that Northerners had listened to the Sai Gon music since as early as the midsixties, quite a bit before Liberation. The Northern audience was aware of all the famous Saigonese singers like Thái Thanh, Lê Thu, Khánh Ly, Thanh Tuyền, Chế Linh. . . . People in the North were listening to this music in private. Because music has no politics and boundary, they were very interested in this kind of music. (Thanh 2001)

Because popular music is a relatively new phenomenon in Viet Nam, many of those who began the movement are alive today. Essentially, living legends of Vietnamese popular music still perform and influence the following generations. Because this group lived a large part of their lives in Viet Nam, the need to reconnect is more acute.

Sai Gon Music Replanted in the United States

Because of the importance of Vietnamese music for the early refugee population and because refugees who had been in the music industry wanted to continue their businesses abroad, sounds of the homeland soon spread through the burgeoning Vietnamese American communities, reconnecting them with the past. Popular music at this time did more than just entertain; it also connected refugees and exiles to the homeland they thought they had lost. This connection ultimately turned into a desire to preserve the Vietnamese culture that existed before the communist takeover. Popular music became important in this endeavor. As John Baily points out:

Music is itself a potent symbol of identity; like language (and attributes of language such as accent and dialect), it is one of those aspects of culture . . . [that] can, when the need to assert 'ethnic identity' arises, most readily serve this purpose. Its effectiveness may be twofold; not only does it act as a ready means for the identification of different ethnic or social groups, but it has potent emotional connotations and can be used to assert and negotiate identity in a particularly powerful manner. (Baily 1994, 48)

During the initial 1975 exodus of refugees, unanticipated departures meant most people left with little more than the clothes on their backs. Few people thought of bringing music with them. In the several years following the emigration, the few people with music recordings such as records and tapes exchanged their wares with others in the community. By 1980 some people had amassed a sizable collection of Vietnamese cassette tapes carried out during the exodus. Dubbing home cassette tapes eventually gave way to more professional operations. Some of the first overseas Vietnamese music producers in the United States had owned music businesses in Viet Nam before the fall of Sai Gon. Phu Nguyen, a longtime Southern California musician, remembers the first few years of resettlement as a time of preservation; the objective was to make quality copies of pre-1975 music (P. Nguyen 2000). This music came predominantly from the war period, so it tended to consist of maudlin ballads of lost lives, love, and country.

During the late 1970s and early 1980s, more Vietnamese immigrants with previous experience in the music industry in Viet Nam reestablished their trade abroad. The Thúy Nga Productions group, for example, had some fame in Viet Nam pre-1975 and continued its craft in France. Once transplanted to France, Thúy Nga's founder, To Van Lai, a former professor in Viet Nam, participated in building the fledgling music house. In 1979 he salvaged in France original tapes of Vietnamese singers, as did many Vietnamese immigrants in the United States. He dubbed them onto cassette tapes and distributed them among the French Vietnamese population (Mui 2001). With a keen sense for the diasporic market, Lai created a division of Thúy Nga Productions called Paris by Night. He explained the reasoning behind its creation:

> The meaning of Paris by Night is this: I used to live in the French Vietnamese community. In the day, this group went to work. They take the train to work, which the French called the *métro*. Then they go home, they go to sleep, *dodo*. After sleep, in the morning, you go to your job called the *boulot*. So your life is three things, *métro*, *dodo*, and *boulot*, over and over again. . . . I wanted to know how a Vietnamese living outside of his country would find entertainment. They go to exercise or hang out at the beach. During the day they go to work, and in the evening they look for entertainment. That is why I came up with the title Paris by Night. Those who lived in Paris needed distractions. Paris by Night is based on the desire for this type of leisure distraction. (Lai 2000)

This kind of thinking shows a clever melding of a Parisian existence with the overseas Vietnamese desire for music. Or as Martin Stokes explains, "Musical images do not just reflect knowledge of 'other places' but perform them in significant ways" (1994, 5), meaning that the types of music that people wanted were the ones that reflected their circumstances and the need to escape their situation and lament their perceived glorious and glamorous past.

Lai explained that by producing outside the overseas Vietnamese music center of Southern California, and to a lesser degree, Northern California, Thúy Nga Productions created the possibility of a global Vietnamese diasporic musical presence. The label initially used male and female singers in France and elsewhere in Europe but then began importing musicians from other parts of the diaspora, particularly the United States. They began producing music videos in 1989 to augment their catalog of records. This move proved to be the most profitable and influential direction the company has taken to date. Success ensued so quickly that a few years later Lai moved headquarters to Orange County, California, the center of the overseas Vietnamese market, where the company has been operating since. Though capitalizing on new video technology, most early PBN videos continue to focus on Vietnamese songs written before 1975.

Considering the circumstances of their departure from Viet Nam and the desire to hold on to their history and sense of nationhood, music from the war years not surprisingly continues to be popular among overseas Vietnamese long after the war ended. So popular and persistent is this genre of ballads that Vietnamese American popular music could aptly be described as a "culture in a bubble,"[7] in which a person's cultural practices, references, and beliefs remain in a certain period or era. In the case of the early the Vietnamese refugees, the Viet Nam War period was that era. C. A. Zwingmann called it "nostalgic fixation," or acute focus on a period's culture caused by post-traumatic stress disorder (withdrawal behavior) and cultural bereavement (strong idealization of reference persons, objects, and situations) (as discussed in Eisenbruch 1991). Indeed, for more than two decades after 1975, the same songs—either Western or Vietnamese songs popular in the nightclubs of Sai Gon during the Viet Nam War—were heard in coffee shops and nightclubs and sold in music stores of the diaspora. The nostalgic use of these songs arose from feelings of loss and desire to maintain the culture.

Songs from Viet Nam involving nostalgic sentiments were soon accompanied by newly composed music in diaspora with explicit themes of a lost nation, patriotism, and the refugee experience. Nationalistic in nature, these new songs carried with them images of a glorious past and hopes of returning to the homeland. So as the first group of refugees, or 75ers, were dealing with the shock of losing their country and having to create a new life in a foreign land, composers like Pham Duy were already reflecting on these conditions. Written in 1977, "Ta Chống Cộng Hay Ta Trốn Cộng" (Are We Running from Communism or Are We Resisting Communism) attempts to answer a question plaguing that generation, especially the men.

Ta chống cộng hay ta trốn cộng	*Are we running from communism or*
	are we resisting communism
Đây là điều ta phải hỏi	*This we must ask ourselves*
Nếu ta sống như con chuột nhắt	*If we live like a little mouse*

Quên đời bằng ly rượu buồn tênh	Washing away our sorrows with wine
Hay vùi đầu trong cuộc đỏ đen	Or submitting ourselves to games of chance
Nô lệ tiền, gái đẹp, gái hoang	Being a slave to money and women
Ta nếu sống như dân ngoại quốc	If we live like foreigners
Quên mình là con của rồng tiên	Forgetting our roots
Quên đồng bào đau khổ triền miên	Forgetting the suffering of our countrymen at home
Ta được quyền đơn độc ngủ yên	Then we can carry on with our lonely lives
Ta đã thắng khi ta vượt thoát	But we won when we escaped danger
Ra ngoài cùng bao bạn đồng hương	Here we are with so many friends
Nuôi hận thù ta nhủ người thương	Not forgetting the crimes against our loved ones
Ta phải về chiếm lại quê hương	We must go back to reclaim our homeland
Ta hãy cất cao lên lời hát	Let us sing in a rising voice
Của loài người yêu chuộng tự do	Of a freedom-loving people
Dân quyền và dân tộc của ta	Human rights and our humanity
Ta phải về xây lại đời ta	We must return to rebuild our lives
Ta chống cộng ta không trốn cộng	We resist communism and do not run from it
Ta và cả trăm ngàn đồng hương	We, you and I and the hundreds of thousands of our compatriots
Ta chống cộng ta không trốn cộng	We resist communism and do not run from it
Mai này rồi ta về Việt Nam mến yêu	One day soon we will return to our beloved Viet Nam[8]

Pham Duy answers definitively for himself that he and his fellow exiles left their country as an act of resistance and harbor hope of triumphant return.

Another participant in the new genre of diasporic music was Viet Dzung, a young refugee musician. Though he like many coming from the 1975 exodus once belonged to the privileged class of Sai Gon, Dzung struggled in his first few years of resettlement in the United States. By the early 1980s his brand of popular music, called *hưng ca*, or renovation music, had become widespread. It spoke to a politically unified community that abhorred the Vietnamese communist regime. According to Dzung, "The Vietnamese American community wants a democratic Viet Nam. So we use our popular music as a tool to fight for what we believe in and represent the community as well as those who remain in Viet Nam and cannot speak for themselves" (Dzung 2005).

In the first twenty years of resettlement, the cultural gatekeepers among the overseas Vietnamese tended to adhere to a staunch anticommunist perspective.

As Thuy Vo Dang finds in her work with San Diego's Vietnamese anticommunist groups, a primary goal of these people is to have the "right" history of Viet Nam and the Vietnamese American experience preserved. This includes a strong anticommunist position on virtually all fronts (T. V. Dang 2005). Consequently, if anyone falls out of line with their views, they pressure the individual or group to take a more strongly anticommunist stance. Truc Ho, director of Asia Music Corporation and Asia Entertainment (Trung tâm Asia), an overseas Vietnamese music company, exhibited this attitude:

> The main purpose of Asia Productions is to gap the bridge between the young and old generations. We try to promote to the new youth. If they want to sing about love and human rights for Viet Nam, I will help them. But if they want to sing about communism, I will not produce them. (Ho 2001)

Almost as soon as the first Vietnamese settled in the United States, they longed for the music scene they had left in Viet Nam. Their desire to find a foothold in the United States manifested itself in the creation of new music venues. Linh Pham, a Bay Area resident since 1973 and a self-proclaimed party girl with a passion for the cha-cha, recalled the musical events she attended during the early years of resettlement in the United States:

> I was young and always looking for a party but nothing was going on before 1975. Right after 1975, when everyone began arriving, we tried to connect with friends by hosting small parties at each other's houses. Then by 1977 it seemed like every month there were community-hosted events at local churches or schools that had live bands and even room to dance. (L. Pham 2005)

These smaller venues gave way to the resurrection of once-popular nightclubs of Viet Nam. Nightclubs with names like Queen Bee, the Ritz, Caravelle, and Lido appeared in Orange County and San Jose, California, as well as other parts of the nation, and became the transplanted locale of one of the favorite pastimes of urban Saigonese. Once considered a lifestyle for only middle-class and wealthy urbanites, now everyone could partake in nighttime entertainment delights. New job opportunities in the United States equalized incomes, but regardless of salary, many Vietnamese Americans put a high priority on entertainment. They spent earnings on such things as nice outfits for club outings and paying high club-entry fees. Club fees commonly ran over twenty dollars, a high price tag in the 1980s. The eclectic popular music played in the clubs ranged from rock to rap, and the dance styles ran the gamut from new wave–inspired movements to the waltz (Dubin and Vanderknyff 1995; Reyes 1999). These spaces became places that Vietnamese Americans could call their own even though they were living far from Viet Nam. Phu Nguyen recalled this time:

We heard a lot of the music at clubs. In the late 1970s, we went to clubs like the Ritz, Tu Do, and a couple other clubs. Friends would come over with tapes. We rediscovered ourselves [as Vietnamese]. Before, we used to listen to KISS, Beatles, Rolling Stones. (P. Nguyen 2000)

James Lull and Roger Wallis describe the eclectic nature of this music scene in their study of San Jose's Vietnamese contemporary music of the 1980s:

In the clubs, for instance, some bands still played mainly U.S. Top 40 favorites while others leaned toward guitar-based rock classics. Still, even hard rock numbers were turned into pop songs, softening the instrumental edge and emphasizing melody and lyrics. Vocalists stayed away from rock conventions such as straining, improvising, and encouraging audiences to sing or clap along. (Lull and Wallis 1992, 225)

Mai Minh Hoang, a teenager and regular at these San Jose clubs in the 1980s, explained their appeal to young Vietnamese Americans: "I once got to go backstage at the Rex [a theater] in Southern California. For some reason, I much preferred these clubs to the mainstream [non-Vietnamese] dance [venues]." Mai was particularly fond of the eclectic mix of music played at these venues:

I liked the ballroom music. I learned to do the cha-cha, rumba, etc. It was odd—a cultural mishmash of Asians doing Latin dances in a smoky nightclub in America. But the couples seemed elegant, transported to a more romantic past. Lord knows they played "Sài Gòn Đẹp Lắm" [Beautiful Sai Gon] enough times. But that was really for the old people. The young people only took to the floor when the DJ came on. It was pretty goofy how we would form a big circle and dare someone to go inside. The dancing was pretty tame back then. People did the Boy George move, or else they did this rowing motion with their arms while they dipped their knees.[9] (M. M. Hoang 1996)

In part, the success of these nightclubs relied on the diversity of the music heard and dancing styles seen. Along with the clubs' intergenerational and Vietnamese-friendly atmospheres, their aesthetic diversity made them a favorite haunt for Vietnamese American families. In the early years of these nightclubs it was common to see young children and teenagers dancing with their parents and friends. Sunaina Maira's study of South Asian American youth culture includes a discussion of ethnic collectivity produced through and in music. She advances the idea that creating hybrid youth culture (re)appropriates culture and contests notions of authenticity (Maira 2002). For Vietnamese American youth, being around other ethnic Vietnamese while enjoying popular music sung in English and Vietnamese helped create a social space for identity formation. Hence, even when parents forbade teenage children from visiting nightclubs unchaperoned, the youths still showed up in large numbers. Mai elaborated on the experience of attending nightclubs with Vietnamese American peers during her teenage years:

> We went all over Northern California in these beat-up [Toyota] Celicas looking for new wave parties—Stockton, Monterey, all over the [San Francisco] South Bay, but mostly San Jose. There would be about nine of us in the car, everyone's spiky or poofy hairdo getting in each other's faces. I was the only one who didn't speak English with a fish sauce accent. We used to always go to the Lido Club. It was our Studio 54. I don't even know how we could have afforded to go. It was fifteen dollars to get in, and we didn't even have IDs to buy the Heinekens and XOs.[10] (M. M. Hoang 1996)

The popular music and the live performances of the singers were a vital element of the whole nightclub scene:

> There would be a live band, sometimes a headliner from Orange County like Lynda Trang Dai, that would do covers of whatever was popular—Madonna, Taylor Dane, the Cover Girls, Will to Power. The female singers were pretty extravagant—the makeup and clothes. It was ridiculous, late-80s cheese. But I'm sure my friends and I looked just as silly in our linebacker shoulder pads. My brothers used to sing and play bass in these kinds of bands, and they dated nightclub divas.[11] (M. M. Hoang 1996)

Teenagers as young as fourteen met up weekly to attend the newest nightclubs or shows. They often had one person old enough to drive and found money any way they could to pay for new clothes and entrance fees. High school kids, for instance, could count on getting in to these clubs even when they were well under the age limit. Word got around that after 11:00 P.M. clubs like Lido let people in free, leading youths to congregate in front of them.

When clubs were not an option for some reason, people looked for privately organized parties in large warehouses featuring a disc jockey or they held parties themselves, exercising their strong urge to see and be seen. Even when venues had gang activity and occasional gunshots, the youths were not deterred from attending weekend dance parties.

In addition to clubbing, Vietnamese American youth identity involved balancing the expectations and conditions of two very different cultures. Mai explained the experience of being part of this subculture in the United States—part of the "1.5 generation" (Chan 2006):

> Why did we go through that whole Lido phase? Because we were the in-between generation. It was a necessary transition. We were teens in America, so we did teenage things. Sneaking out, drinking, smoking, partying.

But we were Vietnamese teens, so we did those things within the context of being Vietnamese. (M. M. Hoang 1996)

Mai related the clubbing experience to other aspects of her Vietnamese American identity:

But it wasn't just the music or the language. For me, being Vietnamese in America also suggested something seedier. I knew so many poor kids. They lived in stinking tenements on East 12th Street [in downtown Oakland, California]. They hung around karaoke bars in the daytime. The guys went to jail; the girls got pregnant. Most of them were on welfare. The Vietnamese I knew were the underclass. They were not the Americanized overachievers, which technically I was. But I didn't know how to be comfortable with that yet. That's why I snuck out, ran away, and spent so much time under the strobe lights at Lido. Because there [at Lido], everyone seemed to belong, if only to some netherworld land of gangstas. At least it was authentic—a world we sort of created; our own little subculture. Come to think of it, Lido Club was kind of like our Cotton Club. Except it was San Jose instead of Harlem. Although the zoot suits were the same.[12] (M. M. Hoang 1996)

Adding to regular nightclub offerings, producers occasionally organized music variety shows. Venues for such shows began modestly in factories and warehouses but eventually moved to convention halls and grander spaces like symphony halls to meet the demands of the attendees. These shows often featured a dozen acts or more. PBN produced some of the more elaborate ones. Their shows had to be grand because fans bought as many videotapes of these concerts as they did the artists' CDs. Lai described the evolution of his shows:

It cost me $10,000 to make the first video because I used local talent. Now [in 2000] when I make a show, I have one hundred airline tickets. I invite people from . . . [Orange County] to [go to] Canada or [to come] from France to here [in Orange County] or [to go from] here to France. Before, I would call people nearby. Those who were far away I did not contact. Before, we had eight songs per video. Now [in 2000] we have twenty-five songs in a program. We have dancers and all sorts of extras. (Lai 2000)

Not everyone could attend such events owing to their high costs and for other reasons like distance, so videos of the events were highly sought and became ubiquitous. Lai described the success of the PBN series:

PBN influence is widespread—in Finland, Norway, Switzerland, Spain. Ask anyone who's Vietnamese living anywhere in the world—even in

Japan—if they have seen PBN. They will say yes. Families view our videos.
The older members buy the videos to the point of collecting all of them,
from the first one to the most current one. (Lai 2000)

These videos are in nearly every home of the overseas Vietnamese diaspora.
Furthermore, although the videos are illegal in Viet Nam, almost everyone living there has at least heard of them. Pirated, black market videos appear in
restaurants, bars, cafes, and many other public places.[13] The home, however,
remains the most popular place to view the videos. This chapter opened with
a family viewing the videos as connoisseurs of the overseas Vietnamese music
industry and its actors. This scenario is played out in millions of homes of overseas and domestic Vietnamese in dozens of nations.

Karaoke bars eventually augmented the nightclub scene. When karaoke
machines first became available, many Vietnamese Americans could not af-
ford them; people had to visit karaoke bars, which proliferated in Vietnamese
American communities. Karaoke bars combined two favorite Vietnamese social spaces: coffee shops and music nightclubs. People seated at coffee tables
wait their turn to appear on large-screen monitors showing Vietnamese American videos with printed lyrics. Most of these rooms are dimly lit and sparsely
decorated. Young women, often in tiny miniskirts, come by to serve expensive
drinks and chat with customers. These jobs exemplify the gender divide in the
labor force (Duong 2003). Though popular among Vietnamese American men,
these establishments were not perceived as family entertainment. Still, any
adult could live out the fantasy of being a famous singer and have raucous fun
with friends.[14] Paris by Night videos in particular showed glamorous Vietnamese Americans in exotic locations singing love songs to their partners. Such images contrasted greatly with the lives of the many PBN consumers who worked
in menial jobs for low pay.

Just as technology enlivened the social aspects of the popular music scene, it
eventually made popular music enjoyment more private by enabling karaoke in
the home. In their essay "'I Want the Microphone': Mass Mediation and Agency
in Asian-American Popular Music," Deborah Wong and M. Elliot observe that
home karaoke usage happened primarily because of the dramatic drop in cost.
Pioneer came out with Laser Karaoke in 1982, the first laser disc machine. Because of its accessibility, it took off immediately, competing with the already
established videotape market (Wong and Elliot 1994). Its accessibility helped
boost the popular music industry through its production of karaoke laser discs.
The popularity of Vietnamese karaoke publications grew dramatically into the
mid-1990s, when Vietnamese music stores had as many karaoke products as
they did CDs, tapes, and videos. The technology allowed many Vietnamese
Americans to reproduce the feel of the nightclub in their living rooms. Karaoke
bars had allowed community members to express their love of popular music;
now this enjoyment could be had in homes.

Internet distribution of sounds and images followed CDs and karaoke machines. By 2005 young people were glued to their computer terminals to watch their favorite popular music videos on the web for free. Many illegally download video clips for repeated viewing. YouTube, the premier video-sharing website, for instance, had hundreds of PBN clips before Thúy Nga Productions removed all unauthorized images in 2009 (Kornhaber 2010). Clarence Dung Taylor, an overseas Vietnamese agent who books talent almost exclusively from Viet Nam for the overseas market, says young people would rather watch their favorite singers for free than pay retail prices for the DVDs or CDs (C. Taylor 2007). Shortly after web-based entertainment was popularized, the older generation joined youth in accessing popular music videos on the web. However, in contrast to watching with friends and family on a large television or singing karaoke in a group, accessing sites like YouTube is usually a solitary activity. One shares videos by e-mailing, instant messaging, or posting the URL of the video on social networks. This starkly differs from the communal, physical closeness experienced in years leading up to the Internet.

Popular musical tastes in the Vietnamese diasporic community also expanded significantly. In the 1980s European new wave music found a long-standing niche in the community. A local musician spoke of that time:

> New wave was so good, and we could handle listening to it and playing it. It was like CC Kat, Modern Talking, Bad Boy Blue, and a whole bunch of other bands. We [Vietnamese Americans] grabbed whatever worked and made it our own. I had a band, and we played this stuff because it was the only way to get to play [for a Vietnamese American audience]. (P. Nguyen 2000)

Attracted by the heavy use of synthesizers and easy-to-understand lyrics, overseas Vietnamese found Eurodisco appealing. Groups that could not find a market in the mainstream American audience were able to pack ten-thousand-seat stadiums full of Vietnamese Americans in San Jose and Anaheim, California (Lull and Wallis 1992).

Desire to create, re-create, or combine musical styles to produce a distinctively hybrid Vietnamese American sound emerged. Many, particularly younger people, hungered for originality because Vietnamese American popular music was perceived by some musicians as a poor imitation of popular Western songs even though it persistently sold well. Phu Nguyen lamented the dearth of new songs circulating in the community in his discussion of the well-known Vietnamese American composer Duc Huy:

> We were able to survive with just the new material from Duc Huy. In the Vietnamese mainstream there was only Duc Huy who wrote good music. He was respected by the overseas community even though some thought his music was too commercial. We had some quality music from the 1960s

and 1970s, but [since then] we [have] just copied [and we] forgot to invent. . . . We didn't support writers of the pop scene [who would have provided us with fresh material]. (P. Nguyen 2000)

Even with the variety of current popular music, some Vietnamese Americans wanted to experience new sounds. They found existing songs uninspiring and the singers lacking talent. Even casual observers could see the excessive attention paid to singers' appearance rather than to their talent, as is consistent with the focus on image and marketing in the mainstream music industry as a whole. When examining Vietnamese American popular music of the 1980s, Lull and Wallis (1992) commented on the scantily dressed singers, such as the Madonna-inspired Lynda Trang Dai, featured on most CD covers at the time. Sky Nguyen, a musician with his own band in the 1980s and 1990s, said:

> The kids grew up thinking of Lynda Trang Dai as their Madonna. Lynda Trang Dai uses her sex appeal instead of her talent. The market is such that, now, if you have the looks and a good production along with a high-tech studio, you can make it. The Vietnamese market just cares about looks since 1975. Like the girls from Asia Productions, they cannot sing. The girls have sounds like a cat's wispy meow. It is not powerful enough to carry, but the studio makes them sound good. (T. S. Nguyen 2000)

The younger generation soon tired of the standards, and many either listened to only the original Western popular music that inspired Vietnamese popular music or stopped listening to Vietnamese music altogether. To Van Lai offered a possible answer for this lack of originality:

> The Vietnamese country is very romantic because life was more carefree. Life was simple, not full of modern-day demands. . . . People were not very modern; they did not even have phones. . . . In the summer, people can see birds on the windowsill. Living like that . . . those people can compose wonderful songs. (Lai 2000)

Life would change drastically for emigrants when they came to the United States. Lai elaborated:

> These same [country] people, when they come to the U.S., they cannot write good songs anymore. They have to worry about monthly bills and other sorts of things. . . . They experience stress, and in experiencing stress, you cannot have romantic inclinations. If you have to think about money all the time, the romance is lost. (Lai 2000)

From popular musical creations that tell an exiled people's stories, to the transplant of Vietnamese standard ballads to the United States, to the appeal of popular Western music new and old, Vietnamese Americans were creating their own cultural identity. This new identity reflected their traditional tastes and incorporated the new experiences of living far from Viet Nam. Even when Vietnamese Americans were heavily influenced by Western popular music, Vietnamese standards remained part of the larger picture of their musical imaginings. The standards represented a time and place that was not to be forgotten and certainly not yet forgotten. For some, the standards represented a particular history that could not be removed.

Some people predict that Vietnamese diasporic music will die within one or two generations as the young forget the language and culture of Viet Nam. Others believe that as long as Vietnamese Americans are seen as the "other" in their host countries they will find their way back to Vietnamese culture, and music is one possible path. Lai explained:

> When we first lost Viet Nam and I had the idea for Paris by Night, everyone said it would only last ten years because the second generation will grow up speaking the language of their host country. I thought that would happen too, but it has not happened. This is because you live in the U.S., for example, taking on its citizenship, language, and so on. You try to speak English, watch American TV, and read American papers to be more American. But as much as you try to be American, you don't quite feel right because you are reminded every day by others that you are different. (Lai 2000)

Facing racial tensions in their host countries, Vietnamese abroad seek a cultural center, something they can call their own away from the homeland (Basch, Schiller, and Szanton Blanc 1994). Lai described the moment when recognition dawns that the cultural base would help overseas Vietnamese reconnect with their country of origin and its music, which turns into a search for artifacts from one's cultural heritage:

> One day you'll see that in your office, the people there don't see you as an American but as an Asian person. This changes your behavior, and you'll ask yourself what is your origin. And at that point, you'll try to find the music of Viet Nam. If you are Vietnamese, you'll begin listening to Vietnamese music, reading about Vietnamese history. . . . Everywhere has good and bad people, and they will discriminate. But we also carry the discrimination in our heads. So at the point when you see that you're not French or American or German, you'll realize you're Vietnamese. . . . And at that point, you'll buy books, music about Viet Nam. Sai Gon fell in 1975, but even now I am able to sell Vietnamese music. It is because the parents buy for their parents, and their kids also are exposed to it. In turn they are used to the sounds. It's like the familiarity they have eating rice or phở [noodle soup]; you cannot forget it. You may like to eat American

food, but you'll have to have Vietnamese food. The music of Viet Nam I
thought would end after ten years of leaving Viet Nam because no one
could speak Vietnamese anymore. But there are still those that return to
speaking Vietnamese. (Lai 2000)

Basch and colleagues maintain that it is precisely this sense of not belonging
that catapults the refugee or immigrant to look elsewhere for cultural validation. The search often entails (re)looking at the home country (Basch, Schiller,
and Szanton Blanc 1994). Thus, Vietnamese diasporic music has widespread
popularity and dominance in the Vietnamese American community because
of Vietnamese Americans' need to have cultural connections; this need fosters
a constant flow of music production.

The popularity of overseas Vietnamese music lasted well into the mid-
1990s, with a resurgence ten years later and another a decade after that, pen-
etrating the black and open markets in Viet Nam and influencing the culture
of citizens there. This music had ongoing influence even though the Vietnamese government maintained such tight control over cultural production in the
country. The next section looks at the political environment in Viet Nam and
the United States after 1975 and surveys how music was produced and consumed by Vietnamese and Vietnamese Americans from 1975 to 2012.

Post-1975 Vietnamese Music

After the reunification of Viet Nam in 1975, the task was rebuilding the nation.
Aware of the importance of cultural control as a political tool during this crucial time, the victorious government made sure cultural production reflected its
social ideals. As Stokes observes, government monitoring of culture is a normal
state of affairs. "The control of media systems by the state, through ownership
of the technology and its ability to exclude through censorship rival systems, is
a tool of social control that few authoritarian states have overlooked" (Stokes
1994, 12). Yet in spite of the level of control that the Vietnamese state wields,
Vietnamese citizens have managed to maintain their individuality and assert
their own desires and personal choices.

Longtime culture critic Nguyễn Thanh Đức recalled:

After 1975 there were some minor changes. The authorities wanted to
return to the traditional music of the people. Rock music was not encouraged. For about ten years [after 1975], youth music was not allowed.
[But] around the 1980s, there were some political songs available. (T. D.
Nguyễn 2001)

Truc Ho, owner of Trung tâm Asia, recalled similar restrictions on music consumption and creation:

After 1975 the Vietnamese government did not let you listen to any kind of music except *Bác Hô* [Uncle Hô] music. You could not play classical, jazz, or rock. The communists had their own ideas and wanted us to listen to revolutionary songs. The revolutionary-inspired music is not about culture but about *đấu tranh*. The climate for making music is better now [in 2001], but music is still controlled by the government. As soon as the composers write anything against the government, they will have a problem.[15] (Ho 2001)

The new leadership believed that sad songs would dampen postwar morale, and thus it required lively songs and songs praising heroes of the revolution and proclaiming love of the newly reunified nation. This meant the government prohibited melancholy love songs popular in South Viet Nam during the war (Marosi 2000; T. D. Nguyễn 2001).

Although they implemented strict controls, government officials could not monitor all the new nation's citizens. Lam Trường, a Sai Gon resident and one of Viet Nam's most famous young musicians in the 1990s, remembered listening to myriad Western and overseas Vietnamese musicians in the late 1970s and early 1980s:

I began listening to music my sister's boyfriend brought over, [including] records of Barbra Streisand, the Beatles, Bee Gees, Carpenters, Christophe, when I was six years old. I listened to all kinds of music to learn from them. Celine Dion, Stevie Wonder, Sting, Lionel Richie, Mariah Carey [was what I listened to after 1975]. I listened to new wave music too, but my interest is in pop. When I listened to overseas Vietnamese music, it was Duy Quang, Duc Huy, Tuan Ngoc, and Khanh Ha; they influenced my musical taste a lot. (Trường 2001)

South Viet Nam had easy access to Western music before 1975, especially during the war period. However, when Sai Gon fell the government forbade Western music and particularly music made by South Vietnamese government personnel and citizens. Trần Diệu Hạnh, a businesswoman, recalled this period:

After 1975 we were not allowed to listen to the music we could before 1975, like the music from the U.S. and . . . [that] made in South Viet Nam. If you did, you would be put in jail. Most everyone had the music in the homes, and if they wanted to hear it, they would play it very low. Everyone feared being caught. If you lived in a neighborhood where everyone trusted each other, you'd play the music more openly, but most even feared their own neighbors. (Trần Diệu Hạnh 1993)

As time went on, people found ways to listen to the music of their choice, as Trần explained:

This [government restriction] lasted for five years [after 1975], after which I began hearing some Western music being played in public places, like ABBA. We were freer to play Western music by the mid-1980s. But not until late in the 1980s did I hear pre-1975 music played in public places. Also, we got some cassettes from overseas Vietnamese around 1986 or 1987 and were exposed to new wave and other new pop styles. Maybe others got it earlier, but I got ahold of these cassettes at this time. Then in 1996 I immigrated to the U.S. (Trần Diệu Hạnh 1993)

The political climate of Northern Viet Nam made it even less likely that one would be exposed to contemporary Vietnamese music with the themes of love, peace, and South Vietnamese resistance, yet music of all kinds found its way there. Thanh Thủy, of Music Fans Company in Ho Chi Minh City, recalled the irony of the North's interest in Sai Gon music while the center of the communist government and the origin of restrictive policies against music from the South: "From 1975 to 1980, Sai Gon music was completely banned in the South, whereas it was enjoyed more frequently and publicly in the North" (Thanh 2001). Similarly, Thanh Lam, a well-known diva of jazz and pop standards in Viet Nam, was able to obtain music from before 1975:

I first heard *nhạc vàng* as a kid. The music was basically really sappy love songs or about a hard life. My father was a soldier for the [North Vietnamese] military, so he forbade his kids to listen to music from the South. But in our neighborhood we continued to listen to the music, so I heard a lot of *nhạc vàng* growing up. Additionally, when I was a teenager, we listened to [new wave] songs like [*singing*] "You're my heart, you're [my] soul. . . ." We got this kind of music from bootleg tapes brought back by those who went abroad. These tapes were pretty rare, and getting originals was even rarer.[16] (Lam 2001)

Music commonly heard while the old South Vietnamese regime was in power continued to have listeners after the fall of Sai Gon, albeit behind closed doors and at low volumes.

Moreover, even though Viet Nam was politically and economically isolated, its people had access to musical favorites of the Vietnamese American community. Beginning in the late 1970s, relatives abroad sent music cassettes back home. By the late 1980s and early 1990s, the citizens of Viet Nam had ready access to pirated videos of shows such as those produced by Paris by Night.

The power of the black market allowed Vietnamese citizens to keep up with global consumer trends through, for instance, illegal acquisitions of music. In 1993 I found Paris by Night videos and other tapes and CDs from the overseas Vietnamese community openly available in the shops of Sai Gon and, covertly, in Ha Noi. When I asked for Paris by Night videos in Ha Noi, a Vietnamese citizen referred me to a small video shop in the old quarter of town. When I entered the store and inquired about Paris by Night videos, the owner stared at me for a few seconds and then asked me to follow her to the back of the store. There, she handed me a paper bag filled with bootleg Paris by Night videos for rental. During that same period in Sai Gon, I found overseas Vietnamese music openly sold in music shops and video stores and heard it in clubs, cafés, and karaoke rooms (field notes 1993b).

In more than twenty years of observing music in postwar Viet Nam, I found a strong presence of South Vietnamese and foreign music there. Living in the outskirts of Ha Noi in the early 1990s, for instance, I was awoken daily by pigs crying in a slaughter yard, UB40, and Los Lobos. The neighbors must have enjoyed the music well enough because I heard the same four or five tunes daily for six months. As in Sai Gon, eclectic musical tastes abounded. Around this same time, *nhạc vàng* was extremely popular among Ha Noi college students. Although it was decades old by this point, young people were discovering it for the first time. Ha Noi residents also enjoyed the music of established local singers like Hồng Nhung and Bảo Yến and newly emerging stars like Thanh Lam, who eventually found popularity in South Viet Nam and contributed to the Vietnamese music invasion. Tight restrictions in the North kept people from fully enjoying music from abroad; nevertheless, they eagerly consumed these cultural productions to the extent that they could.

The musical environment in the South of Viet Nam was quite different: Sai Gon residents were much more captivated by overseas Vietnamese music well into the new millennium. Paris by Night videos were extremely popular—especially in karaoke bars and at home. Most of my interviewees, who represented diverse social classes of the time in Sai Gon, preferred the music of the overseas community, which they claimed had the best singers and the most professionally performed and produced videos. To them, PBN shows looked glamorous and modern compared to the supposedly unsophisticated look of productions originating in Viet Nam. Families were always eager for the next installment of music videos from the United States. Sai Gon residents' musical tastes in many ways mirrored those of the overseas Vietnamese community in the United States. Like their overseas counterparts, residents of Sai Gon enjoyed live shows with performers singing songs popular in Viet Nam before the war: *nhạc tiền chiến*, American pop songs, and Trịnh Công Sơn songs. Music producer Thanh Thủy observed similar trends:

> The period from 1980 to 1990 was when overseas Vietnamese music had the greatest reception among the domestic audience. The whole country was listening entirely to music produced by overseas Vietnamese. Why is this? The first reason is the quality of sound recording. For a long time after *giải phóng* [liberation], there was really no recording facility in Viet Nam. We had no way of making decent recordings of music, voices. There was no studio, performing venues, places where you [could] listen to music. Another reason was out of nostalgia; the local audience craved the

voices of the singers they remembered from the old days. There were no
new singers in Viet Nam who could replace the old singers. There were
only *Việt Cộng* singers who were trained in the opera style, which didn't
appeal to people in the South.[17] (Thanh 2001)

Thanh Thủy confirmed that, contrary to widely held beliefs, people in the
North also enjoyed overseas Vietnamese music:

> The interesting thing is that the Northerners listened to the overseas Viet-
> namese music even more than Southerners because it's something very
> new to them, this style of singing, which is more expressive, soft, and emo-
> tional. Of course, they may not accept this music on a technical level be-
> cause singers in the North were formally trained, whereas many singers
> in the South sang from their emotions rather than technique. But the fact
> is that people were craving music that sounds good, expresses what they
> feel . . . not necessarily music that is very technically competent. There
> was no comparison between the sound recording technology of the over-
> seas Vietnamese and the local music. There was no local recording facility.
> (Thanh 2001)

Viet Nam's efforts after *đổi mới* (renovation) to liberalize its markets supposedly made it easier for Vietnamese citizens to listen to Western and overseas
Vietnamese music. However, the Vietnamese government still today commonly cracks down on the production and dissemination of cultural products
it deems threatening to its established order. For instance, up to 2006 Viet Nam
strictly forbade songs composed by the legendary modern musician Pham Duy.
Even the antiwar songs of Trịnh Công Sơn, a national treasure who remained
in Sai Gon through the end of his life, were censored. Hence, struggling for
personal freedom within the sphere of influence of the communist state meant
in part actively creating opportunities to listen to music suppressed by the state.

Double Music Invasions and the Offensives

The persistence of people in the face of draconian restrictions on cultural production and consumption demonstrates their drive to maintain cultural and
identity affiliation. In this section I discuss how Vietnamese artists in Viet Nam
and in diaspora crossed borders and created avenues for cultural exchange and
even hybrid cultural productions in the midst of powerful influences.

So great is the phenomenon of exchange in the case of Viet Nam and its
diaspora that some have dubbed it the Vietnamese music invasion, in reference to Vietnamese nationals entering the U.S. market, and the Viet Kieu music
invasion, in reference to the rising numbers of Viet Kieu singers returning to
Viet Nam to perform. The double music invasions began with the enormous
popularity of overseas Vietnamese music in Viet Nam. This popularity swelled

when Viet Kieu musicians finally had the opportunity to perform to what was then an essentially brand-new market and myriad new fans. Equally striking is how the diaspora too longed for different sounds and so welcomed music from Viet Nam and eventually demanded to have the singers from there perform in U.S. venues.

The initial novelty of overseas Vietnamese popular music declined with the growing popularity of local Vietnamese artists like Lam Trường, Hồng Nhung, Thanh Lam, Mỹ Linh, Thu Phương, Phương Thanh, and Trần Thu Hà.[18] By the mid-1990s overseas Vietnamese popular music appeared stagnant, whereas homeland Vietnamese popular music was innovative. In the late 1990s CDs such as Mỹ Linh's *Tóc Ngắn* took both Viet Nam and the diaspora in the United States by storm. With its R&B sound and upbeat and romantic lyrics, it was a favorite with many sophisticated listeners in the Vietnamese American community. Young people on both sides of the Pacific were drawn to the sounds of Sai Gon native Phương Thanh in particular. They seemed to have an insatiable appetite for her songs, like "Trống Vắng" (Emptiness) and "Lang Thang" (Wandering). Her appeal to youth is partly because of her raspy, hard-rock voice and rebel image. Of course, many in Viet Nam still enjoyed tunes from abroad, from either the overseas Vietnamese community or others, but those songs did not have the burning appeal of earlier years.

The rise in popularity of singers from Viet Nam began as early as 1990 according to music producer Thanh Thủy. She believes that, when competing with overseas Vietnamese popular music in 1980s, the poor quality of production caused Vietnamese music to fall hopelessly behind. This trend would change with the appearance of Tú Lợi, a wealthy businessman with little understanding of Vietnamese music. What he lacked in training and taste he made up with his keen market instinct. He could sense what people like to hear; he therefore invested in high-quality recording equipment to record musicians of Viet Nam's fledging post-1975 music industry. Similar to the beginnings of overseas Vietnamese music production, the new music that would come to dominate the popular music scene in Viet Nam apparently started in cramped spare rooms of a handful of producers.

These modest beginnings were a springboard for the Vietnamese popular music invasion in the United States. The new music produced in Viet Nam blossomed in the early 1990s; within five years, it had achieved broad popularity within the Vietnamese diaspora. Vietnamese Americans experienced a much-needed injection of new music into the community; the invasion provided more listening choices. By 2005 a second Vietnamese music invasion was characterized by an increase of Vietnamese singers sharing billing with top overseas Vietnamese singers in the United States. Starting in 2006 approximately fifty singers came to the United States annually, according to Clarence Dung Taylor, an overseas Vietnamese music promoter specializing in Vietnamese national representation (C. Taylor 2007).[19] By 2010 Vietnamese nationals were so deeply embedded into the regular lineup of Vietnamese American performers that most audience members just assumed all singers originated from the United States. Adding to the confusion was the growing number of Vietnamese singers, such as Bằng Kiều and Trần Thu Hà, who adopted American citizenship or gained permanent residence by marrying Viet Kieu.

The road to fluid cultural infusion, though, was lined with anticommunist elements within the Vietnamese American community who voiced discontent. Their strong opinions about the types of music that should be produced and consumed led to censorship, which is not limited to Vietnamese living in Viet Nam but extends to the diaspora. Although the United States is ostensibly a democracy, elements of censorship can be found in both its mainstream and ethnic communities. Limits on free expression take place in segments of the Vietnamese American community that are critical of Viet Nam's communist government. Taylor says, "I always have to be careful of the anticommunist elements" (C. Taylor 2007). Even with the increased flexibility, many people in the Vietnamese American community will never accept music originating in communist Viet Nam (Flaccus 2006). The controlling elements may have loosened their grip, but their force has not altogether disappeared. Nguyen Thanh of Kim Loi production company recalled a period of intense reactionary acts:

> Up to 1991, most all overseas Vietnamese listen to the music of artists living in the U.S. . . . In 1991 I sent Vietnamese music to some small stores in the [Vietnamese American] community. But at that time, it was very difficult to distribute Vietnamese music. The stores only wanted to support Vietnamese music made in the U.S. The singers all came from the U.S. It was not until 1993 that I could successfully distribute Vietnamese music in the U.S. . . . In 1993, 1994, and 1995 I tried to get customers in the U.S. used to music coming from Viet Nam. . . . But when I became more active in promoting Vietnamese music, the Vietnamese community here [in the United States] burned my store. In 1998 I got threatening phone calls and faxes from the people who started a fire in my store telling me to stop selling music from Viet Nam. I explained that I am only a musician and tried to get them not to destroy my store. (Thanh Nguyen 2001)

Initially, when Thanh promoted singers from Viet Nam at U.S. venues, he did so at significant risk to himself. He was concerned about the influence of these anticommunist groups.

Not until 2000 did a Vietnamese singer have the courage to perform publicly in the United States. It was sponsored by Kim Loi, and over three hundred people gathered at the opulent Athletic Club in San Jose to watch Cẩm Vân perform. Most heard of the show by word of mouth, but radio stations also announced the event at the last minute. I coaxed my rather reluctant aunt and grandmother to attend the show with me. They told me that they would love to see Cẩm Vân, but because of my grandmother's age and health problems (she was eighty-five at the time), they were afraid of the possibility of violent protestors. Still, we all attended the show and found many familiar faces from San Jose's Vietnamese American community gathered there. From young to old, attendees sat listening to the diva belt out her tunes as they sipped drinks and caught up with friends. Thanh Nguyen, who organized the event, considered the night a success, though not for the reasons expected:

> She [Cẩm Vân] was so lucky no one protested her. She was crying for joy that she was able to perform in the U.S. She was the first Vietnamese to perform in the U.S. [successfully]. We promoted her concert on Vietnamese radio and in the *San Jose Mercury News*. Tickets were going for fifty dollars, which is cheap compared to the hundred dollars we were going to charge for the East Coast concert. Lots of radio and newspaper reporters were there last night.[20] (Thanh Nguyen 2000)

On the heels of a series of successful concerts with singers from Viet Nam in 2000 and early 2001, Thanh promoted another concert in August 2001, held at the Sun Theater in Anaheim. This historic production featured Lam Trường and Cẩm Vân from Viet Nam as well as Yvonne from the United States. Two thousand or so protestors matched the audience in size. Unlike similar events that attracted protesters, however, this one had a visible security presence for the protection of the attendees. Attendees had to drive through streets lined with protesters, but their cars protected them. After driving through the mob for almost ten seconds, attendees emerged surrounded by a fleet of riot tanks and police cars. When the concert ended, guests were escorted through the back of the theater and away from the parking lot, to a spot a half mile from the protesters (field notes 2001). For these anticommunist protesters of the Vietnamese American community, culture imported from Viet Nam is a social evil that requires a social evils campaign paralleling that of Viet Nam's communist government to stop infiltration of evil influences (discussed below).

No Vietnamese or overseas Vietnamese music-production house is safe from anticommunist scrutiny. Even the popular Paris by Night suffered Vietnamese American censorship. In celebration of Vietnamese mothers, in 1997 Thúy Nga Productions released *Mẹ* (Mother), number forty in the PBN music video series (PBN 40).[21] The contents of the highly anticipated PBN video were too controversial for anticommunist groups within the Vietnamese American community. The controversy surrounded clips of a South Vietnamese military helicopter in battle followed by cuts of Vietnamese families running from burning villages during the song "Ca Dao Mẹ" (Mother's Folk Song). Anticommunist groups such as the Front claimed that this sequence depicted the South Vietnamese military as perpetrators of pain and suffering.[22] They and others carried out a full campaign to demand an apology and a recall of all PBN 40 videos.

The Front's newspaper, *Vietnam Insight*, published the following letter of protest in Vietnamese and English on the Internet:

Paris by Night 40's mistakes, especially the portion that portrayed a one-sided story about the Vietnam War in which it presented the people's sufferings and casualties as caused by the U.S.-backed South Vietnam's military action without any showing of the communist North Vietnam's atrocities, aroused anger among the anti-communist Vietnamese community overseas. About 2,000 people gathered in front of the Paris by Night store in Orange County that year [1997] to protest the misinformation and demand the return of their money. Some protestors also said they would contribute refunds of the video to the fund supporting the current anti-oppression protests in Thai Binh and other provinces in Vietnam. The community's outrage across the world has prompted Paris by Night to issue a letter of apology and a promise to edit the portion that distorts history. (C. Trần 1997)

Indeed, because of community pressure, PBN wrote a public apology and reedited the offensive sections of its video. The lesson was clear: de facto censorship within the Vietnamese American community did not allow for the creation of music seen as threatening to the core ideology of anticommunism. Images shown in beloved video productions can come under fire even when no procommunist or anti-American sentiment has been intended, so artists and producers are careful not to cross the line.

Even wearing clothing that can be interpreted as remotely procommunist warrants protest. On July 29, 2007, about one hundred protesters gathered outside the Orange County Performing Arts Pavilion in Santa Ana targeting Tommy Ngo, a Vietnamese American singer. This demonstration came on the heels of a promotional poster in which he was wearing a red belt buckle spelling out "love" with a design of a white star inside the letter *o*. Some people claim the belt resembled the Vietnamese red flag with yellow star in the center (H.-N. Vu 2008a).

Though more sporadic, mass protests in the Vietnamese community against artworks and performances deemed procommunist persist. For instance, in the summer of 2010, Đàm Vĩnh Hưng, arguably the most successful and wealthiest singer in Viet Nam, was met with protests as he toured the United States along with overseas Vietnamese in the billing. The protesters see performers like Hưng as a product of the communist regime or believe that they are in the United States merely to make money off the diasporic community. Hence, well-known anticommunist agitator Ly Tong, dressed as a woman, pretended to present flowers to Hưng while he was performing in California and then attacked with pepper spray when the singer reached down from the stage to accept the flowers ("Dissident" 2010).

Even though by the late 1990s the Vietnamese music invasion was complete, these high-exposure events sent a clear signal to the music industry and to music consumers. This lesson is a continuation of one learned even before Vietnamese refugees fled in 1975. The strong anticommunist view is based on highly traumatic experiences that cannot and should not be forgotten. Viet

Nam never had any pretense of democracy when it came to controlling cultural production, yet its brand of oppression was in many ways comparable to what went on in the Vietnamese American community and anticommunist groups. Viet Nam even had embedded policies that regulated the exposure of certain types of culture, such as its social evils campaign, meant to curb Western and overseas Vietnamese influences in Viet Nam. It included prohibitions against drug abuse, prostitution, gambling, drinking, and Western consumer values (Barr 1997). In particular, Decrees 87-CP and 88-CP of 1995 were enacted to regulate the business and circulation of films, video tapes and discs, and audio tapes and discs; sales and rentals of publications; cultural activities and services in public areas; and advertising, writing, and installation of signboards.

In 1996, in the months leading up to the National Assembly meetings, which take place every five years, a social evils campaign in Ha Noi stipulated covering foreign lettering on billboards. Authorities shrouded the huge Coca-Cola helium advertising balloon outside Ha Noi, for example. They raided music and video shops and confiscated foreign-made products. Because the campaign occurred close to the date of the assembly meeting, observers speculated that the government wanted to show its resolve in controlling cultural exposure.

When word reached the South, music and video store owners ran their businesses carefully for fear of similar raids. Trần Tuấn, a Sai Gon video store owner, commented:

> The officials are really cracking down. We used to pay them a bribe to leave us alone because we rent a lot of overseas Vietnamese and foreign videos, and they left us alone or warned us before a raid took place. Now they take our money and raid us anyway. How are we supposed to make any money with these unpredictable raids? One day they [the police] are here to check out videos [for personal use], and the next day our whole inventory is taken away [in a raid]. (Tuấn Trần 1993)

Often the campaigns boasted of high-profile crackdowns. For example, in 1997 police in Ho Chi Minh City claimed that they burned fifteen tons of banned CDs, videos, magazines, and other items as a show of the Vietnamese government's commitment to flush out culturally threatening items. The contraband consisted mostly of pornographic, violent, and anticommunist materials (P. Taylor 2001, 137). In another instance, in 2000, the nationwide directive 09/2000/CT-TTg went into effect, enacting more campaigns of cultural censorship and control. Examples include inspectors seizing 120,194 tapes, 84,054 CDs, 30 tons of printed matter, 690 video recorders, and 16 gambling machines and deleting 23,000 square meters of "illegal advertisement hoarding" (Vietnam News Service Agency 2000, 36).

The intimidating tactics of the social evils campaigns were meant to convey a message: Viet Nam is an authoritarian state, and consuming anything but sanctioned Vietnamese cultural products threatened its national identity.

Foreigners had to tread carefully if they wanted to continue living and working in Viet Nam. Moreover, locals had to be extra careful, or they could lose their livelihood or face imprisonment. As Blum and colleagues argue:

> We must judge institutions by the extent to which their policies enhance or diminish the freedom of all whose lives they affect. The unity of modern music history comes from the universality of claims to fundamental human rights, which can be realized only through continual dialogue and argument. (Blum, Bohlman, and Neuman 1991, 3)

Given this climate, it was no wonder so few Viet Kieu singers ventured to perform in Viet Nam.

Even so, the number of Viet Kieu CDs appearing in music stores, both state-owned and private ones, increased. By 2000 I easily found CDs including compilations of both Vietnamese and overseas Vietnamese contributors, furthering the Viet Kieu music exposure in Viet Nam and increasing the fan base there. With this easing of restrictions, along with help of the Committee for Overseas Vietnamese, a handful of overseas Vietnamese performers were allowed to sing regularly in Viet Nam and were even billed side by side with Vietnamese singers (Thanh 2001).

Early performers who returned to Viet Nam did so only in the context of the looming sources of influence that I have defined: heavy criticism from anticommunist groups in the United States and unstable policies on culture and Viet Kieu in Viet Nam. Elvis Phuong, having begun his reconnection with Viet Nam as early as 1996, when he made the video *Tạ Ơn Đời, Tạ Ơn Người* (*Thanking Life, Thanking Humanity*) there, was a prime target for people with strong anticommunist views abroad. In 2000, for example, after his first solo show in Viet Nam since 1975, anxious Vietnamese American club owners canceled twelve scheduled U.S. appearances. He recalled:

> Some [Vietnamese Americans] were mad and thought it was political [to sing in Viet Nam], but I'm not about politics. For four years I did not perform in Orange County [because of my performances in Viet Nam]. Radio Bolsa was very critical. They [Vietnamese American club managers] have invited me to sing, but we are not sure. Maybe we will agree soon. I told my audience in the U.S. that I just want to live my remaining days in Viet Nam and maybe be buried here too. So the U.S. audience accepts it. (Phuong 2002)

The point of the protests in the United States is that cultural collaborations with Viet Nam are not acceptable.

Acceptable or not, the trickle of Viet Kieu performers in the 1990s grew to dozens by 2010. Among them are Viet Kieu artists who were too fearful to return to Viet Nam to perform in years past, such as Tuan Ngoc. Others have even bought homes in Viet Nam so they could perform there frequently. They include Hoai Linh, Chi Tai, Huong Lan, and Elvis Phuong (Hải 2010). Thanh Hải, director of a music company who has worked with Viet Kieu singers in Viet Nam, explained their appeal:

> Certain Viet Kieu singers are so popular because they are well-known superstars, and there are so few Viet Kieu superstars left [from older generations]. Even though they have been around for a long time, they also have a newness appeal. People are willing to pay hundreds of U.S. dollars to attend their shows. (Hải 2010)

Again, we see that even in the presence of powerful influences, overseas Vietnamese and in-country Vietnamese may have found ways to cope with pressures from the Vietnamese government and anticommunists within the diasporic communities while asserting their own interests.

Transnational Strategies of Producers, Singers, and Musicians

The double invasion found real success only thirty years after the Viet Nam War ended. Songs, technology, and ideas were, however, being shared long before this exchange of performers began. This section discusses the underground and even overt connections that have created cultural bridges in the past, create them in the present, and will create them in the future.[23]

A common misconception in the Vietnamese American community is that there is a clear distinction between Vietnamese diasporic music and Vietnamese music. Just the opposite is true, because being Vietnamese American means having fluid connections with the cultural products of Viet Nam.[24] One prominent overseas Vietnamese music producer explained that he is careful to limit his contact with Viet Nam, but out of the necessity to find new material, he maintained connections with the music community there. He explained how he avoided criticism from the anticommunists in the community when working with composers in Viet Nam:

> The [Vietnamese American] community does not complain because they cannot differentiate which song comes from a Vietnamese composer and which one comes from an overseas Vietnamese composer. Singers will be criticized because you can see their faces, but songs are harder to figure out because you can't see the face of the composer. (Anonymous 2000)

Producers from both sides of the ocean are anxious to find ways to keep the Vietnamese and Vietnamese American music industries strong. They do so by studying the advantages and disadvantages of both.

The major advantage Viet Nam's music industry has is the country's large population compared to the diaspora; hence, it has a larger pool of strong vocalists and composers. In the 1990s Viet Nam's population hovered around 70 million; in 2012, it is more than 90 million (Central Intelligence Agency 2012). Although its scattered nature makes it difficult to precisely know, the overseas Vietnamese population was 1 million to 2 million in the 1990s and is about 3.7 million in 2010 ("Overseas Vietnamese" 2009–2010).

But Vietnamese American popular music has advantages over popular music produced in Viet Nam: it dominates in technology and style. Based in a technologically advanced nation, the Vietnamese American music industry has had access to the best production technology and techniques available. Vietnamese musicians in the United States are able to experiment with techniques of arranging, allowing them to move years ahead of their Vietnamese counterparts in music production. Even novice musicians can have affordable ministudios in their homes to create popular music and lay tracks at their leisure. Musicians in Viet Nam have very limited access to such equipment and training.

Many Vietnamese singers are aware of these disparities. After a successful concert with another leading Vietnamese diva, Mỹ Linh, sponsored by the overseas Vietnamese humanitarian relief organization VNHELP, Trần Thu Hà noted the benefits of working with overseas Vietnamese musicians:

> I had these preconceived ideas about overseas Vietnamese. I thought they were basically losers because of the few that came back to Viet Nam and created a bad reputation for the others. But when I arrived here [in the United States], my hosts were very kind and the audience was very receptive. Now I'm meeting with local overseas Vietnamese and mainstream musicians and producers to work on collaborative projects. I'm thoroughly impressed with what I've seen. I'm so proud of the overseas Vietnamese community for what they have created in the U.S. in such a short time. My views have totally changed. (Thu Hà Trần 2002)

The United States also dominates in style, although this is a subjective assessment. The U.S. mainstream produces some of the most widely known global popular music—the kind of music that Vietnamese singers, young and old, like to imitate. In the area of Vietnamese language songs, Vietnamese from the new generation grew up watching PBN and enjoying the glamour that went with each show. The organizers of PBN spared no expense to create and maintain a stylish, expensive look. PBN's owner, Lai, explained that a large portion of the cost of a video production is spent on style: "Each song of the video has its own background that costs a lot. Just the background alone cost $70,000 to $80,000 and the lighting costs $100,000 [in 2000]" (Lai 2000). By 2010 PBN shows cost as much as $1 million to produce (Kornhaber 2010).

These high production costs, especially in the United States, have led many Vietnamese Americans to produce their videos or popular music in Viet Nam for a fraction of the cost. Cost savings have become an important motivator for collaborating with people in Viet Nam. One of the additional benefits to making popular music videos in Viet Nam is that the location is exotic and can evoke nostalgia. The Vietnamese American community is fascinated with things from the home country. Vietnamese directors in the homeland bring a fresh look to the videos and work for a fraction of the cost of overseas Vietnamese directors. Additionally, overseas Vietnamese and Vietnamese singers now have the option of performing on opposite sides of the Pacific and hence broadening the market and their fan base.

Shortcomings on both sides have motivated musicians to compensate by borrowing ideas and resources from each other. Overseas Vietnamese and Vietnamese in the music industry have done so for a long time. Though anti-communist zealots in the Vietnamese American community present obstacles for such collaborations, these nevertheless take place regularly. Similarly, although the government of Viet Nam likes to regulate all cultural productions, it cannot stop the collaborations. Hence, the music industry has continually created cultural bridges between Viet Nam and the Vietnamese diasporic community despite these powerful influences.

Collaboration will inevitably produce interesting outcomes and help revitalize the overseas Vietnamese and Viet Nam music industries. This desire to pave the way for new sounds through creative ventures was felt by many overseas Vietnamese youths and young adult musicians. The generation mainly raised or born in the United States, for example, found listening to melancholy music symptomatic of "culture in a bubble" and unappealing. Like other young people, they are attracted to mainstream popular music or renditions of that music in the Vietnamese American music scene.

Given the nature of Vietnamese American music, Tuan Ngoc, over sixty years a musician first in Viet Nam, then in the United States, and then again in Viet Nam, worried about the future of Vietnamese American music and assimilation:

> The sad thing is this: Our children and grandchildren will be as good as the American musicians. But they will not be interested in writing for the Vietnamese American audience because the market is too small. The hope lies in Viet Nam's [artists], but they are not creating either. If Vietnamese American youths can write good songs, that would be great. But will they write for Vietnamese Americans? I believe that the more you stay in America, the more you become an American. You melt into the melting pot. (Tuan 2001)

It seems then that the thing that comforts the community in exile is also what keeps it from creating new sounds. Nevertheless, some are looking to end this paradox. But Vietnamese Americans who have ventured to create their own music complain that they cannot find a market in Vietnamese American communities. Phu Nguyen, a musician who composes and sings his own work in a blatantly Saigonese accent, is unique. Like the English and Irish who prefer American English pronunciations, Vietnamese pop standards prefer the

Northern Vietnamese accent. Phu took the chance of sounding different, but unfortunately, in doing so he failed to find a large enough market in the community. Bands like Phu's rarely get support from the major Vietnamese American production houses. Duy Tran, a sound engineer, musician, and founder of Bflat, a consortium of overseas Vietnamese artists, complained, "I've lost faith in Asia [Productions] and PBN because they have the power to make change, but they won't do it." In reaction to this lack of support for young bands, Duy Tran and others formed Bflat:

> PBN has brainwashed the Viet Kieu community . . . [with respect to] what is good. As a result, we musicians have no chance to have our original works accepted. Our 17th Parallel [rock] band was really hated by the community, and that had a lasting imprint on me. So my work with Bflat is to support artists. Artists are very vain, and I know this. I always push the artists because it's the only way to help them pursue their art. In my compilation work with Bflat, there are a lot of bands that have broken up, but I want to help them feel inspired to take up music again. (Duy Tran 2000)

Bflat's first compilation, *What the Pho?* included eclectic Vietnamese American music ranging from new wave to hard rock. Duy claims Bflat's second compilation, *No MSG*, has two purposes: "to have good music and to promote any upcoming musicians." Duy and his Bflat group have helped promote Vietnamese singers who they believe have "real talent," such as Trần Thu Hà. It seems that with respect to music, Vietnamese American youths have managed to connect with musicians in Viet Nam without the anticommunist-community political baggage carried by many older Vietnamese Americans.

These individuals and groups in Viet Nam and abroad must endure not only the struggle common to all artists but also the added pressures of the major influences identified in this book. Still, they manage to do so while making international crossings, sometimes permanently, to capture new fans. Possibly one of the most notable Vietnamese Americans to return permanently to Viet Nam is the iconic composer Pham Duy. Initially consumed with the loss of Viet Nam and adopting strong anticommunist views during the early years of exile, Pham Duy's longing for home took over as early as 1979, when he wrote "Tiếng Thời Gian" (The Sound of Time):

Có ai nhớ tiếng rao hàng buổi sáng	*Oh, how I miss the sound of the street vendors in the morning*
Tiếng xe máy rú trên đường thành đô	*The screaming sound of motorbikes on the road*
Có ai nhớ tiếng chuông chùa đầu ngõ	*Oh, how I miss the echoes of the bell from the temple near my house*
Tiếng chim hót, tiếng học trò hò la	*The sound of birds chirping, and of kids yelling*

Có ai nhớ tiếng đêm về mùa nóng	*Don't you miss the sound when the night comes in the middle of the dry season*
Tiếng mưa vỗ trên mái nhà lợp tôn	*And the clapping sound of the rain on tin roofs*
Những câu nói tiếng cha mẹ từ tốn	*The calming voice of parents*
Tiếng đôi lứa, tiếng e thẹn chờ hôn	*The hesitant sounds of lovers before the first kiss*
Giờ trong nước câm lặng tiếng rồi	*Now, there's nothing but silence at home*
Giờ ở ngoại quốc xa lạ tiếng người	*And here in a foreign land, just unfamiliar sounds*
Tôi thương nhớ lời nói	*I miss the sweet voice*
Của người yêu hờn dỗi	*Of my lover sulking*
Lời mẹ tôi thường vỗ về tôi	*And the pampering voice of my mother*
Có tôi nhớ tiếng ông bà hàng xóm	*Oh, how I miss the voice of the old couple next door*
Tiếng anh chiến sĩ, say rượu cười vang	*And the rowdy laughter of the drunken soldiers*
Có tôi nhớ tiếng bé đùa ngoài nắng	*Oh, how I miss the voice of children playing in the shade*
Tiếng êm ái, tiếng tôi gọi Việt Nam	*The soothing sounds of Viet Nam*[25]

Three decades after the fall of Sai Gon, in 2006, Pham Duy got his wish and returned to Viet Nam to live out his remaining days. When interviewed by a Vietnamese newspaper about the reasons for his return, Pham Duy answered, "Now, [Vietnamese] society has changed so much, and I want to talk about the contemporary social issues through my music. To do that, I have to come back to Vietnam" (Henry 2005; see also Ninh 2005). Just as Pham Duy no longer knows Viet Nam, the people there hardly know him. Deemed subversive, his music had been banned in Viet Nam for decades. For the few of his songs that did manage to circulate, the composer was listed as anonymous. By 2005 only trickles of his music had legally resurfaced in the country (Henry 2005).

Given its history of believing itself threatened by his music, the Vietnamese government would have been expected not to allow Pham Duy to continue with his craft in Viet Nam. Yet instead of total control, there seems an easing of censorship. By 2010 the Vietnamese government had legalized fifty of his songs, and more are expected to be liberated in coming years (P. Tran 2010). Pham Duy's return did not signal his retirement—quite the contrary. True to his prolific nature, the legendary composer has already begun writing about his return and residency in Viet Nam. In the song "Chiếc Cặp Tóc Thơm Tho" (A Richly Scented Hair Clasp) he wrote:

Thế rồi có ngày hồi hương	*And so one day I went back home*
Cuộc đời trăm phương nghìn hướng	*Life takes you on a thousand paths*
Tạm thời ngừng cuộc lãng du	*For once I put aside my wandering*
Cho qua đi những ngày mưa nắng	*To let the days of storm and sunshine pass*
Ngày đầy hay ngày thưa vắng	*The days, now full, now desolate*
Cho đi theo cảnh đất trời xa	*To travel to a land on the horizon*
Quên đi cảnh đất trời xa	*And forget a land on the horizon*
Thế rồi tôi bước về quê	*And so I turned my steps back home*
Sau nhiều tang thương dâu bể (ề)	*Upheavals without end now past*
Qua bao vật đổi sao rời	*Transformed who knows how many times*
Quê hương mình vẫn là nơi	*The homeland still is just a place*
Để tìm về lẽ sống mà thôi	*To find out only why you live*
Mình tìm ra chính mình thôi	*To find out only who you are*
. . . Thế rồi tôi vẫn còn đi	*. . . And so I still went on*
Trên đường giang hồ đây đó	*On many aimless roads*
Mang theo hương vị quê mùa	*The flavor of the land within me*
Hương nồng từ đất quê ta	*The warm aroma of the country*
Đến từ cặp tóc em thơ	*Coming from the hair clasp of a child*
Chiếc cặp tóc thơm tho	*A richly scented hair clasp*[26]

These lyrics can readily be interpreted as being about having to let go of past animosities to rediscover one's homeland. Thus, the establishment of goodwill among former enemies has been solidified.

Music critic Phi Tran offered a possible reason for the warming of relations between Pham Duy and the Vietnamese government:

> Slowly Vietnamese officials realize that, like it or not, Pham Duy stands at the center of Vietnamese culture as Nguyễn Du stands in the center of Vietnamese literature. . . . Viet Nam needs legitimacy for their regime, and this means defining the identity of Viet Nam and the Vietnamese people. The government sees the new generation rapping or singing canto pop, and they don't understand it. They worry these kids will turn their backs on Vietnamese culture. But they [Vietnamese officials] understand the lyrics of Pham Duy, like "tình ca" [love songs] or the lists of children's songs he's composed.[27] (P. Tran 2010)

Indeed, Pham Duy's work and his decision in 2006 to return to Viet Nam to live permanently have brought Viet Nam closer to the diaspora in a monumental way, via national culture making.

Vietnamese music both at home and abroad has developed in magnificent ways. From preserving pre-1975 music to creating anticommunist protest songs, to creating new sounds, this music continues to evolve. The many covert collaborations of music makers in Viet Nam and in diaspora and creating, disseminating, and enjoying the music have sometimes required dodging political bullets on both sides of the ocean, Many musicians and music lovers have maneuvered through this terrain to create and find the music that expresses their artistic, social, and cultural identity.

Conclusion

> Without the empowerment gained through music, it is impossible
> to keep the past alive in the present, or to recognize and respond
> to the realities that are transforming the present into the future.
> —Stephen Blum, *Ethnomusicology and Modern Music History*

Vietnamese popular music has managed to survive and evolve in Viet Nam and the diaspora since the American War and reunification. These hybrid cultural productions known as popular music have entailed shared cultural history between the global diasporic communities, including the productions' importance in the black market. But this was accomplished because of and in spite of harsh regulations from the U.S. and Vietnamese governments restricting trade and in spite of censorship by Viet Nam's government and anticommunist forces in the diaspora. Viet Nam attempted to protect its national communist identity by blocking pre-1975 music and overseas Vietnamese popular music deemed foreign or foreign influenced. Government restrictions were established after reunification, but people continued to be attracted to tradition-based popular music, including music from the overseas Vietnamese communities.

Through efforts to maintain a culture of anticommunism and hold on to memories of an idyllic past, the Vietnamese American community also greatly affected overseas Vietnamese popular music creations and production. The anticommunist ideology not only added to the "culture in a bubble" phenomenon; it also stalled collaboration between musicians in Viet Nam and those in diaspora. Conversely, while Vietnamese Americans complied with the dictates of anticommunist groups and their ideologies, they were curious about popular music being created in Viet Nam. Overseas Vietnamese business people saw opportunities for expanding musical products for the overseas Vietnamese market in the United States and brought popular music from abroad to the United States. With loosening restrictions from all three fronts—the U.S. government, the Vietnamese government, and anticommunist Vietnamese Americans—overseas Vietnamese found themselves lured back to their home country to perform.

The demand for variety helps popular music products like Paris by Night DVDs to remain popular and Bflat artists to remain in demand. Audiences calling for a diverse array of singers from the homeland and their host country bring about new productions for diasporic communities globally.

Transportation, music, and entertainment technologies allow artists to travel with ease, connect with people abroad more frequently, and view and listen to these different musical developments in many more spaces, like the Internet.

Once seen as two distinctive forms, overseas Vietnamese and homeland Vietnamese music are now increasingly melded by transnational culture flows. I predict that the survival and development of music in both places will require continued collaboration and support for creating new blends and opening up new venues. Reacting to the sometimes static and formulaic productions of overseas Vietnamese popular music, people in the Vietnamese diaspora are actively forming networks that reach Viet Nam to share their creations outside the established overseas Vietnamese music industry. Networks of artists like Bflat offer alternative spaces for musical innovation. Overseas Vietnamese music connections will become more diverse because of transnational links to Viet Nam. The future for diasporic and Vietnamese music looks bright. With the relative loosening of cultural control in Viet Nam and general easing of anticommunist influence in the diaspora, these various sites and styles of music production will allow Vietnamese culture consumers more choices in the future.

3

Social Transformations from Virtual Communities

I ride my bicycle briskly along the gray streets of Ha Noi toward its town center. A young Vietnamese American graduate student in my second session of long-term field work in Viet Nam, I head first, as usual, to the Center for Southeast Asian Studies. Aside from using their resources for research, I also frequently access the Internet with their sole computer. [It is 1996, one year before Viet Nam established its first permanent international Internet connection, so Internet cafés are nonexistent and home computers exceedingly rare, let alone ones with Internet access.] This one computer is my only connection to the information superhighway. One of the first things I routinely do is check postings from a Usenet-based virtual community named Vietnam Forum (VNForum).[1] I and the other international members joined VNForum because of our common interest in Viet Nam.

On this particular day I come across an article written by an overseas Vietnamese high school teacher discussing Hồ Chí Minh's life. The teacher's analysis is thought provoking and evenhanded, a rare state for postings because anticommunist sentiment remains high among the exile community, causing most Vietnamese Americans to criticize the former leader of communist Viet Nam mercilessly in their writing. A week after reading this post, I am taken aside by one of my handlers[2] and presented with a printout of the Hồ Chí Minh piece along with some other random postings on VNForum. "Problematic" portions of the essay in question are highlighted in yellow for my perusal, and my interrogators demand that I explain myself. I simply say, "I did not write that," which is true. Since it is an unacceptable answer, I am threatened with fines and even deportation. (Field notes 1996b)

The event described in the passage above speaks to the obstacles that many in Viet Nam and in diaspora experienced in their initial attempts to connect with one another via the Internet. Creating lines of communication and sharing ideas between Viet Nam and its diaspora had been challenging in the decades following the Viet Nam War. Isolation lessened with developments in information communication technology (ICT) beginning in the 1960s that evolved into the proliferation of Internet access in the 1990s (Abbate 1999).[3] From the early 1990s, ICT aided transnational connections and community-building activities, allowing dialogue where none had previously existed between Vietnamese Americans, Vietnamese nationals, and other interested persons. The Internet gave rise to our current "network society" shaped by religion, cultural upbringing, political organizations, and even social status (Castells 1996).

This chapter examines the first of these transnational virtual communities relating to Viet Nam, VNForum.[4] An influential, moderated Usenet list, VNForum consisted mostly of overseas Vietnamese intellectuals and professionals as well as international scholars and Vietnamese government affiliates.[5] VNForum developed modestly in 1992 through the work of its Vietnamese American founders, Hoanh Tran, a lawyer, and Tin Le, a computer programmer. They facilitated transpacific exchanges, for example, providing training support in the United States for some of the first Vietnamese computer science engineers. These engineers subsequently set up companies with computer servers in Viet Nam and helped the early Vietnamese information technology (IT) community link to the rest of the world.

In addition to building the virtual community through friendly postings and online networking projects, members of VNForum promoted real-world social and political change in Viet Nam. As Barry Wellman sees it, "Internet communication has benefited from and facilitated the social transformation of work and community, from groups in little boxes to globalized, ramified, branching social networks" (Wellman 2002, 95). This chapter discusses a notable sociopolitical movement that emerged from VNForum, the No-Nike labor rights campaign. This movement organized via the Internet and collaborated with the Vietnamese government and overseas Vietnamese for labor rights. It was one of the first acts of international cooperation among these parties. Additionally, we look at how VNForum strategically evolved into Vietnam Business, another virtual community. Having more Vietnamese representation than VNForum, VNBiz better represents the diversity of Vietnamese political thought and the transformations taking place within the country. Finally, this chapter tells how VNForum's cofounder Hoanh Tran, joined a legion of bloggers and used the Internet to reach Vietnamese through the creation of Đọt Chuối Non (http://dotchuoinon.com).[6] This happened during Viet Nam's aggressive crackdown on dissident bloggers within its borders.

Early events in the development of ICT in Viet Nam, the virtual community VNForum, the anti-Nike campaign and its progeny VNBiz, and the eventual development of Đọt Chuối Non taken together illustrate that, despite prevailing political ideologies and forces in Viet Nam and the United States, including anticommunist groups within the Vietnamese ethnic communities in the United States, individuals used virtual communities to transcend national and community restrictions and mobilize people in Viet Nam and abroad. This was done by bringing them together to express opinions and concerns. They in turn created virtual acts that then passed seamlessly from the virtual to the real world, igniting sociopolitical transformation in Viet Nam and the United States. As Christopher Mele notes, "Communities rarely exist exclusively in cyberspace. It is important to investigate the ways in which social groups in cyberspace spill out into the 'real' world and vice versa" (quoted in Kollock and Smith 1999, 19).

The Rise of ICT in Viet Nam and in Diaspora

In 2010 Viet Nam had an estimated population of 89.5 million, and of this, 24 million—27 percent of the population—were Internet users. More than a million had blogs. This was up from 200,000 Internet users in 2000, or only 0.3 percent of the population (Linh 2008; Internet World Stats 2010). Information technology has evolved quickly in two short decades, and now the Internet plays an important role in people's lives globally. "Cyberspace not only assists in the emplotment and mediation of diaspora, it actively keeps the ideology of diaspora alive" (Landzelius 2006, 21).

Immediately after the fall of Sai Gon, refugees who fled had little or no communication with people remaining in Viet Nam. Hoa Newman, who taught Vietnamese language in Monterey, California, before 1975, recalled the confusion of that time:

> I watched the Viet Nam War on television every day. I could not believe what was happening. I [had] visited my parents in 1974 and then in 1975 Sai Gon fell. I kept thinking, "My god, I've lost my country. I can never go back, and I can never see my parents again." Thank god I had a brother who was living in Paris. He successfully maintained contact with my family through letters. So I just sent letters to him and he sent news to my family in Viet Nam. (Newman 2000)

Overseas Vietnamese wanted to maintain relations with each other and friends and family in Viet Nam, but communication was difficult in the early years after resettlement. The earliest communications took place by mail, often routed through third-party countries that had better relations with Viet Nam. By the mid-1980s, families in the United States could notify relatives in Viet Nam of an impending telephone call through a letter or telegram. Family members in Viet Nam would wait at the post office for a call to come in. In 1986 Viet Nam had only nine international telephones, and those had unreliable connections (Grant 1996). Lack of access to new forms of communication technology and more immediate subsistence issues during the lean postwar years meant few owned personal telephones or even considered telephone hookups a priority.

Although communications originating from Viet Nam were equally difficult, those in diaspora had much greater access to technology. Technology had played a major role in the lives of Vietnamese Americans since the first refugees, known as parolees,[7] resettled overseas in 1975. Initially, they were scattered across the United States, but later they were drawn to the temperate weather and job opportunities in California. The majority settled in Orange County in Southern California and in the Bay Area in Northern California. According to the 1990 census, Vietnamese in the San Francisco Bay Area numbered 84,662 (U.S. Bureau of the Census 1993a, 1993b). This number increased to 146,613 in 2000 and 169,099 in 2010, making the Bay Area the second-largest Vietnamese community in the country (U.S. Bureau of the Census 2010b).[8]

In the 1980s Northern California's Silicon Valley housed the emerging microchip and computer manufacturing industries with major companies such as International Business Machines (IBM) and Hewlett-Packard. Many from the growing Vietnamese American refugee population, mostly women, found work as low-level technicians in the high-tech assembly lines of Silicon Valley (Jayadev 1999). Later, as more Vietnamese Americans obtained predominantly science and technology degrees, they found employment as engineers and programmers in some of the many high-tech companies of the region (Saxenian 1999).[9] In 2000 there were about fifteen Vietnamese American chief executive officers among the estimated ten thousand Vietnamese working in Silicon Valley's IT industry (Biers and Cohen 2000).

When Viet Nam plunged into the information age, the government restricted websites that presented information deemed dangerous to the Vietnamese state. The groups and materials perceived as threats then and now include overseas Vietnamese anticommunist groups, humanitarian organizations, religious institutions, and ethnic minorities (OpenNet Initiative 2007). Fearing open access to information by its citizens, the Socialist Republic of Viet Nam (SRV) initially tried to stifle ICT development and then tried to control its rise.

People from around the world and in different industries who wanted to open communication channels in Viet Nam fostered ICT development in Viet Nam. Some of the initial advocates for ICT in Viet Nam included Vietnamese American engineers in the United States and at the Australian National University (ANU) and American expatriate scholars of Viet Nam studies. Since people at the forefront of ICT development lived all over the globe, Internet development in Viet Nam was essentially an international endeavor involving both friends and enemies of the state.[10] Scholars, programmers, and activists worked together to connect Viet Nam with the rest of the world via the Internet. The government, however, had little understanding of ICT; so even as the Vietnamese government promoted ICT development, it did so with the aim of regulating information.

In Viet Nam in 1993, few private homes had telephones. One reason for their relative scarcity was that telephone installation in a home or office cost over one hundred dollars, nearly the annual income of most Vietnamese at the time, and applicants had to wait up to a year for installation. Knowing or bribing an employee of the post office, which oversaw installation, could expedite the process but only a little, because demand far exceeded resources and extensive paperwork was involved (field notes 1993a). In 1993 the country's 180,000 private telephones served approximately one in five hundred residents (Shimbun 1993).

Communication technology thus advanced much more slowly in Viet Nam than in most of the rest of the world, and the country did not have national or international mass communication channels until 1996. Along with ideological differences and logistical obstacles, this lack of communication technology prohibited Vietnamese in the United States from freely creating social networks with Vietnamese nationals. The Vietnamese government considered links with the overseas population to be dangerous, to the point of forbidding the formation of even Vietnamese American groups in Sai Gon. An overseas Vietnamese who had returned to Sai Gon in 1996 to work commented:

> I tried to organize a California Vietnamese group. You know, it would be social, and we could show our Californian pride. Next thing you know, I got visitors from the city police questioning my motives. It was a dream for me to have such a group. But after that visit from the city police, I quickly abandoned any idealistic notion of forming any overseas Vietnamese groups.[11] (Doan Tran 1996)

Information technology and advances in computers directly affected the lives of Vietnamese in diaspora. Much of the development of these technologies took place in Northern California. Vietnamese American computer scientists in Silicon Valley at companies such as Sun Microsystems and at universities such as the Massachusetts Institute of Technology, Boston University, and the University of California at Irvine and Berkeley all came together more than twenty years ago to establish links via the Internet. In 1986 one member of this group, Tin Le, later a cofounder of VNForum, created VietNet, an e-mail list that grew to over one thousand participants in two years.[12] Seven computer servers in Boston supported it. Tin explained his motivations: "We just wanted to connect to each other. It was pretty hard to connect, especially in regions where few Vietnamese resided. We wanted to talk to each other and reach out to one another" (Tin Le 2009). VietNet answered the call to connect.

List administrators encouraged friendly exchanges, but even at this early stage the VietNet mailing list experienced "flame wars" between perceived anti- and procommunist participants.[13] In the worst instances, administrators deleted potentially disruptive postings. In general, participants monitored themselves because in the late 1980s and early 1990s people had to subscribe using a work or school e-mail address, which revealed their identity. The list ran more or less as an open, unmoderated mailing list for at least three years before its administrators moved it to the Usenet group soc.cult.vietnam.[14]

Although many VietNet postings had anticommunist overtones, it was clear to the administrators and those who posted regularly that most subscribers had genuine concerns about the future of Viet Nam. Tin Le was a VietNet administrator from California when he began communicating with Washington, D.C., lawyer Hoanh Tran, who had formed the Vietnamese American Educational Foundation (VAEF) in 1989 to improve relations with Viet Nam and promote development:

> In 1992, the Vietnamese American Education Foundation had five Viet Kieu in charge and fifty members. We shipped books to Viet Nam. Two lawyers and I came back to . . . Viet Nam . . . [to teach] Vietnamese officials like judges and law professors. I had personal friends working with me when I . . . [founded] U.S.-Vietnam Trade Council that were the first to promote relations between U.S. and Viet Nam. [The] Center for International Strategic Studies also had people I knew. They [had] created the China–U.S. Trade Council years earlier. They invited me to join the council to do some early Viet Nam work. We only had fifty members because it was dangerous to do anything with Viet Nam. U.S. military flights [searching] for [troops] MIA [missing in action] were the only way to bring things back [from] Viet Nam. We had Usenet to communicate for our social work, like . . . [donating] twenty tons of books. (Hoanh Tran 2008a)

The VAEF formed at a time of tense relations between Viet Nam, the United States, and anticommunist protagonists within the Vietnamese American community. In fact, the United States lacked diplomatic relations with Viet Nam and continued an economic embargo begun in prewar years. Having learned the potential of the Internet while working as a lawyer for MCI Communications Corporation, Hoanh saw the Internet as the best possible means to sociopolitical change. Tin Le and Hoanh Tran, who first worked together through the VAEF, organized people via the Internet. Members came from many countries, but all had the idea of helping the people of Viet Nam. Although VAEF had worthwhile projects involving an international team, Hoanh felt even more could be achieved. He explained:

> We taught different topics to about fifty people for a few weeks. So what? I want 365 days a year of giving knowledge. So I thought this e-mail thing could do this. I decided to close down Vietnamese American Education Foundation, and [I] shifted our work into virtual space. We don't have to fly anywhere. We just shoot out knowledge. (Hoanh Tran 2005)

The goal of using ICT with people in the home country required convincing Viet Nam to develop its IT industry. Toward this end, Hoanh and Tin sponsored two top Vietnamese IT specialists, Trần Bá Thái and Nguyễn Đăng Việt, to come to the United States in 1993 for further IT training. Hoanh and Tin arranged for the visitors to attend global conferences concerning the Internet in San Francisco and Berkeley and workshops on developing countries' ICT at Stanford University. During Thái's visit, Tin showed him his homegrown Internet service provider (ISP) company and offered extensive technical explanations of ISP operations (B. T. Trần 2009).[15] Tin Le (2009) prides himself for his habit of globally aiding fellow engineers and programmers in their quest to bring ICT to Viet Nam.

This trip to the United States greatly influenced Thái. Though trained in computer science in eastern Europe, he felt it was geographically as well as technologically far removed from the global IT center, Silicon Valley. Thái's exposure to ICT development in the Bay Area became a catalyst for Viet Nam's IT development (B. T. Trần 2009). Thái founded the first ISP in Viet Nam, NetNam, which he ran as a nonprofit until 2000. That year NetNam equitized (became a public company), and Thái became its board chairman (B. T. Trần 2009).

Vietnamese Americans were not alone in promoting IT in Viet Nam. Some of the initial interest came as early as 1972 from Vietnamese students who attended ANU. By the late 1980s Vietnamese students at ANU were using powerful computers but had to leave them behind when they returned to Viet Nam. In the early 1990s Rob Hurle, an American expatriate and computer expert, and Professor Terry Hull, both at ANU, tackled this problem. With introductions from Viet Nam studies professor David Marr, Hurle went to Viet Nam to meet with Vietnamese researchers like Thái and reunite with former students (Hurle 2002).

At ANU in 1992 Hurle used Unix-to-Unix copy program (UUCP) to dial out through the phone system.[16] This handful of scholars wanted to offer access to its digital communication network to Thái in Viet Nam. Hurle "borrowed" an ANU phone line, but data transmission via Telstra, the Australian telephone system, was extremely expensive, and Telstra eventually discovered the theft. ANU willingly paid the bill because ANU's Viet Nam studies professors David Marr and Ben Kerkvliet, also American expatriates, supported Rob Hurle's endeavor (Hurle 2002).

Rob Hurle worked with Vern Weitzel at ANU—another technology expert who supported Viet Nam's ICT development—and the two developed scholarly information on disseminating ICT in Viet Nam with university programmer Matthew Ciolek. This was the working situation when Viet Nam's Ministry of Science, Technology, and Environment sent a team to ANU. The ANU group made a presentation to the Vietnamese officials on ICT for connecting Viet Nam with the rest of the world (Hurle 2004).

The rise of ICT in Viet Nam continued when Telstra sponsored ICT workshops there in 1993. Hurle, along with Vietnamese Australian professor of electrical engineering (and student who benefited from the Colombo Plan)[17] Thong Nguyen, assisted with the workshops. Hurle met Thái in person for the first time at one of these workshops, and they discussed a project to connect Viet Nam to the Internet through UUCP. Nguyễn Thị Thanh Hương, the most accomplished software engineer in Viet Nam at the time, would be instrumental. Hurle worked on one end in Australia and Hương on the other end in Viet Nam. In April 1994 they launched the project. The first communication was between Australian prime minister Carl Bildt and Vietnamese prime minister Võ Văn Kiệt. In 1994 Hurle, who had owned the domain name vn for some time, registered it with the Internet Assigned Numbers Authority under Trần Bá Thái's name (Hurle 2004). Together, Thái and Hurle worked with Viet Nam's Institute of Information and Technology (IIT) to move Viet Nam forward in ICT (B. T. Trần 2009).

Hurle was put in charge of the systems managing Internet communications to Viet Nam and became very wary of potential threats from those who would object to aiding Viet Nam in any way. Hurle, aware of diasporic political tensions around anticommunist issues, commented, "The important thing was that I felt the [anticommunist] Viet Kieu would get ahold of our work and do screwy things to it once they knew how important it was." He explained further:

> I was working on firewalls because Viet Kieus were trying to bomb the systems and tried to shut us down. We had to pay the bill when [anticommunist Internet propagandist] Chân Trần sent bombs [with a false return address of vn]. Unwilling to pay the bill, we stopped her by adding filters.[18] (Hurle 2004)

Hurle recognized that not all in diaspora held antagonistic views of Viet Nam. Of Tin Le, for example, Hurle said:

> I try to keep away from the Viet Kieu community completely. I don't like their politics—except for people like Tin Le and James Do [computer programmer and founder of the Nôm Institute]. I'm impressed with them. Tin Le is interested in networking, like me. Had I known Tin then, we could have done interesting projects together. And there's Thong Nguyen in Tasmania, who was also great to work with. (Hurle 2004)

The handful of people in Viet Nam who supported the advancement of ICT had to convince government officials it was a worthwhile endeavor. Unfortunately, these officials did not fully comprehend the new technology and took their time in approving ICT projects. Moreover, a struggle arose in Viet Nam over who would oversee ICT there. Officially, the state-owned Vietnam Data Corporation (VDC) was in charge of Internet communication in Viet Nam. However, it lacked properly trained engineers and took longer to do the kind of IT work that Hurle and Thái had accomplished for the IIT in Viet Nam. Though IIT was nonprofit and no threat to VDC, VDC wanted to keep tabs on IIT's IT projects. VDC began a hostile campaign against the IIT group. Attempts were made to shut IIT down—including taking away their telephone numbers, making Internet dial-up difficult. The IIT team got around this by changing their numbers and dialing in at different times in different locations. Hurle recalled this cat and mouse game:

> It got to the point where we had someone with a laptop going to a house in 1996, and they would call me with a number, and [then] I'd call them [back]. Also, I [would] put e-mails on a disc and get it over on the first plane possible. People complained about e-mails being delayed, but they didn't know that their e-mails were being flown back and forth. (Hurle 2002)

IIT finally gave the operation to VDC in 1996 and transferred the domain vn to Viet Nam as well. But now, with ICT controlled at its end, the state feared that overseas Vietnamese would send information through the Internet to undermine the government. Although some in the overseas population did try to intervene in Viet Nam's first steps on the Internet, most of VDC's paranoia of harmful overseas elements was unwarranted. Overseas Vietnamese had their own struggles to connect with each other and people in Viet Nam via the Internet to discuss Viet Nam–related issues because certain anticommunists sought to halt such connections. Yet like their Vietnamese counterparts, some overseas Vietnamese found ways to form safe virtual spaces for open dialogue. These efforts began with Vietnamese within the United States and continued with the larger diaspora and eventually with people back in Viet Nam. These connections were accomplished through virtual communities like VNForum.

Vietnam Forum

From their involvement in the VAEF beginning in 1989, Hoanh Tran and Tin Le, the founders of VNForum, learned early about the potential of the Internet. They anticipated that networking via the Internet would foster collaborative projects for sociopolitical change in Viet Nam on a scale much larger than previously. VNForum ultimately became this vehicle, but its origin began modestly. Tin Le experimented first with students and colleagues in the IT field when he developed the news list VietNet. As soon as he opened it to the general public, its subscriber base grew rapidly. At nine hundred subscribers, its founders considered it too large and costly to maintain, so they decided to close it and begin soc.cult.vietnam (SCV) in 1991 (T. Le 2000). At first, SCV was a completely open and unmoderated space. One could very easily use e-mail accounts with fake names to post. Discussions in SCV began with friendly messages from students and technology industry workers. Within months, SCV had generated debates between supposed communist and anticommunist

sympathizers. However, with the lack of accountability, it quickly turned un-
ruly. During its lifetime, SCV's participants used name-calling and made
slanderous accusations against each other. Anh Đoàn, a Vietnamese national
studying in the United States in 2000 discussed his participation in SCV:

> In 1995–1996, many of us refer to SCV as a virtual Vietnamese fish
> market—*chợ cá*. It was sort of a place for people to trade small things—
> ideas—and where "merchants" bickered and argued with one another
> to get what they want[ed]. If you were patient, you could get some good
> news—good products—but it was difficult to see those things. You had to
> pick through a lot to get the good ones. After about one year of this, I was
> tired [of it and] I didn't come back. (Đoàn 2000)

As a watcher of SCV, I noticed that it frequently received eclectic postings,
from personal poetry to testimonials and self-promotional pieces, all side by
side. Even spam (such as mass advertising) found its place on this chaotic site.
On the whole, though, SCV was a place for otherwise isolated immigrants to
discuss contemporary issues of concern to them and their community along
with home-country topics.

Steve Denning, library archivist and activist for Viet Nam human rights
who had been participating in SCV since 1993, believed SCV had a purpose for
Vietnamese Americans:

> SCV is kind of a free-for-all, which has its advantages and disadvantages.
> For example, there are people who use fake names [and] flame each other
> regularly and constantly. On the other hand, you are free to express your
> point of view in the group or post whatever you like to the group. For the
> SCV users' purposes, it is also useful in that the spontaneous nature of the
> group might provide a more candid glimpse into the perspectives of some
> Vietnamese Americans. (Denning 2000a)

Denning was attacked on SCV for his work on Viet Nam–related issues. He
eventually posted a retort to the accusations. Even though annoyed by the slanderous remarks, he believed that SCV allows more freedom of expression than
other virtual sites. The construction and implementation of this online discussion forum is the first Viet Nam–related, virtual community-building project.

Although Tin and Hoanh recognized the appeal of SCV, their aim was to
use the Internet as a vehicle to promote healthy dialogue for social change, and
SCV was not that kind of space. Hoanh explains, "We switched to VNForum
to exchange knowledge and be in front of our computers twenty-four/seven, so
that generates a lot of information. It doesn't cost us the effort [that] running
around, flying around, shipping books for little effects [does]" (Hoanh Tran
2008a). How to create this type of safe and constructive space was an issue.
With the lessons of SCV behind them, Tin and Hoanh sought order and even

control on VNForum. A prospective member had to request to join the new list via an e-mail message and then wait for administrative approval. A code of conduct asked that posts be "messages concerning issues related, or of significance, to Vietnam or overseas Vietnamese communities." It instructed members to refrain from "statements and conduct likely to create disorder, damage the integrity or reputation of the Forum, or harm the Forum or any Forum member in any way" (Tran and Le 1992). When members broke the VNForum code of conduct, administrators responded with sanctions that escalated with each infraction: a private warning, a public warning, temporary suspension, and ultimately, permanent suspension. Administrators enacted these punitive measures several occasions during the life of VNForum. Most often, administrators sent friendly reminders or clarifications of the rules. For example, Hoanh posted this in April 1999:

Dear anh X and All,

Thank you, anh X, for the message from Vietnam concerning potential policies toward Overseas Vietnamese intellectuals. Let me provide everyone a quick response to the message (the original of which is attached). But before I have my comments, please allow me to reiterate our practice here in VNForum. When we discuss about the content of a message, we don't intend to criticize the poster of the message, especially when the poster doesn't claim authorship, as you, anh X, [do not] in this case. So what I may say here has nothing to do with you. You are a mere messenger in this case. Please don't take anything personally. As always, we appreciate good information from everyone.[19]

(Hoanh Tran 1999)

The founders created the code of conduct to ensure that member-agitators of VNForum would not disrupt the flow of correspondence between subscribers. As in Howard Rheingold's description of virtual communities, it is common to establish norms and then challenge, change, reestablish, and rechallenge these norms, as in a "sped up social evolution" (1993, 2).

Tin and Hoanh were confident that they could effectively manage the various elements of VNForum. These included staunch anticommunists who on other virtual communities flamed with impunity. Even outspoken cyberactivist Chân Trần refrained from slander and unfounded accusations on VNForum. Chân is a member of the National United Front for the Liberation of Vietnam (NUFLVN), an anticommunist, humanitarian democracy group that disseminates information on the Internet through *Vietnam Insight*, which Chân edits, and other publications (see Chapter 1). Though Hoanh and Tin attempted to maintain a safe space for debates engaging all sides of the political spectrum, VNForum was still seen by the Vietnamese government as a threat. Hoanh elaborated:

The Vietnamese government tried to shut VNForum down but could not. They even created a mirror Vietnam Forum and tried to be intellectual like us, but they had no members. I knew they could not do it because VNForum was already so popular, and [they on the other hand] had no one to stir a conversation. I don't think anyone knows [what became of this copycat VNForum] because it never took off. (Hoanh Tran 2000)

So even though the Vietnamese Communist Party (VCP) did not officially or openly participate in or recognize VNForum, moderators knew from its inception that members of the party read and contributed to the threads: some messages bounced back to the main server, revealing a sequence of connections back to their origin in Viet Nam. Also, during the early years of VNForum, the Vietnamese government limited Internet access to only governmental and educational agencies. This limitation eventually eased to include a very few home and office computers and, later, Internet cafés. Heeding a call for the "national cause of industrialization and modernization" that is now tied to ICT development, Viet Nam allowed Internet access for its citizens but also monitored their usage and communications (OpenNet Initiative 2007).

Through careful moderation Hoanh and Tin brought together people from diverse and extreme political points of view for discussion. From 1994 to VNForum's final days in 2003, it had a steady stream of approximately three hundred subscribers. But with *gateways*—aliases that fed e-mail to other lists— the number of people reading VNForum was potentially far higher. VNForum had subscribers in nearly fifty countries. That the list had wide geographic distribution of members and that it had been running continuously for over ten years gave people the sense that VNForum was a safe space for the silent majority in the United States and abroad.[20] These characteristics made VNForum an ideal example of a transnational link between Vietnamese in diaspora and in Viet Nam and set the stage for VNForum to create sociopolitical change in both Viet Nam and diaspora. Hoanh observed that whenever there were heated debates about Vietnamese social, economic, or political issues on VNForum, newspaper articles would appear shortly thereafter on how the government was addressing the same issues.

In July 1997, discussions on VNForum revolved around lack of Viet Kieu citizenship rights in Viet Nam. Members shared their feelings and opinions on citizenship policies, and a few critiqued the Vietnamese government for not revising its policies. Most contributors wanted an opportunity for citizenship status in Viet Nam. They argued that Viet Nam needed to recognize the potential of its overseas population and create policies of inclusion to lure overseas Vietnamese investment and participation in Viet Nam's development. They argued that by not recognizing the overseas population as citizens Viet Nam's political leaders could widen an already large schism between the Vietnamese communist party and overseas Vietnamese. Finally, some spoke about this issue in the context of dual citizenship. One post read, "It is in the interest of the country if the overseas Vietnamese, both young and old, don't have to give up their first world citizenship if they want to live in Vietnam long term" ("Viet Kieu Citizenship" 1997).

Arguing on both emotional and legal bases, some members believed that granting citizenship to overseas Vietnamese (or at least not taking it away) would be a positive step toward reconciliation. Members wanted citizenship so that they could buy land in Viet Nam. Some asserted that such incentives would show overseas Vietnamese that the Vietnamese government valued their contributions to Viet Nam.

Following these discussions, some policy changes took place in Viet Nam with regard to citizenship and land ownership. In April 1999 a law went into effect allowing overseas Vietnamese to request Vietnamese citizenship and thus have all the rights of Viet Nam nationals. This law, however, benefited only a small number of overseas Vietnamese who "contributed to the revolution." "Contributed" implies being on the revolution's winning side and excludes the hundreds of thousands of South Vietnamese residents who left Viet Nam for political reasons. In November 2008 the Vietnamese National Assembly passed a law allowing overseas Vietnamese to hold dual citizenship. However, officials judged case by case the perceived contribution and loyalty to Viet Nam. But the vast majority in diaspora who oppose communist rule have no loyalty toward the Vietnamese government, and few were granted citizenship (Đặng 1999; Viet Nam News Agency 2008).

Đặng Hồ Phát, chair of Viet Nam's Committee on Vietnamese Overseas, in October 1999 talked to me about the narrow policies regarding citizenship. Viet Nam needs to deal meaningfully with Viet Kieu citizenship and land ownership policies, he said, but he cautioned that such a complicated and politically charged issue cannot be resolved overnight. He reassured me that the Committee on Vietnamese Overseas had the interest of all overseas Vietnamese at heart, and his committee served as the government agency that would advocate for legislation favorable for them. He added that many overseas Vietnamese from countries all over the world, including the United States, have visited his office asking for more Viet Kieu rights in Viet Nam. He promised gains would be made (Đặng 1999).

Indeed, in 2001 the Viet Nam government announced decree 81/2001/ND-CP, which allowed some overseas Vietnamese to buy one house in Viet Nam. However, ownership is still not easy; to qualify, a person must have long-term investments in Viet Nam, have made recognized contributions to the country, or be an expert or scientist working permanently in Viet Nam. The decree also says that one can qualify by simply wanting to live in Viet Nam, but ownership requires more stringent qualifications in practice. Most overseas Vietnamese who have houses in Ho Chi Minh City in the 2000s are investors and scientists, according to the Ho Chi Minh City Department of Natural Resources and Environment Information and Land, Housing Registration. In October 2006, decree 90/2006/ND-CP permitted overseas Vietnamese to own multiple houses and to give, receive, exchange, and inherit houses. By 2007, however, fewer than one hundred of the approximately hundred thousand overseas Vietnamese who wanted to buy property in Viet Nam had done so, according to official records ("Five Years, Only 100 Viet Kieu Have Houses in Vietnam" 2007).[21]

Given the slow nature of Vietnamese policy making, the real effect VNForum had on policy changes in Viet Nam remains unclear. Though debates on VNForum might not have necessarily resulted in changed policies, having such a forum created an open channel to understanding the desires and needs of the overseas population. Some subscribers of the forum argued that their debates reached the ears of Vietnamese government officials and thus influenced policy recommendations.

De Pham, cofounder of Vietnamese Students Abroad e-mail list, was more skeptical of VNForum's influence in Viet Nam:

> There are a lot of overseas intellectuals who are very enthusiastic [on VNForum] but their topics are not relevant to the mainland Vietnamese. The overseas Vietnamese population does not have [any] influence in Viet Nam whatsoever. They are very naive. They have been out of Viet Nam for so long, and they are not sophisticated enough to know how things run in Viet Nam now. They have a good heart and some resources, but they cannot get too many things done in Viet Nam now. (De Pham 2000)

After a pensive pause, De added:

> Viet Nam is opening up. The government bureaucracy is becoming more transparent with time. So overseas intellectuals can help Viet Nam as time goes by. Right now they are too naive and cannot help Viet Nam. But that will change in the next five years. They can have influence in the future but not now. (De Pham 2000)

In relation to De's remarks, in October 2000 subscribers of VNForum discussed the brain drain crisis, or Vietnamese students not returning to Viet Nam after their training. A Vietnamese national wrote that she believed there were capable individuals in Viet Nam who could aid in Viet Nam's development. She then elaborated on the possible role of VNForum:

> This VNForum is a very appropriate means for networking people. I myself can learn a lot from this forum. How about [we] open a similar one for our brothers/sisters who cannot join in this forum? I have personally talked to many young professionals who have been trained both at home and abroad. They have BRAIN and they have HEART, and they also have to SURVIVE. I am thinking how to get them together. Any solution? (T. S. 2000)

VNForum members from Viet Nam and elsewhere responded with the suggestion of working together on small projects that might lead to larger developmental programs. Translating much-needed technical texts was at the forefront of goals promoted on the list. The discussion was remarkable because it resulted in Vietnamese nationals and Vietnamese overseas actively working together to improve conditions in Viet Nam. Participants were often powerful people or had access to such people and therefore could easily capture the attention of subscribers interested in alternative thinking about Viet Nam issues and national policy. VNForum was exclusive in many ways, particularly because of its elite membership. It was a community in which intellectuals and people with political power could openly discuss programs for progress.

Although VNForum seemed to have a positive influence on information about Viet Nam in the United States and abroad, it had its own set of issues. Tin and Hoanh controlled disruptions on the list instigated by anticommunist groups in the United States and possible encroachment by those in Viet Nam. However, the strong-handed moderation might have factored into the decline in the number of discussions in its final years of operation. Quynh Trang Do (2000), a long-time member of VNForum, believed that toward its end it had been reduced to a mailing list that forwarded published news. She pointed to the regular postings of one of the administrators: "It is his job to disseminate news from Viet Nam and the United States regarding Viet Nam, but that has crowded the screen instead of debates." Steve Denning, a former VNForum administrator who was responsible for posting news, made similar observations: "Though known as a much more undisciplined group, SCV seems to have more of a dialogue going than VNForum on certain issues" (Denning 2000b).

Furthermore, VNForum was not a completely safe space even though it was moderated. Tin received threats related to his work on VNForum from an anticommunist extremist and left the forum for a three-year period between 1992 and 1995.

> I came back to the Vietnam Forum in 1995 as a technical advisor. I was more quiet and tried to stay more low profile. I was aware of not saying things that would bring harm to me or my family. I still am the facilitator, but to do more is like painting a target on my head. (T. Le 1998)

One cannot overestimate Tin's role in maintaining VNForum. He served in a technical support capacity not only for the forum on a day-to-day basis but also for members whenever they needed to create online networks for their social projects. In the pre-Google years, website creation, for example, was a much-sought-after skill. Though at times made uncomfortable in his role as founder and administrator of VNForum, because of the many ways he could assist the forum and its members, he knew the importance of his participation:

> I want to help with VNForum because it's a way to make Viet Nam change. By nudging them [the Vietnamese government] along in their thinking, I'm giving back. Viet Nam lacks a lot of resources. VNForum began with policy recommendations, but we also moved to fundraising for humanitarian projects like flood stuff. It's better to focus on the humanitarian projects because it's easier. No politics is involved, and therefore it's less politicized in the community. (T. Le 1998)

Tin's tone revealed a self-consciousness that comes from a history of being attacked by divisive individuals and groups within the Vietnamese American community. This tension eventually subsided as agitators lost interest or were weeded from the list.

Most of VNForum's active participants seemed cautious about posting regularly at the inception of the forum. But as time went by, people became more comfortable and exchanged ideas more freely. Most posters did not make clear whether they supported or condemned the communist regime, even when they openly criticized the pace of change in Viet Nam. But because the technology the forum used was new and possibly destabilizing for the Vietnamese government, officials had to confront VNForum on some level. Đỗ Qúy Đoàn, a Ministry of Culture and Information official, disclosed in 2000 the government's view that the Internet may be too vast to police and too important to ignore (Hoanh Tran 2000). Some officials initially were quiet observers on VNForum but eventually posted. Hoanh noted their presence:

> After 1997 more Vietnamese [nationals] would join openly, making my prediction [that more Vietnamese nationals would join the forum] five years earlier true. They [Vietnamese government agents] gave up trying to shut us down; they had to join us because if they wanted to connect to the rest of the world, they had no choice. They could not have a forum of their own because who would join them and what would they talk about? (Hoanh Tran 2008a)

The virtual community created by VNForum served as the perfect venue for discussions on controversial topics. But founders and participants had to appear neutral and nonconfrontational because highly influential powers—the SRV and anticommunist groups in the United States—were monitoring them.

No-Nike Campaign for Labor Rights

While dodging direct confrontations in discussions on Viet Nam's development, VNForum also served as a springboard for social justice projects. Most notable of these was the No-Nike labor rights campaign. A member of the six-year-old VNForum, Thuyen Nguyen, began posting concerns about Nike. He had recently viewed an episode of the CBS news program *48 Hours* that exposed substandard working conditions, including sexual harassment and corporal punishment, in a Vietnamese Nike shoe factory with a predominantly young, female workforce ("Nike Shoe Factory Expose" 1996). Thuyen debated with list members Nike's alleged labor abuses in Viet Nam factories. Nike first entered Viet Nam in 1995, contracting with five factories and exporting five million pairs of shoes (Ramos 2006). VNForum Nike discussions acknowledged Viet Nam's positive record for monitoring labor abuses in foreign-owned companies, but the members urged that more needed to be done to improve working conditions ("Nike" 1996).

The e-mails sent back and forth on this subject were not so remarkable in and of themselves. The postings were typical for VNForum: written by well-informed individuals offering their views on Viet Nam–related issues.[22] Thuyen next created Vietnam Labor Watch with friends from VNForum. Their No-Nike website with the red circle and slash over the word "Nike" became a widely recognized symbol of the fight against Nike's labor abuses in Viet Nam (Thuyen Nguyen 2000).

In response to Thuyen's postings, Nike invited him to inspect its subcontracted factories in Viet Nam:

> Nike wanted to assure us that the news organizations were just exaggerating and that Nike factories are great. Therefore, Nike arranged a trip for us to go to Viet Nam and visit factories there in 1997. . . . We . . . paid for our own travel expenses for fear of any appearance of compromise. (Thuyen Nguyen 2000)

This visit found no labor violations; however, suspicious that the Nike-escorted tour had not revealed all, Thuyen decided to investigate again—this time unannounced. With the aid of Ho Chi Minh City labor officials, Thuyen returned to the factories. This second trip revealed a more troubling reality:

> There were two strikes while I was there. There was an incident in which seventy-two women were forced to run four kilometers in the hot sun as punishment for wearing slippers in the work area. I believe thirteen of them fainted and were hospitalized. During the trip, I collected several hundred pay stubs and found that Nike factories were paying below minimum wage and were cheating these workers on overtime pay. I put all my findings together in a report and sent it to Nike. Nike did not seem to care to respond to my findings and were just ignoring us. So eventually we decided to go public with our findings in April 1997. That's when our Vietnam Labor Watch's report made the front pages of many U.S. newspapers. (Thuyen Nguyen 2000)

A swell of Vietnamese American groups and individuals then joined Thuyen's anti-Nike campaign. For example, the student council at the University of California, Irvine, passed a resolution to join the Nike boycott in March 1997. This resolution was supported by student groups, including the Vietnamese American Coalition, and sponsored by the Asian-Pacific Student Union. The University of California, Berkeley, Vietnamese Student Association organized a task force to boycott Nike. During this same year, thirty of the one hundred people picketing the opening of Nike's New York megastore were Vietnamese Americans. About eighty Vietnamese picketed in California at Costa Mesa's Nike Town, and the majority of the picketers at Nike's store opening in San Francisco were Vietnamese (Nhu 1997). This, along with a slew of newspaper articles highlighting Thuyen's efforts, shows how far his project had progressed from the initial posts on VNForum.

Thuyen's actions led to results unprecedented on several levels. It was the first time a Vietnamese American group initiated political action from an Internet list that received international attention. Vietnamese Americans and the Vietnamese government as well as support from mainstream America came together to achieve positive change in the lives of workers in Viet Nam. And most remarkably, Thuyen's endeavors united the fervent anticommunist sentiments within certain sectors of the Vietnamese American community and the SRV, mistrustful of this group. Tin Le, who helped with the campaign's website, believes that the success of the movement stemmed heavily from Thuyen's diplomatic abilities: "Thuyen knew exactly how much to ask and how to ask it" (T. Le 1998). That it took over twenty years of exile before someone could achieve this kind of collaboration underlines Tin's praise of Thuyen.

But VNForum, along with Thuyen, was not immune to criticism. After a long hiatus from VNForum, because of stress and threats to his family from hostile anticommunists, Tin returned and had to ward off attacks from Chân Trần, the well-known anticommunist cyberactivist from the San Francisco Bay Area. Despite having said, "We know that information is one of our weapons. . . . We want to send into Vietnam as much information as we can" (Huckshorn 1998, A2), Chân accused Tin of defending the Vietnamese government in the Nike labor issue. Tin retorted that the Vietnamese government itself first reported the abuses, and these reports contributed to his decision to take action. He elaborated:

> For me, working in Viet Nam to help the poor directly is the only realistic course of action left for people who want to help improve the conditions in Viet Nam. People can work with the Ha Noi leadership if they want to, but this is not my position. NGOs' [nongovernmental organizations'] efforts to improve the daily lives of Vietnamese were criticized by anticommunists as helping the Vietnamese government to oppress its people further, etcetera. People who offered their views to the public were threatened with bomb threats, violence, and so on, by anticommunist groups several years ago. The situation has improved a lot now, but working to help the poor in Viet Nam is still being equated as helping or working with the Ha Noi leadership. (T. Le 1998)

To some, working with the Ha Noi leadership meant fully supporting the government. To others, attacking Nike was comparable to attacking the government, and Nike vice president Joseph Ha exploited this reasoning. On January 11, 1999, he sent a letter to the president of the Viet Nam General Confederation of Labor, Cù Thị Hậu. This letter later appeared in Viet Nam's national newspaper, *Lao Động (Labor)*. The letter targeted Thuyen's group, claiming they had attacked Nike "because Nike helps to create many jobs in Vietnam. Their political objective is to create a so-called democratic society on the U.S. model. A nation should not necessarily apply the model of another nation. Each nation has its own internal political system. Nike believes completely in this" (Associated Press 1999b). The labor rights community came to Thuyen's defense. Four activist groups from President Bill Clinton's anti-sweatshop initiative asked Nike to disavow the letter and reprimand or dismiss Joseph Ha (Associated Press 1999a). To attempt to mend public relations, Nike took action against Joseph Ha (Bissell 1999).

The letter undermined Viet Nam's support of Thuyen's labor rights work. In 1999 Nike employed forty thousand workers in five factories in southern Viet Nam (Associated Press 1999b). Even if the government dismissed claims that Thuyen's group was subversive, Viet Nam had much to lose if it ignored Nike's letter. *Lao Động* published further articles arguing that Nike workers' legitimate complaints had been exploited by "hostile elements abroad" (Birchall 1999). Then Hoàng Thi Kháng, president of the Ho Chi Minh City Confederation of Labor and the most aggressive monitor of the footwear factories, suddenly left the state-run union (Bissell 1999), further evidence that Vietnamese authorities did not want the anti-Nike campaign to jeopardize the company's involvement in Viet Nam. These events dramatically changed Thuyen's effectiveness in Viet Nam. Before the letter,

> [Thuyen] Nguyen had many reliable sources for information on pay and conditions in Nike factories in Vietnam. When Nike said that it was raising wages to a livable level, workers provided Nguyen with pay stubs documenting the wide gap between company claims and workers' reality. When Nike said that it was now committed to dealing fairly with its Vietnamese employees, unionists in Vietnam saw to it that Nguyen got connected up with workers whose experience told another story. (Bissell 1999, 2)

Ultimately, however, with the stream of negative articles in the U.S. press and continued labor group support of the anti-Nike campaign, Nike improved conditions in its Vietnamese factories. The company paid the minimum wage, eliminated the use of toxic solvents, followed Vietnamese labor laws, and (most important) ceased physically abusing workers (Thuyen Nguyen 1997).

The Internet undoubtedly enhanced the possibilities for political activism, and Thuyen took advantage of this to advance labor rights organizing. As Gustavo Lins Ribeiro notes, the Internet has given coalitions a swift and inexpensive means of communication with global capillarity, and data availability that multiplies the opportunities for individuals and groups to denounce, articulate, and campaign. The virtual community that networks is a powerful weapon for generating transnational solidarity on many pressing issues. (Ribeiro 1998, 348)

VNForum was essential to the No-Nike movement, extending its reach globally. The campaign worked with the Vietnamese government and brought in transnational human rights groups, eventually forcing Nike to take responsibility for its labor practices overseas. Moreover, Thuyen's campaign put him directly at the center of the three major influences: American society, as represented by one of its largest corporations; the Vietnamese government; and anticommunist overseas Vietnamese groups. With successful social movements like the No-Nike campaign, VNForum remained relatively influential until its intentional termination in 2003. The evolution of VNForum continued with the creation of another important social experiment, the Vietnam Business virtual community.

Vietnam Business

The closing of VNForum followed the core philosophy of its founders to create positive change in Viet Nam. Hoanh Tran wanted to transform VNForum into a predominantly Vietnamese-run virtual community. He remarked, "Change has to come from inside. I can facilitate, but [I] needed administrators from inside the country" (Hoanh Tran 2008b). Vietnamese administrators, he believed, would help increase the number of Vietnamese participants and ultimately bring positive transformation to the nation. As early as the late 1990s, he approached certain Vietnamese members about taking over VNForum. Some Vietnamese were willing to administer the list, but Hoanh decided to create a new virtual community, Vietnam Business (VNBiz), because VNForum had the reputation of being political and was therefore open to attacks from Viet Nam and overseas. The name VNBiz reflects the community's business-related topics and leaning toward economics issues; however, politics is one of its most important and frequent topics of discussion.

Of the first administrators at the inception of VNBiz in 2000, five were Vietnamese nationals living in Viet Nam, four of whom were women. Three additional administrators included Vietnamese and U.S. expatriates residing outside Viet Nam. The selection of the administrative team took years of networking on Hoanh's part. He had met most of the VNBiz administrators on VNForum and a few others on international visits. All were open to the idea of Viet Nam's development and tolerant of extreme ideologies, whether held by the Vietnamese government or anticommunist groups overseas, two of the three main sources of influence. In VNBiz as with all his other endeavors, he requires transparency in the community; that means posters use real names and thus are accountable for what they write. Indeed, nearly all new members are formally introduced to the "VNBiz family," as he often calls this virtual community.

Keen on making it primarily a Vietnamese operation, Hoanh requested VNBiz be run within the country. However, safe virtual space and reliable communication in Viet Nam proved infeasible, and he based the servers in the United States (Hoanh Tran 2008b). It has had as many as 550 members. The limited number may be due to the predominant use of English.

Administrators actively promote English because as Hoanh explains, "Viet Nam lacks a vocabulary for discussing issues that counter their government's beliefs. It would limit the types of conversations and the flow of postings if only Vietnamese texts could be posted." More important, Hoanh adds, "English allows for an 'international mind-set,'" which is "about opening oneself to new ideas and being rational enough to discern the postings." (Hoanh Tran 2008b). My understanding is that VNBiz wants the progressive leadership of Viet Nam to be aware of its conversations. Hoanh presumes that those with some international exposure and education are more open to constructive discussions about the future of Viet Nam. English is thought to allow this bridge.

With the new VNBiz, its predominantly Vietnamese administrative team to lead discussions and moderate, and its use of English, Hoanh hopes the Vietnamese government will listen to the group's comments. Like VNForum before it, VNBiz consists of well-educated individuals debating and offering policy recommendations that could aid in the development of Viet Nam. Hoanh imagines this goal has been accomplished to some degree, mainly because he believes that the Vietnamese government has read discussions on VNBiz and policy changes followed. Evidence that this happens is seen in the government's actions following VNBiz's discussion on how the global recession affected Viet Nam. In October 2008 in carefully thought-out posts, members of VNBiz suggested lowering interest rates and raising the gasoline tax. On November 3, 2008, the state bank lowered interest rates, and on November 10, 2008, the Ministry of Finance raised the gasoline tax. If this is more than a coincidence, then VNBiz is essentially a continuation of VNForum, a consortium for intellectual debate about the development of Viet Nam, and subscribers act as de facto advisors offering policy recommendations.

As with VNForum, VNBiz fears being thwarted or, worse, losing its usefulness. Always cognizant of the three primary sources of influence shaping their activities, administrators and participants alike promote topics or agendas in the most nuanced way possible. They strive to appear neutral and rational to catch the attention of power holders who can effect change. As of 2012 Hoanh believes that an open enough atmosphere exists in the government for Viet Nam's leadership to consider progressive ideas. But given the seeming exclusiveness of VNBiz, in that many of its participants have graduate-level Western education and extensive knowledge of English, discussions do not reach the masses in Viet Nam, whom VNBiz aims to serve. At the very least, though, VNBiz is trusted and has enough goodwill to bring into its administrative fold Vietnamese nationals and people from outside Viet Nam with influence, no small feat.

The rapid speed of Internet development continues to create many new virtual spaces for the diaspora to engage with Vietnamese sociopolitical culture. Blogs constitute one of these new and important spaces, and members of VNBiz have seen them as yet another channel for making connections and creating social change. The next section discusses the blog *Đọt Chuối Non*, created by VNBiz ex-administrators to continue to circulate their ideas about how Viet Nam can best engage with its citizens and the world.

Đọt Chuối Non

As with the previous virtual communities that Hoanh Tran had helped build, *Đọt Chuối Non* began with calculated intent. On February 7, 2009, after years of participating in VNForum and VNBiz and watching Viet Nam's politics, Hoanh decided to create another safe virtual space for disseminating ideas and information. "Positive thinking is the main theme" of *Đọt Chuối Non*. Hoanh explained:

> I thought that now I should spend time with the larger population in Vietnamese, on an issue I think important for the country—positive thinking. Because of the lingering effects of the war, the totalitarian way of management, the suppression [by the government], weakening of the traditional religious institutions, the collapse of ethics, the rise in corruption and abuses, the paranoia of the government, the distrust of the masses toward social values . . . I thought we need to rebuild positive thinking in the population as the first priority. (Hoanh Tran 2010b)

Hoanh and a Vietnamese engineer from Ha Noi, Nguyễn Minh Hiển, served as the original administrators. A veteran of VNBiz, Hiển was one of the few Vietnamese nationals who had studied and worked in the United States. *Đọt Chuối Non*, meaning "young banana shoot," was created in part to recognize and nurture the positive changes taking place in Viet Nam. *Đọt Chuối Non* posts news from the BBC on topics that have included United States–Viet Nam relations, blogger arrests, freedom-of-press national rankings, and anti-corruption. In addition, as on VNForum and its offshoots, topics of discussion have been controversial. One post in particular spoke of the famous poet Hữu Loan (1916–2010). He fought alongside Hồ Chí Minh's communist army but became disillusioned by the punitive land reforms that ultimately killed his wife's family. Comments to the post expressed sadness, not only over the poet's death but also because of the harsh times under which he had lived. Other posts accused Hữu Loan of being a traitor, which alarmed *Đọt Chuối Non*'s administrators (Hoanh Tran 2010a). With their technical skill, they discovered that the accusations originated from Vietnamese government servers. Hoanh sees these disturbances by such governmental Internet police on blogs like Đọt Chuối Non as another form of governmental control (Hoanh Tran 2010a). Once Đọt Chuối Non administrators realized Vietnamese officials were monitoring the site closely, the group decided to tone down the postings and reverted to feel-good topics like poetry and honoring established national heroes. For the administrators, though, the underlying philosophy remains: Vietnamese citizens should have access to the serious issues in Viet Nam that concern them and others in the international community.

Remarkably, Đọt Chuối Non has not been blocked or shut down. Viet Nam's loosening of Internet access and content creation in the late 2000s allowed citizens to participate in hybrid social networks with blogs like Yahoo! 360°.[23] Through social networks and blogging platforms made popular as of 2005, Internet users openly discussed controversial issues affecting Viet Nam. Topics have included discontent over China's encroachment of the Spratly and Paracels territories and mining of bauxite in Viet Nam ("Vietnam Seeks to Silence Its China Critics" 2009). People who lived overseas could now make direct contact with those in Viet Nam and share ideas in ways and with ease previously unknown.[24]

This atmosphere of free exchange, mutual admiration, and collaboration was short lived. In 2008 the Vietnamese government began systematically harassing popular bloggers in Viet Nam who had once experienced a semblance of open and public discussion ("Việt Nam Tăng Cường An Ninh Mạng" 2009). Other so-called dissident bloggers lost their jobs or were arrested and incarcerated because of their open criticism of Viet Nam's governmental policies. Some in the social network communities took to the Internet to share their disapproval, even while worrying that they would be the next victims in the state's campaign to suppress dissident voices (H.-N. Vu 2009b). In response to the dissident arrests, for instance, Việt Tân (Vietnam Reform Party), the prominent anticommunist organization, launched its Internet Freedom Campaign. It pushed for companies like Google, Yahoo!, and Microsoft to resist giving the Vietnamese government information that could hurt dissident bloggers and urged the U.S. government to call for the release of the arrested bloggers. Đọt Chuối Non began blogging during this confusing time in Viet Nam's ICT history (Viet Tan 2010).

Today, although the Vietnamese government has stepped up the monitoring of bloggers and shut down uncontrollable social network sites like YouTube and Facebook,[25] Đọt Chuối Non continues to survive (Timberlake 2010). But it too has had to make adjustments to dodge governmental restrictions. By 2010, to keep Hiển safe from government crackdown, Hoanh publicly took over as the sole administrator of Đọt Chuối Non, while Hiển remained working in the background. Đọt Chuối Non's ability to remain actively viewed in Viet Nam is also in part because of the commitment of Hoanh and the nearly two dozen

Vietnamese nationals who have assisted in the daily postings of positive information about that country since the site's launch on February 9, 2009. Even with the occasional posting critical of communist Viet Nam, discussions on the site remain relatively noncontroversial. Hoanh hopes for more liberal exchanges if and when Viet Nam eases up on its control over the Internet.

Conclusion

VNForum was established at a time when the Internet was new and home computers were rare. Most members were participating in virtual communities for the first time—when virtual communities existed as social experiments. Hopes were high and opportunity for change was limitless. This was the context in which VNForum, a modest e-mail list run by idealistic overseas Vietnamese aspiring to create positive change in Viet Nam, began.[26] VNForum had members from the United States, including overseas Vietnamese, in addition to Vietnamese government officials and citizens. The group's founders did not want to be harassed by politicized groups or swayed by the three major sources of influence; instead, they wanted the ability to freely express their feelings on any matter. Whereas Barry Wellman has interpreted "network individualism" as acts of individuals fully participating in the many uses of the computer, from commerce to entertainment to business (Wellman 2002), I think this phenomenon is also about the individual rising to form community. Virtual communities like VNForum moved beyond social networking to organize for effective change. Founders Tin Le and Hoanh Tran realized that the Internet was an important tool for this endeavor, but Viet Nam needed to catch up in ICT to enable participation.

The development of ICT in Viet Nam involved dedicated overseas Vietnamese as well as Vietnamese and American expatriates in Australia. Its history is astonishing: "enemies of Viet Nam" reached out to Viet Nam in the late 1980s and early 1990s and continued to in 2012, when anticommunist sentiment still ran high in the diaspora and the memory of the Viet Nam War had not been properly addressed. Also noteworthy is that Viet Nam's ICT industry had to convince a socialist government powered by revolutionaries from a past era to trust in the future of ICT. Vietnamese ICT students and experts and their colleagues abroad helped build a telecommunications bridge from Viet Nam to the rest of the world.

As ICT improved, the influence of VNForum rose. It was the first virtual space in which concerned individuals could rationally discuss the development of Viet Nam and its diaspora. This virtual community spawned a labor movement, the No-Nike campaign, that further enhanced the relationship between Viet Nam and its overseas population. Longtime forum member Thuyen Nguyen used the forum to spread awareness of labor abuses in Nike shoe factories in Viet Nam. His organization and network of labor advocates helped create better working conditions for the factory workers.

As in real-life communities, VNForum brought together like-minded people, and together they experienced battles, protests, reconciliations, resignations, and other significant political events. VNForum's unique capacity for attracting high-quality discussion may very well have in turn attracted the attention of its most important audience, the Vietnamese government. If Viet Nam government officials were paying attention to VNForum, one may argue that VNForum was thus a de facto think tank of and for professional overseas Vietnamese academics, international nongovernmental organizations, international journalists, and Vietnamese citizens to foster change in Viet Nam. The experience on VNForum taught its administrators many important lessons. One was that it was possible for Viet Nam to fully engage in open dialogue for change with foreigners and overseas Vietnamese. So as VNForum faded out, its founders created VNBiz and brought in a mostly Viet Nam–based group of administrators in the belief that change must come from within. Thus, VNForum's legacy continues with VNBiz as founders hand over leadership to residents of Viet Nam.

Keeping pace with Internet trends, Hoanh Tran blogs on *Đọt Chuối Non* to reach Viet Nam's masses. Controversial political discussions ensue, but because of close monitoring by the Vietnamese government, overtly innocuous and positive discussions supplanted more controversial ones critiquing government policies. With the dramatic rise in Internet use in Viet Nam, the state cracked down on its citizens. Many dissident bloggers avoided the dangerous gaze of a totalitarian government, but others fell victim to Viet Nam's efforts to control and limit information (Hookway 2009). With savvy maneuvering, administrators of *Đọt Chuối Non*, as veterans of VNForum, were able to survive. But the solidarity that developed between people in Viet Nam and those in diaspora grows stronger, even though control and censorship have grown in tandem. Transnational virtual communities influence Vietnamese politics and policies both internationally and locally; aided by ICT, communities are rebuilt and new ones emerge and evolve to address the needs and desires of a people and their counterparts in diaspora.

4

Defying and Redefining Vietnamese Diasporic Art and Media as Seen through Chau Huynh's Creations

In January 2009 an art exhibit of Vietnamese American works with the theme of diverse perspectives as expressed freely in art, *F.O.B. II: Art Speaks*, appeared in Santa Ana, in Southern California. A multigenerational group consisting of artists, scholars, students, and community activists organized *F.O.B. II: Art Speaks*, and it was supported by the Vietnamese American Arts and Letters Association (VAALA). The exhibit was a direct reaction to a more than yearlong protest by anticommunist groups against a Vietnamese American newspaper for printing an "offensive" image of an art piece by Chau Huynh and to a recall campaign against the first female Vietnamese elected to office in the United States, Madison Nguyen, arising from a business-district-naming issue. Anticommunist protesters and their supporters shut down the exhibit, but the following day approximately 150 protesters still gathered outside the gallery building to show their disapproval of the exhibit's contents.

The protesters eventually disbanded but not before a dramatic altercation between a few of them and one man, James Du, for showcasing what was reported in mainstream press to be a "communist flag." In actuality, the flag was not one of communism but rather a Chau Huynh–created quilt consisting of different-size South Vietnamese and North Vietnamese flags woven together. James Du's "unity flag" so offended the protesters that about a dozen of them beat him, causing the police in attendance to handcuff and remove him for his own protection. (Field notes 2009)

A portion of this chapter was originally published as Kieu-Linh Caroline Valverde, "Creating Identity, Defining Culture, and Making History from an Art Exhibit: 'Unfinished Story: A Tribute to My Mothers,'" *Crossroads: An Interdisciplinary Journal of Southeast Asian Studies* 19, no. 2 (2008): 35–62.

I counterprotested to begin an open dialogue, but before anything could be exchanged, I was beaten. (Du 2009)

Meant as a vehicle to open dialogue between diverse groups within the Vietnamese American community, *F.O.B. II: Art Speaks* instead represented yet another instance of how alternative views are suppressed. Exhibit organizers did not want to give in to the protesters but were forced by the city to shut down the exhibit three days early. Despite this, they believe the exhibit was an overall success. "While it has been a difficult process, in the end, we were able to celebrate the enduring power of art within this community," proclaims cocurator Lan Duong [Duong 2009]. But instead of programs and celebration on the last day of the exhibit, Lan Duong sits on what was to have been the performance stage, witnessing artists pick up their pieces to take home. If art speaks, so can it be silenced. (Field notes 2009)

An impetus behind the exhibit and James Du's one-man protest described in the passages above was the artist Chau Huynh. She is notorious for a controversial reworking of three pedicure basins painted entirely in yellow with three red stripes, symbolizing the former Republic of Viet Nam (South Viet Nam) flag. First publicly displayed as part of a student exhibit at the University of California in 2006, the image of one of these basins alone made her infamous within the diasporic community in the United States. When disgruntled Vietnamese Americans saw the *Pedicure Basin*, they protested in front of the largest Vietnamese American newspaper, *Nguoi Viet Daily*, in which the image was first published in 2008.[1] Segments of the Vietnamese American community, known for their anticommunist fervor, took special offense at Chau's art and claimed it showed lack of respect for the memory of a lost country. They also labeled *Nguoi Viet Daily* as communist for its decision to publish the photograph.

In 2012, nearly forty years after the United States withdrew from Viet Nam to end the second Indochina war and thirty-seven years after the fall of Sai Gon, images from that period still provoke extreme emotions. Many who experienced the war and its aftermath have not been able or willing to let go of the raw memories of those experiences; others who were born well after the war ended and now live far from the home country also find the war and its aftermath fraught. The struggle of these groups for representation emerges in art and art's media portrayal. In this context I discuss the works of Chau Huynh and the publication of her art pieces in *Nguoi Viet Daily*. The protests against the perceived symbolism behind the art and the backlash to the protests are my starting point for exploring emerging forms of Vietnamese diasporic culture and political ideology that were previously hidden.

This chapter focuses on Chau Huynh's life and motivation for her works. I discuss the *Pedicure Basin* controversy itself and *Nguoi Viet Daily* and staff involvement resulting in the more than yearlong protest because art, and places that display art, can shape what is acceptable cultural production in society. This is similar to what Timothy W. Luke suggests when speaking of museums as "highly political agencies, which become engaged in authoritatively allocating scarce cultural values by helping define who means what to whom, where, when, and how" (Luke 2002, 67). Cultural production and, very importantly, the media outlets that disseminate and validate the works, then, become the focus for shaping the political, cultural, and social landscape for relatively recent immigrant groups like Vietnamese Americans. Besides offering a narrative to help explain how cultural struggles develop, I dissect the reasons for these struggles and what the reasons imply about the future of identity formation for Vietnamese Americans overseas. Finally, I offer an argument for how this new environment of creation and discontent has allowed new struggles for voice and representation within the Vietnamese American community to emerge.

The Artist and Her Creations

As Chau Huynh herself did, we may wonder how an art student's senior exhibit, consisting simply of seven handmade quilts and one installation, became the focus of an international controversy for Vietnamese in diaspora. Now a mother of two, Chau came to the United States as an international bride in 1999.[2] Her husband, an overseas Vietnamese, had spent years courting her by flying back and forth from the United States before she agreed to marry him.[3] It took years because, among other things, they had very different political points of view. Chau recalled:

> I was raised communist and my dad was a party member for a long time. I really knew nothing about those who left Viet Nam. I was taught that the North liberated the South, and even when living in the South, no one told me any different. In looking back, I think no one dared because they were afraid [of the Vietnamese communist government]. . . . My husband, on the other hand, grew up in a very anticommunist family who fled Viet Nam. So whenever he tried to tell me things like Hồ Chí Minh was a bad man or communism hurts the Vietnamese people, I got very angry. I loved him but I could not believe the things he said. We had to agree not to talk about politics in order to get along. . . . My mother then finally allowed me to marry and leave with my husband when he promised her I'd be able to continue with my art studies in the U.S. (Huynh 2008a)

Chau's political beliefs initially did not change when she resettled in the United States, but her curiosity about the experiences of overseas Vietnamese led her to ask many questions:

> I first learned about the boat people and the horrible stories about the Vietnamese communist government from my parents-in-law. I then interviewed a lot of people that I knew and even acquaintances too about

this topic. From them I learned that the stories my in-laws told me were all true. . . . I didn't want to believe it, but it was clear that I was not told the whole truth while living in Viet Nam. For a period after this realization I too became angry and very anticommunist. I didn't even know about the South Vietnamese flag or what it looked like; can you imagine? I cried for both [the former Republic of Viet Nam and the current Socialist Republic of Viet Nam] flags. Now I accept that Viet Nam is still a part of me and I'm proud of my own background as well as my husband's. (Huynh 2008a)

The idea that people from different backgrounds could come together and try to understand each other inspired her *Marriage Quilt*. Chau sewed together Republic of Viet Nam (RVN) flags with SRV flags in varying sizes side by side.[4] "The flags represent the union between me and my husband," Chau explained (Huynh 2008a). While making the quilt, she knew she wanted to make more to pass on to her children and future generations. James Du, mentioned at the beginning of this chapter, purchased the original quilt. He dubbed it the "unity flag" and then used it to counterprotest the *F.O.B. II: Art Speaks* incident and to promote dialogue between Viet Nam and its overseas population. Chau made another, similar quilt at the request of her husband, and it now hangs in their home.

Chau's early home life involved some intensely defining moments. One was her father leaving the family when she was only seven years old. Recalling that day, Chau said:

He left my family and took with him the only possession of value we had at the time, an electric fan. I will never forget the image of my father carrying out that fan. Now I think maybe that fan meant a lot to him too, some sort of important memory perhaps. I've learned to let go a lot of the pain related to my father. I created the *Fan Quilt* as a way to try to love my father again. (Huynh 2008a)

Though the pieces in the exhibit represented all of Chau's family, she dedicated the show to her mother and her mother-in-law. Thus the title given to the exhibition: *Unfinished Story: A Tribute to My Mothers*. For her own mother, who still lives in Viet Nam, she created a quilt representing the period when Chau was nine years old and her mother was hospitalized with leukemia. The hospital did not allow visitors, so Chau wrote letters to her mother, who was particularly fond of one of those letters. In it, Chau asked about her mother's health and wished for her mother's early release from the hospital. She wrote that she had painted a picture, "Coming Home from the Market," and asked what her mother thought of it, whether it was beautiful or ugly. Chau remarked on the amazing inner strength of her mother during her illness:

You know, hospitals were really bad back then. If you had leukemia, it basically meant you won't live long. It was a miracle, but my mother got through that and still lives until this day. She claims that after reading my letter, she said to herself that her kids needed her and vowed to get better to return home to them. (Huynh 2008a)

When Chau's mother returned home, she framed the special letter and showed it off to guests whenever they visited. The framed letter embarrassed Chau, but it also served as a reminder of an intensely sad time in her life, when she almost lost her mother. Many years later Chau created a seven-by-six-foot quilt replica of the handwritten letter. Chau explained:

> I created the quilt because I figured I had cried so much already thinking about the time my mother was sick; I didn't want to cry anymore. I thought if I created a quilt of my letter, then the sadness and tears would be in the quilt itself, and therefore I don't have to cry about it anymore. (Huynh 2008a)

For her mother-in-law, who also had been very ill but then died, Chau had an equally cherished tale. Chau loved it when her mother-in-law told stories about Viet Nam because this history was all new to Chau. While in the hospital with cancer, Chau's mother-in-law began the story of the Hue massacre of 1968. She described vividly the carnage that turned the ponds red. From this image Chau created a quilt depicting a beautiful lotus pond with the odd distinction of having red fabric representing blood flow off the quilt canvas itself. Her mother-in-law passed away before she could finish telling the Hue massacre tale, leaving Chau with an unfinished story.

As a tribute to her memory, Chau created *Connections*, involving three pedicure basins painted yellow with three red stripes in each to signify the RVN flag. Yellow electric cords from the basins converge to a red electric socket. The image of just one of these basins made Chau Huynh infamous overnight. She explained her inspiration for the creation:

> When I first arrived in the U.S. my mother[-in-law] got me a job in a nail shop where I worked for one year before going to art school. I witness[ed] the women working seven days a week to keep the community alive [economically], send their kids to college, and remit money back to Viet Nam. Even though they [nail salon workers] are anticommunist, they continue to help out their relatives still living in Viet Nam. My mother-in-law was just like the other workers. She toiled in the nail shop for 26 years washing the feet of about fifteen customers per day using basins like the ones I painted for the exhibit. She put four of her kids and myself through college and sent home money to her family too. I created the basins as a tribute to her hard work and devotion to her family. (Huynh 2008a)

When asked what was the meaning behind the title *Connections*, she said, "I called the installation *Connections* because the basins represent the women working in the nail shops and the cords to the socket represent their connections to Viet Nam through sending back money [remittances] to their families" (Huynh 2008a). In 2010 alone, overseas Vietnamese remitted over $8 billion to Viet Nam (VNS 2011). Remittances have been an important economical component for Viet Nam, and its leaders have repeatedly thanked overseas Vietnamese for their contributions ("Overseas Vietnamese Are Integral Part" 2009). So Chau's mother-in-law was a part of this powerful economic force.

Given these explanations, *Pedicure Basin* does not seem intended as communist propaganda, as certain members of the Vietnamese community had claimed. Nevertheless, it was provocative enough that when a photo was printed in a popular Vietnamese overseas paper, *Nguoi Viet Daily*, it created a maelstrom. Some believed this cultural production disseminated through a popular ethnic newspaper threatened to destabilize anticommunist ideology. Chau was virtually unknown to Vietnamese Americans before photos of her works were printed in *Nguoi Viet Daily*, two years after she debuted the *Unfinished Story: A Tribute to My Mothers* exhibit. Shortly after the photos of *Pedicure Basin* appeared, leading anticommunist blogs using Vietnamese, such as *Take2tango* (no longer available), began ad hominem attacks on Chau, calling her names, criticizing her physical looks, and using sexual epithets. Most of the anti-Chau comments were along the lines of Chau having no talent, that she was a communist agent sent to the United States to create controversy within the Vietnamese American community, and that she was mentally unstable or physically ill. A vast number of posts used degrading, sexist terms. Posts also claimed she purposely tried to defile the South Vietnamese flag. In one such post on a Vietnamese American site, Vietsoul.com, someone with the screen name Philato wrote a lengthy piece calling for Vietnamese Americans to take action against Chau and *Nguoi Viet Daily*:

> The responsibility to protect and respect the United States is the responsibility of all citizens of South Viet Nam. Whoever lives in the United States has to be careful and should not just raise the flag everywhere, then let the flag get weathered and tattered like the ones we usually see in front of some commercial markets.[5] (Philato 2008)

Opponents even attacked her on the comments section of her personal Yahoo! 360° blog, resulting in her closing the blog to public view. This cyberbullying took its toll on Chau:

> You know, when I had my exhibit, I think I may have [had] subconscious [motivations in] not advertis[ing] to the Vietnamese American community. Even if I [had] expected this kind of backlash two years after the exhibit, I could not have imagined the magnitude of negativity towards my work. I actually was scared for the first couple of days after the protests.

Luckily, I had my family, friends, and professors there to support me. I
have a good support system. (Huynh 2008a)

Chau was not without supporters within the Vietnamese American community
either. *Viet Weekly*, another popular ethnic newspaper in Southern California,
ran a series of positive, in-depth articles about Chau. In the paper's online forum discussing the articles, there was name-calling but also a fair number of
Chau supporters who were critical of the protesters' tactics. An anonymous
poster wrote, "Opposing communism does not mean you can do anything you
want like a bunch of mafias" (Chống cộng không có nghĩa là muốn làm gì thì
làm như một lũ mafia). The post continued:

> If the Vietnamese people are fighting for freedom and democracy, then a
> picture or pedicure basin is the wrong target for doing so. They [protest-
> ers] speak up for "personal" ideas of freedom using the laws of a civilized
> country like the U.S. that completely respects and protects absolutely [the
> people's freedom]. When the "personal" ideas are forced to follow com-
> munists or communism, then you have the right to oppose.[6] (Anonymous
> 2008)

Additionally, in an article from *Xoài Vàng*, the publication of the Vietnamese Studies Association at the University of California, Berkeley, Christine Le
writes:

> Although the reaction from the Vietnamese community in this case is a
> bit more extreme [than anticipated], it also suggests the limitations that
> can be placed in a country in which freedom of speech and expression are
> its main values. . . . I used to think that art was the one thing that could be
> purely peaceful since it allows one to express an idea in whatever medium
> one pleases, but I guess that still depends on perspective. (2008, 2)

Arguably, the artist's intended meaning had little significance to the larger audience. This recognition of the power of art and the need to define and control
certain forms of culture production through media outlets led to the protests.
However, there is more to this controversy, and so I explore the mechanisms
of the controversy itself to uncover its deeper causes and the motives behind
the creation of art, media representation, and the protesters' discontent. Let us
begin this exploration with the *Nguoi Viet Daily News*.

Nguoi Viet Daily News

Nguoi Viet Daily News is the oldest and most reputable Vietnamese-language
newspaper in the United States. It was begun modestly by a former South Vietnamese journalist, Yen Do, who came over with the first wave of Vietnamese

refugees in 1975. With a meager savings of $4,000 and financial help from old school friends and colleagues he knew while in Viet Nam, in 1978 Yen was one of the first to set up shop in the center of what is now Little Saigon in Westminster, California (Brody 2003).

From the start, *Nguoi Viet Daily* was unique compared with other Vietnamese press before it. Inspired by the French newspaper *Le Monde*, whose journalists own the paper, Yen's business model calls for 40 percent of profits to be reinvested in the company, 40 percent paid out in dividends to workers, 10 percent to go to community projects, and 10 percent to go to humanitarian projects in Viet Nam (Brody 2003). He always made sure the paper was more like a tight-knit family than a business. Workers shared the profits equally during prosperous years and felt the pinch during lean years. As a journalist-activist, Yen's role included helping new Vietnamese refugees and immigrants decipher American society, through *Nguoi Viet Daily* articles, while developing their own ethnic community.

But even with the best of intentions to please and help members of the Vietnamese American community, Yen quickly realized that *Nguoi Viet Daily* would always face scrutiny from those within this same community, particularly the anticommunist groups. He attributed much of this to how the press operated in the former South Viet Nam:

> Most everything relating to the Vietnamese has been a consequence of the Cold War—during which the fighting was very heavy on ideas and on propaganda. . . . So when they came here [to the United States], the refugees could not agree about anything . . . the values, the way of argument, the rationale, the prejudices shaped their thinking that everything was a communist plot. (Quoted in Brody 2003, 64)

Nguoi Viet Daily staff was subject to threats, protests, and arson when they or the paper expressed ideas that were not perceived as anticommunist enough.

In 1989 when the paper printed pictures of Hồ Chí Minh's tomb, 150 people protested (Tran and Silverstein 2006). In another incident, *Nguoi Viet Daily*'s delivery truck was firebombed in front of its office because a television station affiliated with the paper showed CBS footage of Viet Nam containing Hồ Chí Minh's image and the SRV flag. The show benignly used the images along with a popular song about the loss of South Viet Nam, but still this was used by competing newspapers as evidence of Yen's treachery, and he and *Nguoi Viet Daily* fell victim to more extremism (Brody 1994, 2003).

The largest and most damaging protest took place in 1994 when the United States lifted the economic embargo on Viet Nam, making way for the thawing of relations and formalization of diplomatic ties that came one year later. During this period Vietnamese Americans began returning to Viet Nam for a variety of reasons, including visiting family they had not seen in decades. Yen took a public stance when he defended Co Pham, president of the Vietnamese

Chamber of Commerce, against criticism for traveling to Viet Nam. Furthermore, Yen broke a code of silence in Little Saigon when he told the *New York Times* that he believed much of the protest against Co, a doctor, was motivated by other Vietnamese American physicians wanting to discredit him to his patients. For this, approximately three hundred people descended on *Nguoi Viet Daily* demanding an apology from Yen. He refused but eventually resigned as editor when protestors threatened to boycott the paper (Brody 1994).

So, by the time the Chau Huynh art controversy appeared, *Nguoi Viet Daily* had already experienced several episodes of interethnic strife. Yen, who passed in 2006, was replaced by his daughter, Anh Do (Tran and Silverstein 2006), who inherited the legacy of protest. But while some things remain the same, such as attacks by anticommunists, others change, such as methods to deal with them. The Chau Huynh controversy revealed some new methods.

The Controversy

In its January 2008 Lunar New Year issue, *Nguoi Viet Daily* published a photograph of *Pedicure Basin* by Chau Huynh, then a master of fine arts candidate at the University of California, Davis. Managing editor Hao-Nhien Vu (2008a) first learned of Chau Huynh's exhibit with the controversial *Pedicure Basin* from her Yahoo! 360° social network blog. Chau had written in English a personal statement explaining that *Pedicure Basin* represented her hardworking mother-in-law, whose sacrifices earned her money to put her children through college and send money back to relatives in Viet Nam. Impressed by the artwork and Chau's story behind her creations, Hao-Nhien asked her to translate a blog entry describing her art into Vietnamese for publication in the *Nguoi Viet Daily*. The Vietnamese translation, along with a photo of *Pedicure Basin*, was published in the New Year's edition of *Nguoi Viet Daily*. The following month, *Nguoi Viet Daily* printed a lengthy interview with Chau, in which she spoke openly about several subjects: her communist background, the meaning behind her art, and the hope that there would be better relations between people in Viet Nam and those in the diaspora ("Mẹ Chồng Tôi" 2008a).

Some in the diaspora were outraged by the photo of *Pedicure Basin*, claiming that the art piece showed a lack of respect to their former RVN flag. They apparently viewed the intended meaning behind it as irrelevant. Both the artist Chau and *Nguoi Viet Daily* came under fire for supposedly having some sort of connection to communist Viet Nam. Protesters began picketing in front of *Nguoi Viet Daily* on February 26, 2008. For about a week, on average twenty protesters were in attendance. Protesters set up a Hồ Chí Minh effigy and displayed large images of *Nguoi Viet Daily* editors who they felt were responsible for publishing photos of *Pedicure Basin*. The protesters even presented two duplicates of Chau's *Pedicure Basin*, but they painted their basins to look like the SRV flag instead of the RVN flag. In the basins they placed cutout images of Chau, her mother-in-law, her mother as a young woman, her sister, her father, and Hồ Chí Minh. These images are believed to have come from the Internet and newspapers with stories about Chau Huynh (Huynh 2008b; H.-N. Vu 2008a).

The protests resulted in the recall of the New Year's edition in which Chau's article appeared, and the eventual firing of two of the top editors and the managing editor, Hao-Nhien Vu, of the *Nguoi Viet Daily*. The replacement managing editor assumed the position with an apology, calling the article a mistake. However, the protests continued through much of 2010, though with much less fanfare than in previous months, raising the question of what the protesters ultimately wanted. In late spring 2008, when the controversy was still at full intensity, protest leader Doan Trong Nguyen (2008) spoke to this question: "We protested page 194 [on which the *Pedicure Basin* photo appeared] of the New Year edition of *Nguoi Viet* [*Daily*]. . . . The bucket [pedicure basin] is a dirty thing, and to put the flag there says the flag is a dirty thing. But we respect the First Amendment, so we don't care about the person who made the bucket. We blame *Nguoi Viet* [*Daily*] for printing it." But as Doan's further comments below indicate, the protesters' gripe with the *Pedicure Basin* image was also a convenient platform for exposing the perceived politics of the *Nguoi Viet Daily*—obtaining political control through cultural control:

> *Nguoi Viet* [*Daily*] manipulates . . . the [Vietnamese American] people. Now, we let the [Vietnamese American] people decide the future of *Nguoi Viet* [*Daily*]. My job is to show the propaganda and give evidence about *Nguoi Viet* [*Daily*]. We initially asked *Nguoi Viet* [*Daily*] for a public meeting so they can explain to everyone why they printed the picture [of Yen Do and Vietnamese government officials], but we don't need that anymore. We already have evidence [of *Nguoi Viet Daily*'s connection to communism]. (D. T. Nguyen 2008)

The picture of Yen and Vietnamese government officials Doan referred to is one of two 1998 photos of the now deceased founder of *Nguoi Viet Daily*, Yen Do, with Vietnamese government officials in the United States. The two images in question included one of Yen and former consulate general Nguyễn Xuân Phong posing together with a Hồ Chí Minh portrait and an SRV flag in the background. The other picture was taken with the prime minister of Viet Nam, Nguyễn Tấn Dũng (who was still in office as of 2012). When asked what these pictures could mean, Doan replied that Yen Do might "have been a spy, an agent, or even a high-level Communist Party member" (D. T. Nguyen 2008). *Nguoi Viet Daily* representatives steadfastly defended their founder with the explanation that journalists often appear in pictures with those they interview. Besides, they were not sure the images were real; the images might have been doctored (Schou 2008).

When asked to state the ultimate goal of the protestors, Doan Trong Nguyen simply claimed it was "to expose *Nguoi Viet Daily*." He then quickly added, "But we don't want to ruin *Nguoi Viet Daily*." When asked whether the protests would stop if it were proved that *Nguoi Viet Daily* was not tied to communist Viet Nam, he answered, "That's for the people to decide. If the truth comes out, it will be the end of *Nguoi Viet Daily*" (D. T. Nguyen 2008). To make better sense of these issues, we must tease out the forces that create situations like the ones narrated.

Conflicting Forces

The controversy around Chau's installation and the *Nguoi Viet Daily* shows the continued efforts of certain Vietnamese Americans to produce their own reality away from the home country. A deeper understanding of the overseas Vietnamese experience requires consideration of how groups such as the anticommunist protestors and other members of the Vietnamese American community function within the sociopolitical order of their home country and their host country. These three—anticommunists, home country, and host country—powerfully influence the lives of people in the diaspora. Central to this analysis is a consideration of how these three forces work separately and in combination to dominate the lives of the overseas Vietnamese and how the latter then respond to those forces.

Community members whose ideas diverge, even in the arts, threaten the anticommunist base. Divergent ideas disseminated through media can potentially influence people's thoughts and actions. Media then, must be controlled. Thus, when Hao-Nhien Vu, the managing editor of *Nguoi Viet Daily*, decided Chau Huynh's art was valid, he inadvertently legitimized it and challenged the views of extremists in the diasporic community. Action perceived as having been influenced by Viet Nam threatens staunch anticommunists. The fear is that if members of the community are influenced by alternative ideas, they will not subscribe to a unitary history—that of losing at the hands of the communists. With the fall of Sai Gon, there remain only symbols of a time long gone. The South Vietnamese flag, strongly representing the lost nation, is one of the most potent of these symbols, and every potentially defiant act against it accrues monumental costs.

Controlling media is the frontline of the struggle to maintain an anticommunist ideology. The offensive art, some protesters argued, was only a secondary target because the newspaper is ultimately responsible for displaying communist images that counter the forces of anticommunism. If *Nguoi Viet Daily* is a communist-run newspaper, then the communist government of Viet Nam has infiltrated one of the most reputable overseas Vietnamese media outlets. This is unacceptable, and for many exposing and shutting down *Nguoi Viet Daily* is a worthy cause.

Because the newspaper depends heavily on advertising revenue that comes from Vietnamese American businesses, protest and boycott effectively disrupt revenue. Publishers of another well-read paper, *Viet Weekly*, know this all too well. Its founder, Le Vu, a boat refugee whose background is in engineering and computer science, began *Viet Weekly* as a direct reaction to what he perceived as anticommunist suppression of free speech. Almost immediately his choices of articles, in particular allowing an opinion piece from a former Viet Cong guerrilla, made Vu a target for protestors (Schou 2008). At the protest's height, an estimated one thousand picketed the office. Vu, however, remained steadfast, refusing to change the nature of the paper (Ortiz 2007). The protestors, though fewer over time, continued their protest for another eleven months, causing the paper to lose advertisers and cut down the number of printed pages.[7] This protest coincided with the *Nguoi Viet Daily* protest regarding Chau.

Ironically, the nearly yearlong *Viet Weekly* protest prompted Vu to seek advertisers directly from Viet Nam to fill the advertising gap (Schou 2008). Newspapers like *Viet Weekly* and *Nguoi Viet Daily* had originally had policies to not accept advertising even related to Viet Nam, such as from Vietnamese American businesses that sold Viet Nam–made products or travel services to there. Because of need for revenue and increased recognition of connections with Viet Nam, in 2006 *Nguoi Viet Daily* adjusted its policy to allow Vietnamese American advertisements for such services as visa application assistance for Vietnamese international students. Since 2009 the paper has accepted advertising from Viet Nam, such as for dental care services for the consideration of visiting Vietnamese Americans (Dinh 2011).[8]

The previous discussion has examined anticommunist attempts at censorship for fear of Viet Nam dominance and how institutions like the press comply with or resist these forces. Will anticommunist groups succeed in silencing free speech in instances like this, or will different voices rise to the surface? This I discuss in the following section.

Protesting the Arts

Protests are not exclusive to political issues, as art also has important political and historical meaning. This has included museum exhibits in Southern and Northern California with art from Viet Nam as well as art seen to depict offensive communist images and propaganda. For example, in the summer of 1996 when the Smithsonian traveling exhibit *An Ocean Apart: Contemporary Vietnamese Art from the United States and Vietnam* arrived in San Jose, it was met with protest. With no anticipation of controversy, the exhibit creators had included a component to showcase Bay Area overseas Vietnamese artists. Nguyen Qui Duc, a well-known journalist and cultural critic, was invited to guest curate. In the process, Duc found some interesting differences and similarities between artists in and out of Viet Nam. "I discovered they [overseas Vietnamese] reached back to their history and experiences (war refuge, boat journey, cultural difficulties, nostalgia). The museum curators and I didn't set out to directly show differences between artists inside and outside [Viet Nam]; we simply wanted to show there was a thriving art scene within the local Vietnamese American community. It all got lost in the protests" (Q. D. Nguyen 2009).

Indeed, approximately three hundred Vietnamese American protesters claimed the exhibit displayed blatant communist symbols (Sherman 1996; Dubin 1997). They did not succeed in closing down the exhibit, however, as they had three years earlier for a traveling exhibit of paintings by North Vietnamese about the Viet Nam War. That exhibit was canceled in Minneapolis and San Jose in reaction to protesters who characterized the exhibit as communist propaganda (Dubin 1997; Sherman 1996). Overall, Duc has fond memories of curating *An Ocean Apart*: "Looking back I am happy I had the chance to do it, if only to present images and voices from those living outside [Viet Nam]" (Q. D. Nguyen 2009). Even more, Duc set a precedent for being one of the first Vietnamese Americans to work on a national museum exhibit and bringing overseas Vietnamese art into the mainstream.

Exhibits like *An Ocean Apart* began shortly after Viet Nam and the United States normalized relations in 1995, opening doors for cultural exchange. The changed political climate also birthed the Meridian International Center's traveling exhibit *A Winding River: The Journey of Contemporary Art in Vietnam*. The exhibit consisted of artwork that included seventy-five contemporary works from fifty-three Vietnamese artists. Having its first opening in 1997, in 1999 it traveled to the Bowers Museum of Santa Ana in Southern California, home of the largest Vietnamese American population. The museum hosted the exhibit in part to serve this population but instead fell victim to protest by anticommunist groups, which believed the paintings were propaganda showing the oppressive SRV regime in a favorable light and called for the exhibit to close. Initially, Bowers Museum staff tried removing some of the more offensive images, such as *Young Woman Forging Steel*, with a woman in a North Vietnamese uniform, but ultimately left the exhibit intact, and the exhibit continued with its original curatorial intent (M.-T. Tran 2009). This incident showed that those displaying Vietnamese art in the mainstream still had very little understanding of the political pitfalls in dealing with the Vietnamese community's anticommunist elements. Art for art's sake did not take into account the continued pain and loss of the protesters, for whom freedom of expression does not extend to the arts.

In 2000 Pacific Bridge Gallery cofounders and curators Geoff Dorn and Beth Gates exhibited forty collage, digital imaging, and oil pastel works of Hồ Chí Minh's image done by an American veteran of the Viet Nam War, David Thomas. Many Vietnamese community members felt this much more blatantly controversial exhibit was a direct affront to their suffering as refugees. Before the show began, they warned that they would protest. True to form, the protestors came in droves the day of the opening and stayed on for the length of the exhibit (field notes 2000).

The curators felt strongly about standing behind the artists and their creations. Geoff Dorn explained:

> I'm always fascinated by the way the Vietnamese government hides behind Hồ Chí Minh as a communist symbol. They have the mausoleum and put him on display. Then there are those that left Viet Nam who really hate him. Abstract art presents dialogue around these issues in a way that only art can do. (Dorn 2008)

Dorn and Gates admitted in retrospect that they were naive to think that images of Hồ Chí Minh, arguably the most recognizable symbol of a communist Viet Nam, would bring about dialogue with anticommunist Vietnamese Americans. Also, they did not realize a large anticommunist protest just a year earlier had left momentum. That protest began with video shop owner Truong Van Tran, then a thirty-seven-year-old refugee who had come to the United States in 1980. Truong decided to hang the leader's image and flag at his storefront, claiming, "I like Ho Chi Minh and I have a right to" (Feldman 1999). In reaction, angry anticommunist protesters gathered in the thousands in front of his store for a five-day demonstration.

Interestingly, Truong had the image and flag displayed for quite a while without any repercussions. Closer investigation revealed that Truong sought reaction to his provocation. When he initially received none, he sent letters to community leaders. A prominent human rights advocate in the community elaborated: "Even after the letters were sent, we didn't care. But then one radio personality took it upon himself to make a huge deal about it. He really helped flame the situation, and pretty soon people got very angry about Tran's act" (Ngo 2008). When protesters appeared at Truong's store, his landlord, Danh Quach, filed an injunction against him. "He is causing a public hazard and people are losing business. . . . That's not how we do business," Danh Quach proclaimed (Mai Tran 1999). Orange County Superior Court judge Barbara Tam Nomoto Schumann issued a preliminary injunction against hanging the communist flag and Hồ Chí Minh image. She held that Truong broke his lease agreement, which prohibits him from creating a nuisance (Tessler, Yi, and Weinstein 1999).

At times the protests turned violent. Truong was beaten and taken to the hospital when he attempted to leave his store. Truong's attorney, Ron Talmo, was kicked by protesters when his identity was revealed by protest leader Ky Ngo. Reporters covering the protest helped physically shield Talmo from attacks (Winn and Jang 2004; Tsang 2003). Amid controversy over freedom of speech versus public discontent, the judge reversed her ruling, explaining that she had no choice under the free-speech guarantees of the First Amendment. When Truong returned to his store to hang again the poster and flag, he found a crowd of 150 protestors (Reuters 1999). The number swelled into the thousands as community members angry and hurt by the images joined anticommunist groups, curious passersby, and even tourists during the typically busy Lunar New Year period. The ruling would have stood except that police raided Truong Hi-Tek TV and VCR store and seized two thousand videotapes suspected of being pirated. Virtually all such stores contain similar contraband, so exposing Tran in this manner was clearly an attack. Tran's corporate landlord, Terra-Bushard, then shut down the store ("Shop Owner" 1999).

The Hi-Tek controversy has the dubious honor of gathering the most anticommunist demonstrators; however, the *Nguoi Viet Daily* situation remains the longest-running anticommunist protest. The organizers' motivations remain unknown because of their unclear messages. One may wonder why, while indicting Chau's work, they focused much of their protest on the publication *Nguoi Viet Daily* rather than on Chau herself. We also may wonder why the protesters asked for concessions but then continued to protest even, for instance, after the editors responsible for running the *Pedicure Basin* photos were fired and an apology was delivered. One thing is clear: such protests do meet with success.

The small group of people protesting in front of *Nguoi Viet Daily* managed to get themselves a great deal of press coverage. Their demonstration tactics included disrupting *Nguoi Viet Daily* business with noisy chants and visual materials. Examples include maintaining three small protest trucks outside the paper's headquarters that carried enlarged images condemning *Nguoi Viet Daily*. The trucks became a fixture, including a trolley with a fifteen-foot statue of Viet Nam's ancient heroic figure, Trần Hưng Đạo, in a warlike pose. Indeed, protest leader Ky Ngo explained that like Trần Hưng Đạo the protesters would not stop until the battle was won. "We want to create a monument right here [at the *Nguoi Viet Daily* office] to show that we will be here forever protesting [*Nguoi Viet Daily*]" (Ky 2009). Most impressive was the resiliency and dedication of the leaders and protesters, no matter how few. Like clockwork, daily they arrived and left the protest location, as if it were a job.

Whether these tactics will remain an effective and predominant form of political action within the diaspora is unclear, but the crossroads of demographic change and political diversity discussed above seem likely to eventually change the ways of doing politics in the diaspora.

Climate for Action and Change

Chau Huynh's actions may be a sign that we are at a crossroads. Chau's case is unusual, simply because she was the first to openly display images of the SRV Vietnamese flag alongside the RVN one. The act of painting the South Vietnamese flag on *Pedicure Basin*, without a second thought about how it could be perceived by anticommunist groups, was unprecedented. It is clear to anyone connected to the Vietnamese American community that anticommunist ideology has long limited the types of cultural, social, and political productions acceptable in the community. People who grew up in the United States in a household of Vietnamese immigrants are very likely to be aware of this, but Chau is different in many ways.

Chau's father was a Communist Party member who reentered the former South Viet Nam from the North. Her formal education consisted of radical propaganda that systematically erased not only the history of emigration after 1975 but also the history of the South from the Viet Nam War to the present. Having lived in Viet Nam most of her life, she did not know about, let alone understand, the political beliefs of the overseas population or their real motives for leaving Viet Nam. When she began her life in the United States, she worked in a nail shop for a year and then entered the university. Unfettered by unspoken rules that included careful self-censorship to avoid all possible symbols of a communist Viet Nam, Chau was sheltered in her art community, away from ethnic enclaves. Liberated, Chau created taboo images with abandon.

In stark contrast, her contemporaries in the United States take on the history and memories of trauma of their parents and elders as their own, commonly referred to as "postmemory" (Hirsch 2008). Long Nguyen, an Asian American artist, created *Tales of Yellow Skin*, a series of painted dismembered body parts, including a life-size boat textured with human organs to depict the war and refugee experience. Irrespective of the artists' personal politics, these are the images more commonly accepted by anticommunist groups.

Even now, when Chau is fully aware of the consequences of her actions, she is unabashed and resolute to carry on as an artist without fear, though these events have clearly affected her work. Ironically, during the height of the controversy in 2008, while working on her master's, in her studio was an ethereal installation made of white cheesecloth, with incense sticks forming the outlines of a boat that took up nearly all of her ten-by-ten-foot studio. It does not take much to understand this was a tribute to the experiences of the boat people from Viet Nam. "It's my way of honoring those that died in the seas," Chau explained (field notes 2008a; see also Huynh 2008b).

But along with the beautiful life-size fishing boat made of cheesecloth were stark paintings using primary colors and caked-on layers of paint. In the jumble of colors I could spot images of the SRV flag. What could have motivated her to go from a work that brings thoughts of peace and serenity to such bold art that incites anger and anxiety? She defiantly confessed, "Those protesters and their negative comments about me first hurt and scared me, but now I only feel angry. I cannot think of peaceful things when I'm full of rage. These paintings are the manifestation of my rage." Shortly thereafter, Chau burned her ethereal boat to "make room for more art" (Huynh 2008b).

Chau, previously somewhat free of the anticommunist aspects of the diasporic community, now found herself affected by the sentiments and tactics of that part of the community. Her initial isolation from those forces did not prevent her from experiencing pain and loss later. She must now work hard to remove the inhibitions placed on her by her confrontations with the protesters. Thus, in the end, those who deploy fear and intimidation within the

Vietnamese American community are at least partially successful in muzzling new ideas, but in doing so they bring creative, artistic, and political stagnation to the community.

The Chau Huynh controversy stirred the imagination of the Vietnamese American community, as seen so clearly with the *F.O.B. II: Art Speaks* exhibit described at the beginning of this chapter. In direct reaction to the intolerance displayed by the Chau Huynh and *Nguoi Viet Daily* protests, the exhibit included over fifty artists from Viet Nam and the United States with diverse perspectives. Curator Lan Duong, an assistant professor at the University of California, Riverside, commented, "I am not trying to be the voice of anyone or [any] group but I want to offer a place for . . . artist[s] to come together and move ahead as a block" (Duong 2009). Duong and her cocurator, Tram Le, explained the purpose of the exhibit:

> For too long, the Vietnamese community has defined *political* to mean either "anti-communist" or "pro-communist," with the former being the only acceptable label in this "community." Moreover, if the artwork contains any symbols, colors, or images relating to this kind of politics, it is propaganda. *F.O.B. II: Art Speaks* seeks to expand on these definitions because as long as we subscribe to this dichotomous ideology, we continue to allow two things: (1) those outside the community to see us as overzealous protestors with only one way of thinking and (2) ourselves to live in a constant state of fear of saying something that is considered "too procommunist" or "not anticommunist enough" or whatever is the "wrong" statement/sentiment/belief/ideology, etc., or else we will be shamed out of the community. Only when we let go of these limiting definitions of *politics*, *art*, and *community* and dialogue together can we truly move on to the process of healing and strengthening our community in a lasting way. (Duong and Le 2009)

Meant to end self-censorship and simultaneously open dialogue from various groups, the exhibit ultimately became a target for anticommunist protesters (M.-T. Tran 2009). This time the unacceptable communist symbol was Brian Doan's photograph of a young woman in a red tank top with a yellow star (representing the Vietnamese communist flag) standing next to an ostentatious golden bust of Hồ Chí Minh and a cell phone. My interpretation is that this represents modern day consumerism in Viet Nam and the questionable values that clash with the original images of a materially modest Hồ Chí Minh. Doan himself has said the woman's attire and the Hồ Chí Minh bust represent communist propaganda while her gaze reveals her dream and desire to leave Viet Nam (M.-T. Tran 2010). As with Chau's art, though, which is not exactly procommunist, none of this mattered because communist symbols still warrant protest.

The City of Santa Ana, where the exhibit was held, demanded the exhibit be closed because of the city's alleged inability to provide sufficient crowd control during the protests. The gallery's lack of city license was conveniently trotted out when *F.O.B. II: Art Speaks* organizers would not comply with the city's demand. Furthermore, state assemblyman Van Tran wrote a letter demanding the exhibit stop showing because of a lack of sensitivity toward the Vietnamese American community. Despite the exhibit's early shutdown the first day of protests, the protests continued the next day, as narrated above. Furthermore, Ly Tong, considered a hero in the more extreme anticommunist groups, entered the closed exhibit under false pretences and defaced two paintings. Besides spray painting Brian Doan's work, he attached female underwear and a feminine napkin to show how "dirty" the art was (H.-N. Vu 2009c).

The vandalism, and in particular the use of the female objects to show ultimate insult, indicated the attacks had taken on sexist and even ageist characteristics. Opponents of the exhibit began using sexist vulgarity, for instance, to attack the organizing group, who were all women. Cocurators Tram Le and Lan Duong received numerous messages on their private cell phones calling them names such as "prostitute." Ysa Le, director of VAALA, the sponsoring arts organization, was shocked by one such attack during the press conference to announce the early closing of the exhibit. While sitting alongside the cocurators, one board member, and a contributing artist—all women—Ysa remembers vividly a woman from the crowd dressed in the traditional *áo dài*, appearing extremely demure and feminine, who screamed profanities at the speakers, calling them *con đĩ*, or "whores." "I just didn't expect that language coming from her," Ysa lamented (Y. Le 2011).

In addition to, and more than, sexist attacks, Ysa experienced hostility based on generational differences. Ysa recalls that ethnic newspapers printed statements along the lines of "What do these kids know about communism; they are too young anyway. Their parents must have been too busy to properly teach them about the atrocities of the war" (Y. Le 2011). Additionally, Duong said, even though they had made all attempts to respect and honor the lost and the suffering of many in the community in the exhibit itself, critics still referred to them as children ignorant of and insensitive to the experiences of the war and its aftermath. They demanded, along with the shutdown, an apology from the women (Tram Le 2011; M.-T. Tran 2010).

Another such generational melodrama played out in the community and press when Brian Doan's father, Han Vi Doan, demanded and then pleaded for his son to take down the controversial piece during the show. Han Vi Doan had been an intelligence officer for the South Vietnamese Army and spent ten years in the Vietnamese communist reeducation camps before qualifying for the HO Program, which allowed former South Vietnamese soldiers and their families to immigrate to the United States (see Chapter 1). Opponents of the exhibit were especially critical of Brian Doan's perceived disrespect for his family and the pain he caused his father. Though sympathetic to his father's suffering, Brian chose to continue displaying the image, resulting in their estrangement (Bharath 2009b). Brian Doan and the cocurators, Tram Le and Lan Duong, respect the history of the refugee experience, which they share, and they ask only for respect for their endeavors to represent their and others' thoughts through art (M.-T. Tran 2010).

Whether the exhibit was a success is debatable, but Lan Duong seemed optimistic even in the aftermath of the shutdown: "While it has been a difficult process, in the end we were able to celebrate the enduring power of art within this community" (Duong 2009). Of the fifty-plus artists who participated in the exhibit, none backed down during the protests; all stood behind their creations, even standing up to public denunciation by their parents (Chang 2009).

Of the many different forms of bravery, withstanding strong tides of coercion within the Vietnamese American community is one. When Hoa-Nhien Vu was relieved of his position as managing editor of *Nguoi Viet Daily*, it could very well have slowed him down or ended his career. He admitted defeat yet found a new route in a more liberated form of journalism: a blog. He named his blog *Bolsavik*, chosen clearly as a swipe at anticommunists, and it is now a favorite among Vietnamese Americans. With a tone of exuberance unique among those attacked by anticommunist groups, Hao-Nhien said of his decision to blog:

> It was not a difficult decision to blog because I believe there are many in our [Vietnamese American] community well assimilated in our society and [who] appreciate freedom of the press and like that the writings are not sugarcoated. I decided to appreciate writing the truth. Like that Jack Nicholson movie [*A Few Good Men*], when he said, "You can't handle the truth!" There are enough people aware of the hard political facts. People know about the issues I bring up, but the only difference [between them and me] is I'm not afraid to write about it. So what I write, everyone knows, not just the *Bolsavik* [myself]. (H.-N. Vu 2008a)

Hao-Nhien described his time as editor of *Nguoi Viet Daily* as a balancing act. When it came to choosing a topic to write about, Hao-Nhien asked himself, "Will this be bad for anticommunism?" He explained further:

> Stories like investment in Viet Nam (like Intel—two billion) [were] newsworthy and there was pressure not to print it, but I did it anyway. Sometimes it is buried in the middle of the paper in small print. If I keep printing stories about investment in Viet Nam or doing charity work in Viet Nam, people in the community may think I'm a communist. These people think I should only print negative aspects of Viet Nam. And I agree there are problems in Viet Nam like the environment, and that should be printed too. (H.-N. Vu 2008a)

When asked why this type of censorship exists in ethnic press, Hao-Nhien offered this:

The community is not used to the idea of an objective press, coming from a war where both sides are trying to control propaganda efforts for the cause. Some even lived under communism [and] saw how their papers run. This may well be the best reason to explain things. (H.-N. Vu 2008a)

Hao-Nhien Vu showed courage in the face of tough intimidation tactics. He does so in the heart of the Orange County Vietnamese ethnic enclave and even blogs on topics that many find unacceptable. But taking to the Internet and creating a blog was just one form of resistance. Now some have taken legal action to deter protesters.

For instance, though *Nguoi Viet Daily* fired its editorial staff and formally apologized to the Vietnamese American community for printing a photo of the controversial *Pedicure Basin* installation, that did not placate the protesters, who continued their strike. Its chief editor, Anh Do, then got an injunction that limited protestors' activities.[9] The paper alleged a variety of infringements, including harassment and intimidation of *Nguoi Viet Daily* employees. Early successes included injunctions against certain protesters and limitations to their activities (Bharath 2008a, 2008b). One injunction banned protestors from "making threats of violence against the newspaper's customers and employees; assaulting with bullhorns; following or stalking anybody; acts of vandalism or damaging any real property belonging to the newspaper, its employees or customers and trespassing" (Bharath and Mickadeit 2008). On April 8, 2008, a preliminary injunction prohibited protesters from making threats and using bullhorns. Following that, on May 12, 2009, the Westminster City Council approved timed parking on the streets near the *Nguoi Viet Daily* office (Bharath 2009a). Protest leaders admitted the injunction made it difficult to demonstrate. Protesters continued to park their trucks with large propaganda posters but had to frequently move their vehicles, including the trolley with the Trần Hưng Đạo statue (Ky 2009).

To add insult to injury, in the summer of 2009 *Nguoi Viet Daily* rehired Hao-Nhien Vu as an editor. But far from making an issue of the rehire, *Nguoi Viet Daily* and Hao-Nhien have remained quiet about it. Though his responsibilities were many, he was given the simple title of editor. "*Nguoi Viet* [*Daily*] doesn't want to put my name too prominently out there because of the controversies from before," Hao-Nhien explained (H.-N. Vu 2009c). When asked whether returning to the paper meant returning to the same forms of censorship, Hao-Nhien seemed pleased with his new duties: "I'm still careful about what to report. The big difference is now I get to report on issues that I feel are important, and so I am okay with letting go of other issues. I can live with that" (H.-N. Vu 2009c).

In May 2009 Ky Ngo and two other protest leaders, Trong Doan and Cung Tran, settled a lawsuit originally filed in February 2008 by *Nguoi Viet Daily*. The lawsuit accused the men of "harassment, intentional infliction of emotional distress, violation of right to privacy, interfering with a business, nuisance, and trespassing" (Bharath 2009a). The three men are now prohibited from protesting at *Nguoi Viet Daily*, but a handful of other protesters congregated daily outside the office until 2011, well over two years after the protest began (H.-N. Vu 2011).

This victory for the embattled paper marked yet another break with formerly accepted political actions. It seems using courts to deal with protestors is not isolated to the *Nguoi Viet Daily* incident but rather the beginning of a trend. The protests of *Nguoi Viet Daily* supposedly began over a "communist" art piece intended to insult exiled Vietnamese from the former South Viet Nam. *Nguoi Viet Daily*, by choosing to print an article about Chau Huynh, the piece's creator, therefore must also be communist. This kind of simplistic premise and conclusion is at the core of a vast majority of red-baiting in the Vietnamese American community. Perpetrators are fully aware of how to use red-baiting to harm their opponents politically, economically, and socially, and victims have suffered without recourse. This pattern has changed in recent years as victims have filed defamation suits against their accusers.

In a journal article, Linda Võ documented one such case, involving the hiring and firing of Kim-Oanh Lam-Nguyen in 2007 for the position of superintendent of the Westminster School District. She was to be the first Vietnamese American superintendent of an American school system, but the school board changed its mind only one week after offering her the position. Kim-Oanh never received an explanation, other than the assertion that she was not qualified. The claim made very little sense considering Kim-Oanh's vast experience teaching at K–12 and university levels and activism for immigrant and refugee students. Her time as a Garden Grove School District trustee and as associate director of the Center for Language Minority Education and Research attests to her qualifications. Her outreach to Latinos and Asian Americans and ability to speak Vietnamese, Spanish, and French made her a favorite with parents. Her ardent supporters staged protests, and community leaders, educators, and politicians from across party lines and diverse backgrounds rallied around her cause. Even so, the board members did not reverse their decision (Võ 2007).

However, board members themselves later leaked the information that local community activist Sinh Cuong Cao called them after hearing about the job offer and told them that Kim-Oanh was a communist. This information presumably persuaded two board members to change their votes, resulting in a 3–2 decision to rescind the appointment (M.-T. Tran 2009). The daughter of a colonel in the South Vietnamese military, Kim-Oanh took the matter to court. "Mr. Cao's slandering negated all that my father stood for and damaged our family reputation," Kim-Oanh said. "The decision to seek legal action is one way to prevent incidents like this from happening again" (M.-T. Tran 2009). Kim-Oanh later amended her complaint to include "malice," meaning the false labeling was made recklessly with the intent to cause public scorn. Cao initially denied telling the board Kim-Oanh was a communist but then changed his story, saying he really did not know her and thus could not have malice. He added that the communist label is no longer considered slanderous and therefore not actionable. Both arguments proved detrimental to Cao's case because the jury thought making statements without proof supported the slander argument and they knew how denigrating the label is in the Southern California Vietnamese American community ("School Candidate" 2009). The slander case was eventually thrown out on a technicality (Nelson 2011).

Using the courts to defend against red-baiting is a noteworthy trend of historical significance. For example, community leader Tuan Joseph Pham of St. Paul, Minnesota, found himself on the defensive after lowering the South Vietnamese flag during a 2004 visit by a bishop from Viet Nam who requested to not have political symbols in his pictures. Soon after, some labeled Tuan Joseph a communist and protested outside his market, driving customers away and ultimately forcing him to close his business. As a former South Vietnamese soldier who suffered two years in a communist prison, seventy-three-year-old Tuan Joseph found the accusations hurtful. He filed a defamation suit against seven protesters. Tuan Joseph was awarded $353,000 in damages when the Minnesota Supreme Court ruled in his favor. Afterward, Tuan Joseph noticed that the name-calling and protests within his ethnic enclave had ceased (M.-T. Tran 2009).

Like Kim-Oanh Lam-Nguyen and Tuan Joseph Pham, *Nguoi Viet Daily*'s leadership filed lawsuits to protect the newspaper. These outcomes arguably constitute a pattern of successful legal action against the once apparently unstoppable onslaught of red-baiting. Similarly, Hao-Nhien's use of a blog as a medium for alternative thought has led many to herald him as a harbinger, bringing truth and information. Finally, Chau Huynh's wholehearted ownership of her art has led to dialogue on free speech, representation, and community identity. These actors are all highly visible manifestations of the so-called silent majority in the community. They and others like them help make it possible to imagine a diverse Vietnamese American population.

Conclusion

While untangling the *Pedicure Basin* controversy surrounding Chau Huynh's 2006 exhibit, *Unfinished Story: A Tribute to My Mothers*, and the exhibit's connection to the *Nguoi Viet Daily*, I observed that the Vietnamese American community lives in a state of fear. Fear of not adhering to anticommunist dogma, in particular, has placed most Vietnamese Americans in a Foucauldian state of self-monitoring. The ethnic enclave essentially serves as a prison and the rabid anticommunists as its guards. Because of the consequences of straying from the dominant ideology, the disciplined individual practices self-control even without the physical presence of guards (Foucault 1977).

The worst part of the situation is not that people live with the fear of being called an enemy of the community, or having aggressive protestors at their doors, or being closely watched and judged in everything they say, do, or produce. The worst part is that the fear the community has endured is so long-lived that it seems normal and expected; the fear and the resulting intimidation are rarely openly questioned.

Ironically, the anticommunists themselves are also afraid. At the very core of all of the protests lies fear, fear that one's history and experiences will be forgotten and one's suffering will not be remembered. It is counterintuitive: by alienating the people who can help us better understand the special history of the refugee experience, the fearful may initiate their own demise. The effort to hold on to *one* truth, history, and experience effectively brings the community to a standstill. People with alternative ideas and ambitions are forced underground, there to create under the shadow of fear.

With fearless people like Chau Huynh and Hao-Nhien Vu, media outlets like *Nguoi Viet Daily* and *Viet Weekly*, and those involved in the arts like organizers and artists of *F.O.B. II: Art Speaks*, a truer picture of the full diversity of the Vietnamese American community emerges. Individuals like Anh Do, Tuan Joseph Pham, and Kim-Oanh Lam-Nguyen showed their bravery by confronting their tormentors using the legal system. The trend of successes on the legal front results from the new and defiant ways that those in diaspora face historical fears to create change for the future. As Chau remarked after I asked whether she would follow the same course knowing beforehand all the controversy her art would cause, "Of course I would. I'm not going to leave the mess in the community for my children to have to take care of" (Huynh 2008b).

5

Whose Community Is It Anyway?

Overseas Vietnamese Negotiating Their Cultural and Political Identity: The Case of Vice-Mayor Madison Nguyen

On an uncharacteristically sunny and warm early winter day in February 2008, council member Madison Nguyen calls a press conference at her campaign headquarters in her recall election. Easily spotted in the crowded room, Madison wears an impeccably tailored, stylish, and form-fitting gray suit as she scurries about with a huge grin. As community members and journalists enter the room, she greets them warmly, pausing for the occasional whisper in her ear by her chief of staff, Louansee Moua, and her campaign manager, Melanie Jimenez, both as youthful as Madison Nguyen.

The room is filled with Vietnamese American journalists, many of whom had written extremely critical pieces on Madison's performance as a council member, and a few of whom came under attack themselves when they praised her. As the press conference begins, Madison comes to the podium, where she succinctly announces the release of her free, thirty-minute Vietnamese-language DVD highlighting the accomplishments of her three years as council member. Although she does not explicitly say as much, the documentary is clearly meant to convince the Vietnamese American public not to recall her. After the DVD announcement, one of the event organizers introduces a "very special guest." He is Madison's sixty-seven-year-old father, a former soldier in the Army of the Republic of Viet Nam. Dressed in a modest suit and wearing spectacles, Nho Nguyen begins speaking to the press in Vietnamese in defense of his daughter and presenting evidence she is not a communist. (Field notes 2008b)

t is difficult to imagine that a controversy over the naming of a business district would erupt into a full-scale recall election, but because she did not support their choice of the name Little Saigon for a San Jose business district, a group of Vietnamese Americans determined to oust a council member. As in the case of the artist Chau Huynh and her controversial *Pedicure Basin* installation, divisive politics led the Vietnamese American community to attack council member Madison Nguyen with slander and accusations of corruption. Madison's ability to keep her seat in the end signaled a new beginning for the Vietnamese American community—a significant recognition that there is diversity of thought in the diaspora and a willingness to expose malicious acts against individuals.[1]

With three generations of Vietnamese in the United States since the end of the Viet Nam War, it may seem strange that anticommunist sentiments remain so strong. Indeed, *community* in relation to Vietnamese Americans has become almost synonymous with holding staunch anticommunist views. Few are openly procommunist in any form, and other, more pressing issues exist, especially for the younger generation, including creating a place for themselves as Americans in the United States and negotiating a complex relationship with their home country, Viet Nam. Because perceptions and understandings vary greatly depending on each individual's connection and conceptualization of the Viet Nam War experience, it seems that Viet Nam truly is more than a war and even more than a country.[2] It has become not just one but many "imagined communities" in the Benedict Anderson (1983) sense, in which collectives imagine themselves as belonging to multiple communities. The image of Viet Nam can be and has been manipulated to form enforced realities, but when not everyone subscribes to these realities the struggle for real and perceived history begins.

This chapter examines the cultural and political struggles of Vietnamese Americans for political representation and dominance within the contemporary Vietnamese American community. This struggle includes coping with continued relations with the home country; adjustment to the host country; and the need to mediate divergent ideas within the ethnic community, felt particularly by staunch anticommunists. These three factors are sources of influence constituting a framework that can be used to uncover the causes of friction within Vietnamese American communities. Friction arises from residual sentiments surrounding the war—including anticommunist ideology, loss, and sorrow, which in turn hinder reconciliation with the country of origin and acculturation in the host or birth country. Additionally, class, generation, and gender have emerged as points of contention among community members.

I focus on one key figure—San Jose vice-mayor Madison Nguyen—who, despite a strategy of openness and compromise, found herself in a battle with members of her Vietnamese American community over representation in the naming of a business district and a recall campaign against her by those in her ethnic community. The naming debate culminated decades of political action and brought to the surface the true feelings of the silent majority and what it wants for the future of Vietnamese American politics. Madison's case is important as it marks a major episode of political events and uncovers generational conflict, gender discrimination, and power struggles. The outcome of her controversial decision as a council member offers a starting point for exploring the emerging forms of Vietnamese diasporic culture and political ideology, which have been alternately accepted, suppressed, or oppressed by local, national, and international forces. Despite—and sometimes because of—these multiple influences, overseas Vietnamese innovatively maneuver through difficulties and carve out cultural and political identities. Besides offering a narrative of how cultural and political struggles played out, the Nguyen controversy reveals the reasons for these struggles and what they imply about the future of identity and community formation for Vietnamese in diaspora.

Community (at) War and Peace

In K. M. MacQueen and colleagues' (2001) definition, a *community* is a group of people with diverse characteristics who are linked by social ties, share common perspectives, and engage in joint action in geographic locations or settings. The key characteristic of community is that it is a grouping that distinguishes itself from others. Hence, according to Anthony P. Cohen (1985), a community simultaneously has internal similarity within itself and differences from other groups. These differences include physical, racial, religious, and linguistic characteristics.

Friction among members of a community appears when some presume that there is only one way to think, relate, and act to maintain the cohesiveness of the community. However, difference within the community is as important a characteristic as similarity. Scott Peck's (1998) *The Different Drum: Community Making and Peace* presents the idea that the community-building process is deliberate and based on knowledge and application of set rules. The process goes through four stages: (1) In pseudocommunity, members are cordial with each other and present the most favorable aspects of themselves. (2) Chaos appears when people move away from the superficiality of the pseudocommunity stage and attempt to form an organization that relies on a facilitator for leadership. But organizations are not ultimately community, and (3) emptiness arises when people move on from attempting to fix, heal, and convert, and they acknowledge their own woundedness and brokenness, symptomatic of all humans. (4) True community then forms when people respect and listen to each other's needs, showing compassion for and understanding of fellow members of the community. Maintaining a sense of community in the later stages is the true challenge. Getting to that state of true community is the present challenge for Vietnamese Americans, as seen vividly in the case of Madison Nguyen.

The Politician and Her Dreams

At the press conference in this chapter's opening, all eyes were on Madison's father as he took the podium to speak in support of his daughter:

My name is Nho Nguyen, and with me is my daughter, Madison Nguyen. We are here to share with you something I have kept to myself since the day my family and I escaped from Viet Nam by sea. I was a soldier for the Army of the Republic of Viet Nam. After many years in the army, I was honorably discharged. I still have my discharge papers, and I brought those papers here today. When I left Viet Nam, I took with me the [former South] Vietnamese national flag. I believe that this flag represents a nation that is always close to my heart and holds the memories of my home country. As a soldier, I will never forget my country, and this flag represents my political identity. (Nho Nguyen 2008)

Madison's father lamented that though he wanted to protect Madison when critics unfairly attacked her over the years, he kept silent so that Madison would be "independent and experience life's lessons on her own." However, after the most recent accusations of her being a communist, he had to speak up to say that his family has no connection to communism. He added that Madison, who came to the United States as an infant, sees the United States as her home and wants, with all her heart, to help the Vietnamese community (Nho Nguyen 2008).

Her father ended his speech with a symbolic gesture: offering Madison the flag. Father and daughter then carefully opened a package to reveal the tattered, handmade flag that the elder Nguyen had kept with him since the fall of Sai Gon. Cameras flashed nonstop for several minutes as Madison and her father posed with the flag and his military discharge papers (field notes 2008b). This display seemed rather dramatic as an effort to dispel perceptions of Madison as a communist and traitor to the Vietnamese American community. Yet her current situation was far removed from her phenomenal rise in politics, a rise that had compelled members of the Vietnamese community to dub her a "golden child" (H.-N. Vu 2008b).

Madison burst on the political scene seemingly overnight, but in reality her rise was years in the making. Her involvement in the San Jose community began while a graduate student, when she directed a Vietnamese American youth center. Then in her midtwenties, she was a determined young scholar with a passion for social justice. She came to prominence when she organized a hugely successful voter registration drive for thousands of Vietnamese Americans in the city. The rest of San Jose would take notice of her when, as a junior school board member, she waged a dramatic campaign against the San Jose police department over the wrongful killing of a young Vietnamese American mother, Cau Thi Bich Tran. The effort resulted in a settlement for the slain woman's family, one of the largest in the city's history (M. Nguyen 2009b).

Madison was only a toddler when her parents and she and her eight siblings escaped by boat from Viet Nam in 1979. Their resettlement in the United States proved challenging at first:

My family worked in the fields picking fruits when we first came to Modesto in the 1980s. Each one of my siblings [and I have] had to labor since we . . . [turned] fourteen; no one got off easy. Working among other migrant farm workers taught me the lessons of hard work, perseverance, and determination. (M. Nguyen 2008)

Prospects for a better life might have seemed slim for the family except that her parents stressed the value of education to their children daily. The message had a profound effect on Madison:

> Even at a young age I knew going to college was the only way to leave the fields. Therefore, college was not optional. It was a necessity if you wanted a better life. Eight out of nine kids in my family attended and finished college. My eldest sister didn't go to college only because she got married very young. With the pennies my parents saved working in the fields, they put eight of us through college. (M. Nguyen 2008)

Though education provided a pathway to prosperity, Madison never moved far from her working-class roots. She majored in history and minored in education at the University of California, Santa Cruz. She recalled her college years:

> [In college], I learned about the different social movements in American history. So when I learned that there was a public demonstration for workers' rights and fair wages in Watsonville and Salinas, I would drive down Highway 101 to participant in these marches. I spent many more weekends fighting for worker's rights than most college students. I got involved because, coming from similar circumstances, I could relate to these workers. (M. Nguyen 2008)

Balancing education with activism, Madison sought to make change as an educator. She was admitted to the prestigious graduate program in social science at the University of Chicago. After earning a master's degree there, she decided to pursue a doctorate and focus on the Vietnamese American diaspora in her research. Since San Jose held the largest population of Vietnamese in the United States, she returned to her alma mater, UC Santa Cruz, for graduate study.

Upon returning to California, Madison quickly became involved in the Vietnamese American community as an organizer. She founded the Vietnamese American Center, where she and her staff provided after-school academic assistance to students and training in parenting skills to parents. This experience helped her better understand the lives and daily workings of members of the Vietnamese American community. She noticed then that although Vietnamese Americans as a whole do well economically and are able to send their children to top universities and establish strong social networks, they lacked in other ways. She observed they did not have a "political voice." Madison stated, "The obvious reason was that, as typical immigrants, they were more concerned with taking care of themselves and achieving economic stability. They didn't register to vote, or if they did, they tended not to go to the polls"

(M. Nguyen 2008). Recognizing the need for proper representation of the community, Madison set out to create change:

> So there I was, a graduate student looking at the social fabric of the Vietnamese Americans as whole and how to assist them to get more involved politically. The discrepancy in political representation was a major void, and I wanted to help fill that void. Since many Vietnamese Americans did not register to vote, I helped organized a concert called Rock and Vote, which [was] modeled after MTV's Rock the Vote. With this campaign we registered approximately five thousand new voters, many of whom were Vietnamese Americans. (M. Nguyen 2008)

Very much in tune with her generation, she found inspiration from the video music channel MTV. Her youthful energy and effective organizing skills with Rock and Vote received attention from enough people that, when a seat opened on the Franklin-McKinley School District board of education, many in the community encouraged her to run. So she put her education on hold to run for political office.

With the same energy and enthusiasm she had put into the Rock and Vote project, she began an aggressive grassroots campaign reminiscent of the way she had successfully registered new voters: talking to people directly herself and relying on volunteers. For her school board run, small groups of volunteers grew to legions of supporters within weeks. Madison beamed when she recalled the race: "I had volunteers ranging from middle school kids to many Vietnamese elders who spent their weekends knocking on doors campaigning on my behalf. The energy was definitely there" (M. Nguyen 2009b).

Although she had received some exposure from the Rock and Vote campaign, Madison felt like a "relatively new face" running against three incumbents. Because she was new to city politics, fund-raising efforts proved challenging, particularly in her own ethnic community:

> The Vietnamese Americans I approached were reluctant to give money to something they didn't even understand completely. The first visit where I asked for one hundred dollars from individuals and business owners was met with rejection. Still determined, I came back to the same people and asked for half the amount, fifty dollars. Still they resisted. Out of desperation, I visited them a third time, asking for any kind of donation, ten dollars, five dollars, anything. At that point they had already seen my face a few times and were impressed with my persistence. Some either felt sorry for me or recognized my determination, so they eventually contributed ten dollars each. (M. Nguyen 2008)

Madison believes that her strategy—visiting and speaking with as many people as possible and requesting only small donations—boosted her name recognition in the community.

With her campaign well under way, it became clear to many community observers that Madison was more than just a school board candidate; she had become a symbol of the coming of age of Vietnamese American politics in the region. Madison's campaign lawn signs began to disappear only a week after being installed. Rather than being evidence of pranksters or dirty politics, however, the thefts turned out to be the work of schoolchildren looking for souvenirs of the campaign. Madison reminisced:

> I was touched by what they did, because these students felt proud to have a Vietnamese candidate vying for a seat on a local school board. Some even took the signs simply because they also had the surname Nguyen; so placing the sign on their walls at home inspired them. (M. Nguyen 2008)

This type of support helped Madison get out her message and eventually win the school board seat. She received far more votes than the incumbent, who placed second. When asked what critical factor secured her victory, Madison said:

> One of the primary reasons I won was because our team had such a successful voter registration campaign prior to the election. Many Vietnamese Americans in the district were proud that they could vote for one of their own in an election. We had a relatively high turnout among Vietnamese American voters, as well. Of course, my landslide victory caught me by surprise because I thought that if I had come in third [winning the third open seat], I would be completely ecstatic. The overwhelming support of the Vietnamese community was breathtaking and historic. (M. Nguyen 2008)

Although only a junior politician in a relatively low-level political office, Madison quickly became the trusted public servant for all issues ailing the Vietnamese American community. The most compelling concern was the wrongful killing of a young Vietnamese American mother by a police officer:

> When the Cau Thi Bich Tran incident happened, it sent a huge shock wave throughout the Vietnamese community. People everywhere were upset that a San Jose police officer shot an innocent Vietnamese woman inside her own kitchen. The mainstream media did not do a good job with its minimal reporting. A few community leaders called me and asked if I could take the lead in approaching the San Jose police department to find out what actually happened. (M. Nguyen 2009b)

Creating her own definition of the duties of a school board member, she decided to take special interest in this case. In calling for aid, Madison recalled,

> these community leaders that sought my help regarding Cau Thi Bich Tran understood that, as a school board member, I was not in a position

to influence city officials in this particular case. However, they also re-minded me that the Vietnamese community didn't have anyone else who held an official political position. I was the only one they had. So I couldn't resist, but the decision to get involved had nothing to do with my politi-cal position, it was a social justice issue. I had always been an advocate for social justice. The incident was important to the Vietnamese community. It was important to me. (M. Nguyen 2008)

For the effort, Madison organized and mobilized approximately three hun-dred people, mostly Vietnamese, who marched from the victim's house to San Jose city hall and then to the San Jose police department to demand a public apology from the chief of police. They also demanded police reforms, including more police training in cultural sensitivity, foreign-language capability among newly hired officers, police use of tasers, and more transparency in police rec-ords. Madison was instrumental in helping Cau Thi Bich Tran's family win nearly $2 million from the San Jose police department for her wrongful death.

This victory and her good record on the school board launched Madison into the position of president of the school board. With her new success, re-spect, and name recognition in the community, it was no surprise that when a San Jose city council seat unexpectedly opened (a resignation resulting from corruption allegations), Madison was identified as a viable candidate. She was a reluctant politician again, but the same reasoning that had previously swayed her convinced her to run: if she failed, she could simply return to school.

Madison's city council race, which resulted in a tough run-off with another young Vietnamese American woman, Linda Nguyen, was historic on many lev-els. Vietnamese American voters in the community knew that whomever they supported would become the first Vietnamese woman elected to a city council in the nation. On election day, Madison made history in San Jose by winning 63 percent of the vote. Her campaign and victory made her a sensation not among only Vietnamese Americans but also non-Vietnamese constituents. She stood out as a unique Vietnamese American politician who crossed generational, ethnic, and racial lines. Transcending these boundaries made the victory even sweeter, she recalled. It was "joyous," "historical," "delightful," as many people attending her victory party attested.[3]

When asked how she won so decisively, Madison once again pointed to her grassroots operation: "We walked precincts every day just to make sure people know me and learn of my message" (M. Nguyen 2008). Though reluctant to discuss the pitfalls of her campaign, she said things got "messy" with the op-position:

It was the first time I experienced any kind of negativity from members of the Vietnamese American community. They wrote in papers and went on radio calling me a communist and focusing on my physical appearance. I found all of that very hurtful. (M. Nguyen 2008)

In his study of Madison's 2005 campaign, political scientist Christian Collet (2006) reports that her popularity was in part because of her modest beginnings and intellectual background. Collet documents that Vietnamese Americans tended to speak of Madison as an individual, whereas Linda Nguyen was often tied to her wealthy developer father, Son Nguyen. Although Madison remained popular, just over two years into her city council position she found herself in the middle of a politically damaging controversy over the naming of a San Jose business district where many Vietnamese businesses are located.

The Controversy—Little Saigon

The Little Saigon controversy began when factions within the Vietnamese American community asserted very strongly that a business district up for naming by the city should be named Little Saigon. They demanded the name mostly on grounds of national symbolism, branding, and popular support. Other considerations influenced Madison to propose what she regarded as a diplomatic and fair compromise based on popular names advocated by her constituents. When Little Saigon proponents did not get their choice, they mounted a negative campaign, accusing Madison of, among many other things, being a traitor to her ethnic community, being a communist, having dirty dealings with business developers, and illegally counseling her fellow council members to vote her way on the naming issue. Despite weekly rallies against her at city hall, endless name-calling, and a media onslaught, Madison maintained her position on the naming issue. Her opponents forced a recall election.

These events are widely viewed as a charged ethnic dispute involving a segment of the Vietnamese American community that wanted to name a business district Little Saigon and Madison Nguyen, who believed in compromise and who won the support of a majority of her fellow council members to name the commercial area the Saigon Business District. Proponents of the Little Saigon name said their preference was the only way to represent overseas Vietnamese and their experiences as refugees fleeing a communist-controlled Viet Nam. I look deeper, beginning with the question of how Madison Nguyen, elected with an outpouring of support from the Vietnamese American community, found herself in a fight to save her political career only two years into her term—a fight begun by members of the very same community.

During the recall campaign, Madison confided to me that the contention had taken a toll on her. When asked why she stayed in politics if the cost was so great, Madison sighed and answered, "Where do I begin?" The answer lies at the beginning of her run for the city council (M. Nguyen 2009b). When she ran for city council, she promised her ethnic community that if elected, she would make sure two things happened. The first was to build a Vietnamese community center with $2 million she had helped raise for that purpose. The second was to get the City of San Jose to recognize the contributions of Vietnamese commerce by formally recognizing the businesses' location as a business district.

Speculation within the San Jose Vietnamese American community is that, with the community center project, some already felt Madison was not complying with wishes of some ethnic leaders. John Vu, Vietnamese American blogger and proponent of the Little Saigon name and recall campaign, reported that "the community was in uproar when she made the decision on who would be on the board and running the center without consulting the community." So when the business-district-naming issue came up, they perceived Madison's explanations as more lies to mask her true intentions (J. Vu 2008a).

For Madison the designation of a commercial area was important because it meant that businesses, particularly small ones, could receive city improvement grants. As a grassroots politician, Madison's instinct was to get input from the Vietnamese American community on what to name the new district: "I wanted to be inclusive and give the community a voice, and so I opened up the discussion to name the business district. . . . We had a couple of community meetings, and mainstream news covered it" (M. Nguyen 2008).

Proposed names for the business district designation included Vietnamese Business District, Saigon Business District, New Saigon, and Little Saigon. When a news article appeared on a Vietnamese website discussing the business-district-designation project, some Vietnamese Americans took notice. In the first of many misunderstandings around the naming issue, members of the Vietnamese American community circulated the idea that Viet Nam media had learned of the business-district-naming meetings before the diaspora had, failing to notice that the articles were direct translations from Associated Press articles. Madison noted that these readers and numerous Vietnamese American language presses asked, "How come Ha Noi knew about this meeting and we didn't?" Her opponents were convinced she never intended to include the community in the naming process and that she had settled on a name on the basis of personal and economic gain (J. Vu 2008b). Such allegations would mean a huge conflict of interest warranting investigation, but the city never investigated Madison.

Rumors of Madison's connection to Ha Noi escalated when it became public that she had become engaged to a Vietnamese international student, Terry Tran.[4] The ambiguous political nature of Vietnamese international students in general and Terry's unknown background troubled Madison's foes. The Vietnamese American press then incorrectly reported that Terry belonged to a powerful communist family. Stories circulated that he and Madison had had a lavish wedding with forty Vietnamese officials in attendance. "Nothing could be further from the truth," Madison explained:

I had a small wedding with family members and really good friends at a friend's house. We had originally put a down payment for a five-hundred-guest reception, but we were concerned that some people might be upset that they were not invited since they were also big supporters of my campaign. Also, I did not want my wedding day to turn into a political event. (M. Nguyen 2008)

To complicate matters, the Vietnamese president at the time, Nguyễn Minh Triết, was visiting the United States during the same period as Madison's wedding. This coincidence caused some members of the community to speculate that Madison's close relations with the communist party included following their bidding to name the business district (M. Nguyen 2008).[5]

Undaunted by the new attacks, Madison planned a community meeting about the naming issue:

> [At] the first meeting [on August 15, 2007,] the [Vietnamese American] advocates for the name Little Saigon came with signs and said they would not support me and that they will call me a communist unless I name the business district Little Saigon. I opened up the meeting with this protest going on because I believe in the politics of convincing, not politics of fear. At the meeting I explained the process that included surveying [residents and business owners within] a thousand-foot radius of the Story Road shopping area[, the center of the business district]. At this point the protesters wanted to know the names of the people and businesses that did not want [the] Little Saigon [name]. They threatened to pay them a visit. I was shocked, because these threats were being made in an open forum. They [the Little Saigon proponents] did not understand the surveys were anonymous and the council doesn't give out information of survey participants. This was too much like communist Viet Nam [with its lack of privacy around politics]. (M. Nguyen 2008)

Madison intended the meetings to help the Vietnamese Americans in attendance better understand the process behind naming a business district:

> During the closing remarks of this meeting, I thanked everyone for attending. I explained the process thoroughly. After my concluding remarks, the room was completely silent for a few minutes. Then all of a sudden one person screamed, "Đả đảo Madison" [Down with Madison]. The rest of the audience joined in, with some adding that I was a communist, and started yelling, "You know what you did; you're a traitor and a liar." (M. Nguyen 2008)

Opponents claimed it was not so much the content of her words that troubled them but rather "her condescending tone, disrespectful manner and gesture" (J. Vu 2008a). A particular meaning behind the name of Little Saigon also appeared. Little Saigon advocates claimed that that name alone represented the refugee experience, freedom, democracy, and nationalism. Most of all, it represented anticommunism. Hence, not supporting the name Little Saigon meant not believing in these ideals. Madison's opponents immediately uploaded to YouTube local news segments reporting on the issue and a video of the meeting in which Madison explained the city's general process for naming a business district (though the exact protocol was unclear). These video clips were touted as proof of Madison's disrespect for the community and proof that she had not been open in the process.

The pro–Little Saigon movement had a substantial elderly representation who were particularly outraged about the naming situation, although some from the 1.5 generation lent their support to the Little Saigon name.[6] One of the most outspoken of this latter group, Dan Pham,[7] confessed that his involvement was not because of a personal connection with the name Little Saigon per se; rather, he felt compelled to aid the older generation because, without fluency in English and understanding of American institutions, they seemed to lack a voice in the political process. However, he had his own reasons for protesting as well, which mirrored those of many Little Saigon supporters:

> [First,] supporting the Little Saigon name allows for a consistent [commercial] branding of the name since it has been used in places in Southern California like Santa Ana, Garden Grove, and Westminster as well as in Northern California, like San Francisco. Second, it is a political branding that will help us redefine the political position of the community as anticommunists and political refugees. The name Little Saigon unifies us [Vietnamese Americans] with established communities like Japantown, Chinatown, Little Havana, and so on. Last, it connects me with fellow [overseas] Vietnamese, and it will help the next generation to do the same. I embrace the name Little Saigon on an intellectual and emotional level and support the intentions behind fighting for it for the older generation. (Dan Pham 2008)

Though passionate in his support for the name and its proponents, Pham's personal ambivalence regarding Little Saigon was a common reaction heard in over two dozen formal and informal interviews I conducted on the significance of the name. When asked if the name Little Saigon *always* represented anticommunism and the refugee experience of Vietnamese Americans in San Jose as they claimed, answers got complicated. Some adamantly believed in the symbolism of the name. However, when asked why they would fight for the name only now, when hundreds of shopping centers, stores, and community organizations and centers have existed in San Jose since the end of the war without the name Little Saigon attached to them, there was no clear answer. Even 1.5- and second-generation opponents of Madison Nguyen answered that they had no emotional ties to the name. They explained that their disagreement with Madison had more to do with her character and actions as a politician than the importance of the name Little Saigon; supporting the Little Saigon naming effort exposed Madison's motivations.

Specific names notwithstanding, the idea of ethnic place making to preserve cultural identity and maintain a sense of community in a racist society has real merit (Aguilar-San Juan 2009). When a people can associate a name with a space that inspires these sentiments, it makes the geographic place all the more important and meaningful. Without a doubt, Little Saigon as a name has symbolic cultural, economic, and nationalistic value and is widely recognized in the U.S. mainstream, Viet Nam, and Vietnamese diaspora. Yet the meaning behind the name, what it represents, and commitments to it vary according to each person. It does not hold the same meaning or value for everyone in the community. For instance, compared to other names, it may have more cultural significance in Westminster, Southern California, where Little Saigon is a designated commercial center and tourist attraction recognized by the city and known worldwide as the de facto capital of Vietnamese living in diaspora. This does not hold true in all other areas with Vietnamese commercial strips, though. Vietnamese in the San Jose area, for example, have had businesses there since about 1975. At any point in the last thirty-five years, merchants or residents near the business centers could have named whole commercial areas Little Saigon or even informally called a section of the city Little Saigon, but they had not. Hence, given the very recent fervor to name the business district Little Saigon, I argue that the cultural and economic significance of Little Saigon for Vietnamese Americans in the San Francisco Bay Area generally, and San Jose specifically, was motivated in large part by political discontent.[8]

Because of the strong tensions within parts of the Vietnamese American community in the area, Madison carefully weighed which name to back on the basis of communications from her constituents. After hundreds of phone calls, e-mails, and letters, she made her selection: "I chose Saigon Business District as a compromise. Fifteen prominent Vietnamese American organizations wanted New Saigon. To appease the New Saigon and Little Saigon supporters, I chose a name that they both shared, Saigon. Representatives of the New Saigon people were fine with the compromise. Little Saigon supporters were quite upset, to put it mildly" (M. Nguyen 2008). The discontent steadily grew. "Five days before the vote I had a press conference. One of the protestors threw back my own campaign shirt," Madison said. Despite such incidents, Madison believed she was doing a good thing for the community. But more than that, she wanted to represent everyone in the community, including non-Vietnamese residents, and not just a particular few.

In early October 2007 at the second community meeting on the naming issue, approximately one hundred protestors appeared. Madison recalled the feeling of excitement in seeing all the Vietnamese American faces present. "This was good because we usually get about three Vietnamese attendees at community meetings." But then Madison heard shouts of "There she is; she's the traitor." Attacks grew personal. As Madison recalled:

> When I was walking to my chair at the community meeting, this older lady was screaming at me. It really hurt my feelings, especially since I knew the lady. She's in fact about my grandmother's age. I turned to her and said in Vietnamese, "I know you. You helped me with my campaign.

I went to your house with *Tết* gifts. You know me. Why are you being this way? You can speak with me nicely. You don't have to use these rude words." The woman just said, "I won't talk to you anymore," then turned away.[9] (M. Nguyen 2008)

Every time Madison thought she was being helpful to the community, she found herself under attack by some of its members. Madison had called the meeting to discuss the business-district banner. "It looked really nice, and I even fought to have the South Vietnamese flag included in the banner," she said and added, "Still, the protesters shouted, 'We just want Little Saigon. We don't want the banners. We will protest the businesses'" (M. Nguyen 2008). Madison felt betrayed and baffled by such strong opposition to a project that she had spearheaded to honor her own ethnic community.

At this point, it might have seemed logical for Madison to reconsider her stance or at least reconnect with her constituents to consider the name Little Saigon and appease the protesters. This did not happen. So proponents of the Little Saigon name grew impatient with Madison. They organized the Committee for Little Saigon (CLS) and continued a media blitz of negative attacks against her while restating their support for the Little Saigon name. Barry Hung Do, spokesperson for the newly formed CLS, explained the importance of the name Little Saigon:

> Only Little Saigon always represented the Vietnamese American identity. We don't want the name Saigon because that is the name of the former capital in Viet Nam, not here. Why with such a reasonable request did Madison not agree to name it Little Saigon? We have to ask why . . . , and maybe it has something to do with [her connection to] the [Vietnamese] communists. Maybe the Vietnamese do not like the name Little Saigon. (B. Do 2008)

Madison Nguyen's name was now firmly linked to communism, a label she and many others on her behalf reject.

The vote for the name finally came on November 20, 2007, at city hall. By most estimates, approximately eight hundred people arrived at city hall, but only three hundred were allowed to enter because of capacity limits. The vast majority of people allowed in and those who had to wait in the rotunda shouted in protest against Madison. When asked why there was so little public support for Madison at the council meeting, she conjectured:

> I was told by several people that Little Saigon supporters harassed them because they refused to hold the Little Saigon signs. A lot of people left before the meeting began because they felt intimidated by these types of harassment. Most people who left are young and 1.5-generation Vietnamese. The Little Saigon supporters were aggressive, and they went around

and ripped up all the signs that did not read "We support Little Saigon."
(M. Nguyen 2008)

Inside the hall, attendees were allowed to voice their opinions of the name.
Most came to the podium to express their preference for the Little Saigon
name; others boldly called Madison names, blaming her for not doing what
they wanted. Expressed opinions started off rational but then escalated to passionate anticommunist statements and the linking of ideals of freedom to the
name Little Saigon. Many attendees were above middle age, with an impressive
showing of seniors, but there were also some young people. Madison was especially struck by one of these young speakers:

> One of the twin girls who regularly attended community meetings and
> helped me with my campaign spoke about her parents' struggles against
> communism and escaping Viet Nam to only experience it again in the
> United States. She compared the [security] guards at the [city council]
> meeting to the communists who tried to control her parents. If you didn't
> know that she was born in the United States and had never experienced
> the aftermath of 1975, you would think she was there when the commu-
> nist government took over South Viet Nam. (M. Nguyen 2008)

Even with the overwhelming number of Little Saigon supporters present, council members still voted eight to three in favor of Madison's name recommenda-
tion, Saigon Business District. It was a bitter victory for Madison because she
believed that the protestors, though clearly a very strong presence at the meeting, did not represent the majority of the Vietnamese American community as
they had repeatedly claimed. Interestingly, during deliberation some of Madison's colleagues began lecturing the protestors, coming to her defense. They
argued that she was one of the hardest-working council members they had ever
known and that she always strongly advocated for the Vietnamese community.

For months following the vote, many Vietnamese residents of San Jose
spoke their minds and some even took to the streets. Little Saigon supporters
not only bombarded the Internet with blog entries and video clips criticizing
Madison Nguyen; they also began a weekly protest outside city hall. Calling it
Black Tuesday, in a reference to Black Friday, for the day South Viet Nam fell to
the communists from the North in 1975, bands of protesters, averaging about
twenty each time, held up banners and shouted anti-Madison slogans. These
city hall protests culminated in a large rally reportedly attended by approximately two thousand Vietnamese Americans from across the nation (Molina
2008). On February 15, 2008, a flamboyant veteran from the South Vietnamese
air force, Ly Tong, volunteered to go on a hunger strike until the name Little
Saigon was chosen.[10] But his was not the only voice present.

The general population also chimed in on the controversy. On the website
of the *San Jose Mercury News* in the comments section, emotions ran high after

Little Saigon–related stories were published. Some postings expressed support for the Little Saigon movement, believing its proponents' assertion that the name represents the Vietnamese American community. Many more, however, displayed frustration over the matter; to them, there was no difference between the names Saigon and Little Saigon, hence, they saw the controversy as petty ethnic melodrama. Racial tension arose when other demographic segments of San Jose, predominantly Latinos and whites but also other Asian Americans, began efforts to reclaim San Jose as a multiethnic city that should not have ethnically demarcated business districts. At times, people posted comments containing racial epithets directed toward Vietnamese Americans on Little Saigon–related articles. For instance, in reaction to an editorial I wrote highlighting the issue of red-baiting and media's role sensationalizing controversial issues like Little Saigon, comments ranged from agreement with my interpretation of the controversy to personal attacks against me (Valverde 2008). Some aggressively claimed that their understanding of Viet Nam's history and the experience of refugees was the only correct one. The comments evolved into a battle of words among the posters themselves. For example, Eddi Chu of Monta Vista wrote:

> Viets go back to Vietnam! If people really consider themselves American they should stop being hyphenated Americans. This is the problem: NO assimilation, no respect for what America represents. These immigrants and 2nd and 3rd generation Viets are not American so long as they represent or fight for ethnic separatism. These starving Boat People should be glad they were allowed to settle and prosper here. These people didn't even have a written language until the Portuguese and the French colonized them. Mostly the Viets were a bunch of backward hill tribes living in huts and digging around for roots to eat.

The pattern of comments my editorial received was repeated for most of the *San Jose Mercury News* reports on the issue.

At the March 4, 2008, council meeting to discuss the naming issue again, both supporters of the Little Saigon name and those against were present. Both sides were given fifteen minutes to make group statements. Little Saigon proponents once again claimed that they represented the majority in the Vietnamese American community in wanting the name and that Madison's actions were based solely on the interests of developers. On the other side stood supporters of alternative names or those who generally supported Madison and wanted a peaceful resolution to the naming issue (field notes 2008c).

Little Saigon advocates made an impressive showing; several hundred were given an opportunity to state their case. The vast majority simply said, "I support Little Saigon." The few who elaborated on their support seemed to hold a particular set of assumptions about Madison. Many who took to the podium used misquotations and unsubstantiated rumors as the basis to attack her. Approximately one-quarter spoke in support of Madison and offered an array of alternative names for the business district. By the end of the meeting, following Madison's lead, council members rescinded previous decisions regarding the naming issue. They acknowledged that the city lacked a structured process for naming business districts. Even though they dropped the naming issue altogether, the council expressed optimism that, with feedback from residents and business owners in the district, they could revisit the naming issue at a later date. It is unclear why council members decided unanimously to rescind the name Saigon Business District. It seems likely that they wanted to free themselves from the controversy that had plagued city hall for over half a year (field notes 2008c).

By 2:00 A.M. on the night of the meeting, nearly everyone had received time at the podium. Before the council deliberated, Mayor Chuck Reed addressed the audience. He said that, as a military veteran, he found being called a communist by Little Saigon supporters on the basis of his actions on the naming issue extremely offensive. He further asserted that intimidation tactics were not the way to do politics. Madison followed with a statement addressing some of the remarks directed at her:

> There has been a steady stream of dissidents to the vote [of the council]— Vietnamese men and women who felt that I had somehow betrayed the community and conducted myself in an undemocratic manner. As understandable as the passions are behind these feelings, the methods employed by a fraction of this population are unacceptable. I can accept differing opinions. I can accept the fact that some disagree with the decision. I can accept all the criticisms because, in an open and democratic society, everyone is entitled to his or her opinion. Although I can endure the personal insults, abuse, and accusations that have arisen from this situation, I cannot tolerate the attacks to my colleagues, to my staff, and to my family. I am also disheartened by the insinuations that the process of municipal government is somehow an undemocratic one. Additionally, I regret that what was meant to be an economic development project has turned into a stream of political upheaval. However, now is the time to bring closure to this issue and move our community toward a peaceful resolution. (M. Nguyen 2009a)

Nearly two weeks later, on March 26, 2008, the City of San Jose, with support from both Mayor Reed and Madison, made a deal with the proponents of Little Saigon. The city agreed to allow proponents to hang banners with the name Little Saigon at their own expense.[11] Although the group treated this agreement as a victory, they continued their efforts to recall Madison.

Recall Campaign

On April 22, 2008, the Recall Madison Nguyen committee submitted paperwork for a special election, and on October 9, 2008, it had gathered enough signatures to qualify for the March 3, 2009, ballot. The recall attempt was soundly defeated that day, voters rejecting it by 55–45 percent. Madison Nguyen's victory can be attributed to some basic facts: she raised twice as much money for her no-recall campaign than her opponents; all the San Jose council members and the mayor supported her; other high-ranking politicians throughout the state endorsed Nguyen, including former mayor of San Jose Norman Mineta and former mayor of San Francisco Willie Brown Jr.; a cross section of San Jose groups, including the San Jose Silicon Valley Chamber of Commerce and South Bay AFL-CIO Labor Council, supported her; and non-Vietnamese and Vietnamese alike supported her (M. Nguyen 2009b; Woolfolk 2009).

Madison's biggest battle was to keep her spirits up through the long campaign. That proved a challenging task, as she conveyed to me:

> Sometimes, driving through my grandmother-in-law's neighborhood for a visit, I'd see rows of "Recall Madison" lawn signs. I get sad. These are the same people I work hard for daily so they will have better housing and pride in being Vietnamese in San Jose, and they hate me. (M. Nguyen 2009b)

Madison always seemed upbeat about her chances of beating the recall. When asked how she could maintain such confidence she replied, "I have my campaign manager and chief of staff to worry and be conservative about our chances of winning. If I don't remain upbeat and optimistic, we'd all be depressed and nothing gets done" (M. Nguyen 2009b). Her confidence was warranted considering the cross section of support she received during the recall. This was most apparent during her victory speech at the AFL-CIO office in San Jose on March 3, 2009. Approximately 250 people—young, old, middle-aged, black, white, Asian, and Latino and an equal number of men and women—were in attendance as Madison addressed the crowd:

> I didn't even cry when a thousand people came down to city hall to yell and scream at me, and here I am, speechless. I really have no words to describe how grateful I am for all the work that you've done. This is the American dream for me. And this is bigger, way, way bigger than when I won in 2005. This election, this campaign, has brought out so many people from all walks of life, from all parts of the community, from different parts of the city, county, and state. And I really don't know what I've done to earn such support, but I will never forget it. Thank you so much. Thank you. Thank you. (M. Nguyen 2009a)

Overwhelmed but relieved by her victory, Madison pondered what her accomplishment meant for the future of Vietnamese American politics.

Conflicting Forces and the Power of Protest

The controversy around Madison Nguyen, the Little Saigon naming issue, and the recall campaign exemplify the tension in the continued efforts of Vietnamese Americans to produce their own reality away from the home country. This tension stems from the relationship the diaspora has with Viet Nam, the United States, and anticommunist members of Vietnamese American communities and it leads to conflict between genders, generations, and classes. Along with the usual quest for fame, power, and money, these conflicts complicate the actions and perceptions of the diaspora. Challenging anticommunism has historically resulted in retaliation from anticommunist Vietnamese Americans, including threats, violence, slander, exclusion, and protest. As illustrated in the case of the Little Saigon campaign, these protests and threats of further action have met with relative success.

As the United States and Viet Nam moved closer diplomatically and economically, U.S. government support for Vietnamese American anticommunist groups declined, and these groups consequently redoubled their efforts in promulgating their anticommunist beliefs. Evidence of this trend emerged clearly in 1999 during the single most controversial anticommunist protest in Vietnamese American history to date, the Hi-Tek incident, in which thousands of Vietnamese Americans protested Truong Van Tran, who hung a Hồ Chí Minh image and flag of Viet Nam at his Hi-Tek TV and VCR shop in Orange County, as discussed in detail in Chapter 4. The Hi-Tek incident showed that neutrality was not an option for politicians. Anything short of a strong stance against communism made one vulnerable to anticommunist attacks. Such was the case when Westminister councilman Tony Lam, under city attorney advisement, stayed away from the Hi-Tek controversy. Approximately two hundred protesters moved their fight to Lam's restaurant after the Hi-Tek store closed (Mickadeit 2008). Politicians who took office after the Lam incident not only learned to support anticommunist protests; for self-preservation some even joined in the protests. Orange County supervisor Janet Nguyen and Westminster city councilman Andy Quach went so far as to fly to San Jose on several occasions to speak at a city council meeting and local community events in support of the Little Saigon name.[12]

Having found success in earlier protests, anticommunist groups continued to go against international diplomatic currents by strongly opposing Vietnamese influence in the United States. For instance, in May 2004, the U.S. State Department made a surprise announcement to city officials of Garden Grove that the vice president of the National Assembly of the Socialist Republic of Viet Nam, Nguyễn Phúc Thành, wanted his motorcade to drive through the city's Little Saigon section. One-third of Garden Grove's population was of Vietnamese descent, and many held very strong anticommunist sentiments. Garden Grove's city council unanimously backed a resolution stating that "the City Council does not welcome or sanction high-profile visits, drive-bys, or stopovers by members and officials of the Vietnamese communist government" (Lehner 2004, A12). Just weeks later the City of Westminster followed with a similar resolution, cowritten by Vietnamese American council member Andy Quach. Quach defiantly said, "It doesn't matter what the commies or the State Department say; we on the council are responsible to our constituents in Westminster" (Agence France-Presse 2004). Although not legally binding, these resolutions served as a symbolic message to Viet Nam and the diasporic population that anticommunist sentiments remain strong in the U.S. Vietnamese diaspora.

Showing how the diplomatic tide had turned, the U.S. federal government, a former ally of South Viet Nam, sided with the Socialist Republic of Viet Nam instead of supporting the city councils' resolutions. The U.S. government publicly expressed disapproval of the resolutions, saying they would offend the Vietnamese government and interfere with future bilateral agreements (Lehner 2004). Viet Nam embassy spokesman Bạch Ngọc Chiến said the council members were "blinded by hatred" when they passed the bill and their actions were "not consistent with American and Vietnam hospitality" (Lehner 2004, A12). He said:

> Those who favor and advocate such a resolution . . . do not serve the interests of the majority of the Vietnamese people, and they are making a desperate attempt to hinder an irreversible trend of contacts and exchanges between the government of Vietnam and Vietnamese people living in the U.S. (Haldane 2004, B1).

In the end, the so-called no-commie-zone resolutions did not hurt relations between Viet Nam and its overseas population or between Viet Nam and the United States. Most important, despite the belief that added pressure by anticommunist groups would curb trade, nothing in the resolution addressed the trading of goods and services. The incident showed where the United States stood when presented with the choice of supporting an old ally (former South Viet Nam) or a new one (Socialist Republic of Viet Nam). Still, the resolution allowed anticommunist groups to at least boast government support at the local level and even appear to be the majority voice in the Vietnamese American community.

When such groups began protesting Madison Nguyen in 2007, they already had a string of successes. The mainstream press had consistently identified anticommunist groups as the core of the community without considering whether there were alternative points of view. The eye of the press had been caught by groups that seemed caught in a time capsule and that offered images of aging radicals literally waving flags. As Nhu-Ngoc Ong and David Meyer (2008) note, less dramatic political action just does not have the same mass appeal. Anticommunists within the Vietnamese American community have thus far been quite effective at creating and winning political fights through intense protests, boycotts, and harsh rhetoric. Politicians, merchants, scholars, organizers, artists, and journalists have been intimidated by such actions. For example, young Vietnamese American scholars often confide to me that they are torn about research topics that involve fieldwork in Viet Nam for fear their parents would disapprove. So they have to decide whether to conduct the work in secret or abandon it altogether. Even seasoned academics choose their words carefully in writing and speech to avoid unnecessary controversy. Politicians, even Madison Nguyen, support bills recognizing the South Vietnamese flag as the official heritage flag for Vietnamese living in diaspora. These are just a few examples of actions made in response to fear of retaliation from anticommunist groups.

Who instigates these protests? The answer is some in the diaspora who desire importance. A good portion of the Vietnamese population who left Viet Nam, particularly during the 1975 wave of refugees, came from wealthy and politically powerful families. Many of these men and women came to the United States with nothing and had to start at the very bottom economically and socially. For many who are older, the climb back to normality proved challenging (Kibria 1993). Desires to lead, maintain the respect of the community, and enjoy financial security linger among these people.

I conducted background research on a handful of these people, and patterns emerged. Most are middle-aged or older and male. After arrival in the United States, they tend to have served as leaders of an organization but to have been ousted or become irrelevant to the group; they tend to have unsuccessfully run for public office, and they tend to come from well-established families of the South Vietnamese regime with very high expectations for their success. Dan The Hoang (2009) spoke of one of these leaders:

> He hates Madison's guts because he is a nobody. He once led an organization but was stripped of his title of president after twenty-eight days. He's hopped from one organization to another but gets nowhere. He's very ambitious, but he knows he cannot be Madison, so he wants to bring her down.

Leadership can also take the form of bold acts, as in the case of former fighter pilot Ly Tong. His fame came from his claims that he flew over Sai Gon in 1992 and 2000 and dropped leaflets calling for an uprising. Both times he was reportedly arrested, once in Viet Nam and once in Thailand. He also claims to have flown over Havana, Cuba, in 2000, also dropping leaflets calling for revolution, but he was apparently not arrested. In recent years Hao-Nhien Vu, political blogger at *Bolsavic* and editor of the largest Vietnamese ethnic paper in the United States, *Nguoi Viet Daily*, and other members of the Vietnamese American community investigated Ly Tong's many claims and media reports of heroism. Inconsistent claims and dubious logistics cast doubt on Ly Tong's supposed actions. Still, Ly Tong played a prominent role in the Little Saigon controversy.

In San Jose, Ly Tong supposedly went on a hunger strike from February 15, 2008, to March 13, 2008, to support the Little Saigon name. He ended his hunger strike when the city allowed, but did not endorse or finance, banners in the business district area displaying the name Little Saigon. Shortly thereafter, he attempted to lead protests against *Nguoi Viet Daily* in Orange County, California (see Chapter 4), but became involved in a power struggle with other protest leaders there. In January 2009, he vandalized art pieces at the *F.O.B. II: Art Speaks* exhibit (see Chapter 4). In 2010 he openly maced a well-known Vietnamese singer while the latter toured in the United States. Many doubt most of Ly Tong's claims of protest; nevertheless, many Vietnamese Americans consider him a hero.

Orange County Register journalist Deepa Bharath, who covers Vietnamese American issues, when asked what motivates the protest organizers answered, "People gain notoriety and status as a protest leader. These leaders protest full time. I cannot pinpoint [their] motives [to protest], but there is lots of prestige in being a community leader" (Bharath 2008a). For individuals who have lost their position and power in Viet Nam, this is a quick way to get instant respect from a handful or more of their compatriots. Ong and Meyer (2008), who looked at Vietnamese American protests occurring from 1975 to 2001, note that most protest leaders have been quick to take credit for their efforts. Some have even boasted that they could outdo themselves in future protests.

For those who achieved some success as community leaders, it seems only a consolation prize for their ultimate unachieved dream, to hold power in Viet Nam. Some maintain connections to Viet Nam through economic collaborations, nonprofit or humanitarian work, and other nonpolitical endeavors. But for the public figures who openly oppose the Vietnamese government, it seems their connection to Viet Nam is more tenuous, lacking in any substantial links. This is not always the case, however. Although rarely discussed openly, Vietnamese government officials have directly and indirectly approached certain influential Vietnamese Americans to build diasporic alliances. From my conversations with these Vietnamese American leaders, I learned that they mostly believe these interactions with Vietnamese representatives imply that Viet Nam is relatively open to change and inclusive of diasporic participation. Sometimes these overtures are simply oral assurances, but they sometimes also include more formal and public displays of friendship such as *bằng khen*, or certificates of praise.[13] Most important, political influence from Viet Nam is no longer merely anticommunists' paranoid fear.

These overtures make it understandable that some within the Vietnamese American community, though it is thousands of miles from Viet Nam and outside its realm of direct influence, harbor fears that Viet Nam will take hold of the diasporic community. Some from the anticommunist camp have capitalized on knowledge of Vietnamese soft rapprochement with its diasporic community. During Madison's reelection campaign in 2010, for example, her opponents on the Recall Madison Nguyen committee fully supported her challenger, Minh Duong, another Vietnamese American in his thirties. As part of their campaign, they created a DVD, "Sự Thật Đã Được Phơi Bày" (The Truth Was Exposed), in which they claimed that many of Madison's more high-profile Vietnamese American supporters had long been doing business in Viet Nam and a handful received "certificates of praise" from the Vietnamese government (Recall Madison Nguyen Committee 2010).

As Viet Nam develops economically, drawing the diaspora toward increased visits, investments, and other vested interests in the home country, the concern arises that Vietnamese economic influence abroad will lead to cultural and political control of the diaspora. Economics is seen as another realm within which to attack one's opponents in diaspora. It is well known in the Vietnamese American community that red-baiting often occurs to eliminate business competitors. Accusing a storeowner of being a communist, for example, has resulted in loss of business for the accused. Storefront protests compound the effects of such accusations. Economics was a factor in the case of Madison Nguyen. Many people who wanted her recalled did so because they believed she was supporting large business developers by preferring Vietnam Town as the name of a development project in the business district, as a part of a quid pro quo. No evidence has surfaced to support these claims, and Madison pushed for the name Saigon Business District as a compromise with many groups that liked some form of the name Saigon. Madison knew the name would meet with resistance, and when it did she did not waiver. She said, "I knew that if I'd supported the name Little Saigon, I probably wouldn't have to endure all the insults and abuse by this group. But I struck a compromise because I did what I thought was fair and objective" (M. Nguyen 2008).

Business documents have disclosed that a wealthy business developer, Son Nguyen, father of Madison's competitor in the council seat runoff, Linda Nguyen, owns the rights to the name Little Saigon Plaza and plans to develop shopping centers in San Jose and Sacramento (Sherbert 2009). These facts suggest that for some parties economics underlies this political controversy. When discussing the question of who does business with Viet Nam and whether economic competition influences anticommunist acts, my business informants provided consistent answers: People in diaspora regularly engage in business deals with Viet Nam, and commercial endeavors exist. They happen frequently, legally, and sometimes openly.

Barry Hung Do, spokesperson for San Jose Voters for Democracy, the leading group in the recall effort against Madison, explained it this way: "Now there's a lot of communist Vietnamese doing business here [in the United States], and some Vietnamese here doing business with them. . . . [W]e don't want them doing it in front of us. We don't want to see it" (Do 2008). For Barry, Madison's supporters are businessmen with lucrative contracts with the Vietnamese government. The U.S. government should curb these connections, he thinks, but if it does not, then anticommunist Americans need to fill the void. Barry even cited the legislation the cities of Garden Grove and Westminster in Orange County, California, have passed that requires Vietnamese communist dignitaries to make public their visits to the cities.

Although the no-commie-zone, Hi-Tek, and other controversies found support across generational lines, mostly first-generation Vietnamese sided with the anticommunist demonstrators and younger people were either critical of them or expressed more ambivalence. As directors Lindsey Jang and Robert C.

Winn revealed in their documentary on the Vietnamese American community and the Hi-Tek incident, *Saigon, U.S.A.*, the older generation tended to focus on the negative aspects of communism, which they personally endured during the war. The younger generation, on the other hand, were more focused on connecting with their families and understanding their histories. However, they found doing so difficult given the language barrier and cultural differences, having been born or raised in the United States. When it was time for them to define their political and social identities in the United States in terms of activism, they met with the disapproval of their parents and others in the older generation (Winn and Jang 2004).

Such was the case when a University of California, Irvine, student activist, Bao Quoc Nguyen, organized a protest during John McCain's visit to Asian Garden Mall in Westminster, California, during McCain's 2000 bid for the Republican presidential nomination. Bao and his group of student protesters attended the rally to speak against McCain's reported use of *gook*. McCain explained that he had meant only his captors in the communist Vietnamese prison camps when he said, "I hated the gooks. I will hate them as long as I live" (Fan and Mangaliman 2000). This term is universally seen as derogatory toward all Asian Americans, and yet this presidential candidate used it publicly, initially without apology even when he was made aware of the historical and social implications of its usage. Many at the rally were McCain supporters and misunderstood Bao's intent; they verbally and physically accosted him and his fellow student demonstrators. Attendees at the rally tore up the signs and T-shirts that read, "I am not a gook," urinated on the students, and pushed them onto the busy boulevard (Tsang 2003). Much of this is documented in *Saigon, U.S.A.* When interviewed about the incident, Bao commented that the older generation tends to say that there is too much freedom in the United States, whereas he believes that there is not enough (Winn and Jang 2004).

The Little Saigon, no-commie-zone, and gook issues were not the first in which some Vietnamese American groups tried to hold on to the past while dismissing others with new ways of thinking that emphasize the present and the future. For example, many Vietnamese Americans, especially from the first generation, believe the U.S. presence in South Viet Nam was a good thing. They wish only that the troops had stayed instead of retreating in 1973, contributing to the fall of Sai Gon two years later. Once settled in the United States, many of these Vietnamese refugees believed that the Cold War would continue. That sense of continuity ended abruptly when the United States and Viet Nam normalized relations in 1995. In the younger generation, however, many are more engaged with current international developments, including the second Iraq war, and they even question the U.S. imperialist roles then and now (Espiritu 2005).

Generally speaking, the older generation wants to speak for a history that needs preservation, whereas the younger generation calls for recognition of the realities of current conditions. In many ways, the Little Saigon naming issue had similar generational dilemmas. The San Jose Voters for Democracy representative Barry Do (2008) asserted, "The community campaigned and helped put her [Madison Nguyen] in office, and she doesn't listen to us." According to Confucian values, in which elders are to be revered and their words taken without question, Madison's actions might be viewed as disrespectful. But Madison, who understands her duties as a younger member of the Vietnamese American community, is surprised that separating culture from mainstream politics is not always an easy task for community members. "I hope they understand that, by electing me, I will make decisions based on input from different groups in the community. I cannot make decisions based on just one particular group or organization" (M. Nguyen 2008).

The older proponents of the Little Saigon name have demanded on several occasions that Madison apologize and "do the right thing" by choosing the name Little Saigon so they can accept her again as their daughter. Her unwillingness to adopt the role of the older generation's child whose duty it is to listen and do as they say has angered her opposition. Madison explained:

> Change is the future for our generation and the generations that will come after us. Many of us are educated in Western schools and are more accustomed to the American ways of life. But that doesn't necessarily equate to our lack of understanding of our own culture. I have deep respect for what my parents have gone through to bring me to this country, just as I have respect for what the Vietnamese community in San Jose has given me and those who have paved the way for me to get to where I am today. My family's story is not any different from a lot of Vietnamese families who came to this country by boat. Viet Nam is our homeland, but the U.S. is also our newfound home. In order to move toward upward mobility, we need to learn the politics of compromise rather than harbor the politics of fear. We are no longer living under the communist regime. We have laws in this country that will protect us. We have the freedom to express our views, even when they result in disagreement. But that's the beauty of this country. We can agree to disagree without fear of retaliation. (M. Nguyen 2008)

Madison tried to keep her values growing up as a Vietnamese American but also attempted to appease those who followed more traditional Confucian ways of thinking. As Chung-Hee Sarah Soh explains in her discussion of Korean female politicians in Korea, this strategy is effective in a Confucian society:

> For a Korean woman in politics, the persistence of the hierarchical Confucian ideas about the proper role and places for men and women further hinders her professional efficacy and leadership style. She has to exercise her *nunch'i* (tact) to behave in ways appropriate to her gender and yet, at the same time, keep up with the happenings among male politicians in order to act effectively as a professional in the patriarchal democracy. (Soh 1993, 80)

Clearly, generational differences and acculturation levels play a crucial role in the conflict.

Generational power hierarchies, however, represent only one Confucian standard that many Vietnamese American families consciously and unconsciously abide by; gender is another. When Madison won her council seat, as a young woman she did not fit the usual characteristics of an ethnic community leader. Vietnamese American leaders tended to be male, senior, and part of the first wave of Vietnamese refugee-immigrants. So instead of redefining how a leader looks, they inserted Madison back into the Confucian order. She became the daughter, sister, and in some cases bride of an ethnic population, or as the saying goes, *làm dâu trăm họ* (bride of a hundred families). But this symbolic assimilation and support came with certain expectations. As a subordinate family member, she was expected to obey the elders.

As a single woman, Madison was subject to Confucian control of her sexual identity. Madison may have known this too, so even though she openly discussed her refugee experience, seen as an asset in distancing herself from communist affiliations, she kept her intimate relationships private. This virginal and simultaneously available persona helped Madison gain the support of the male-dominated infrastructure within the Vietnamese community. But when her engagement to Terry Tran became known, the same parts of the community that initially supported her became indignant. To justify the outrage of losing their sexual control over Madison, Vietnamese diasporic ethnic news that spoke for a segment of the community accused her of keeping Terry secret because of his connections to the Vietnamese government. Madison continues her efforts to undo these perceptions, and respected community members and Terry have attempted to dispel the myths, including speaking on television and in radio spots.

The realities of gender and class struggle overlay the three major influences—constituted by the U.S. government, the Vietnamese government, and anticommunist Vietnamese Americans—to factor significantly into how political actions take place and how overseas Vietnamese maneuver through these complicated terrains. The struggle for identity is complicated by a series of interconnections that requires peeling away many layers to unveil complex understandings.

Climate for Action and Change

Even a casual observer of the Vietnamese American community can decipher the apparent changes that have occurred in the community over the years. First, the idea of community has evolved. Increasingly more Vietnamese Americans recognize that, like the United States as a whole, the Vietnamese American community represents diverse experiences, identities, and historical viewpoints informed by different conditions of departure from Viet Nam, periods of arrival in the United States, ages at arrival, and educational levels (Lowe 1991). For example, according to an *Orange County Register* poll from 2000, voter registration in the community has been about evenly split between Democrat and Republican (Collet 2000). Vietnamese American political beliefs range from strongly conservative to fervently socialist, with a large majority hovering somewhere in between. Many in the community see themselves as integrated Americans, and the third generation is nearing voting age. There is no longer an essential contradiction between being anticommunist and, for instance, visiting relatives in Viet Nam annually. So the time is ripe for change. Next, I examine the motivations of community members who wish to change and discuss the segments of the community in which change is taking place.

Although it may appear that members of the Vietnamese community were always unified by anticommunist campaigns, this was not always the case. For instance, the no-commie-zone issue was the first that exposed substantial community views countering the anticommunist stance. When the no-commie-zone controversy began, Thuy Reed wrote in the *Los Angeles Times*:

> In voting yes on the so-called "no-communist zone" resolution, the city councils in Garden Grove and Westminster have inadvertently made this silent majority in Little Saigon more silent. The measure will give the new citizens the impression that the "government" is condoning the acts of hardened anti-communists, whose tactics might be considered a violation of civil liberties in the American mainstream. (Reed 2004, 1)

These sentiments were echoed again when Vietnamese American studies scholars jointly published an op-ed piece in the June 2004 *Orange County Register* responding to the resolutions:

> Non–Vietnamese Americans, and even many Vietnamese Americans, may think that the Vietnamese American community is united behind such an act. This is not so. Many Vietnamese Americans have no wish to continue the fight against communism, but are very reluctant to say so, since an extremist element in the Vietnamese American community resorts to protests, shouting, and even violence to quell any such disagreement. The turn to legal action, however, shows that the Vietnamese American community is maturing and that it is attaining a political power and voice that it lacked in the past. What disappoints is the fact that a new generation of Vietnamese American and other elected officials choose to fan the flame of hatred as the most convenient way to get votes rather than work to represent the diverse interests of their constituents. Many of us have long started redefining our relationship with Vietnam through our work, travels, commerce, and social connections. Most of us have done so

quietly, but it is time to speak out forcefully against the McCarthyist anti-communism of some Vietnamese Americans. (Nguyen, Do, et al. 2004)

VietUnity, a group with socialist leanings, also spoke against the resolution: "[We are] Vietnamese and Vietnamese Americans committed to the struggle for global peace, justice, and self-determination. We represent an important progressive voice within the broader community of Vietnamese Americans that has been silenced and repressed by the dominant political ideology of our fellow community leaders" (VietUnity 2004). In response to the resolutions, they wrote an open letter:

> We believe that this resolution further increases divisions between the government of Viet Nam and our Viet community here, while diverting attention from the greater domestic issues that our community should be uniting around. The resolution creates unnecessary barriers for Vietnamese Americans interested in really helping our motherland recover from the devastating effects of war as well as from the years of being isolated from the global economy due to the imposed U.S. trade embargo. (VietUnity 2004)

These first public showings of diverse perspectives represented a slow percolation of discontent within the Vietnamese American community coming into view. The frustrated tones of the letters expressed the idea that, thirty years after the Viet Nam War, overseas Vietnamese clearly have differing relationships with Viet Nam, the United States, and each other. This diversity is best seen along generational lines and time spent in the United States or by acculturation level. All the scholars of the *Orange County Register* op-ed were Vietnamese Americans who came before or during 1975 as part of the first wave of Vietnamese Americans, 1.5-generation Vietnamese Americans, or non-Vietnamese scholars.[14]

Madison Nguyen is a unique politician. When most Vietnamese Americans were either apolitical or interested in only ethnic politics, she worked her way into mainstream politics, as a community organizer, a school board member, a city council member, and eventually the vice-mayor of San Jose. Having grown up in the United States, working in the fields there and attending top U.S. universities, Madison crossed both class and racial lines. She is also charismatic, able to motivate support. Many in the Vietnamese American community who do not understand the political system or how to garner broad support are puzzled by how she has advanced in American mainstream politics. Dan The Hoang, long-respected community leader and considered by many an elder statesman, explained it this way:

> The older generation look at Madison and they ask themselves, "Why is it her and not me that had that position?" They either did not think to start from the beginning to pay their political dues or if they thought of it, they

were not able to do it. It's not easy getting people to vote for you. But she did it, and that bothers them greatly. (D. Hoang 2009)

Dan The Hoang offered another possibility for the generational and gender friction—envy from the predominantly male senior population and their perceptions of Madison:

For the older generation, they see Madison as someone not from the local area who found upward mobility through mainstream politics by getting elected as a government official. They say, oh my god, we want one of ours to move up like that. They are puzzled as to how Madison succeeded and so many before her failed. They perceived she rose to power overnight. What they don't understand is, as someone who grew up in the U.S., she understood the government system and started at the very bottom as a school board member. (D. Hoang 2009)

In the following months of weekly protests and city council meeting demonstrations, these groups used red-baiting tactics to get their way. In the process, they alienated many Vietnamese Americans living in the Bay Area. In an unprecedented event in Vietnamese immigrant history, over eight hundred Vietnamese American professionals, laborers, leaders, and activists calling themselves Our Voice signed an open letter asking for the end of intimidation tactics by the protesters and calling for peace and support for Madison Nguyen (Our Voice 2008). The letter was printed in the Vietnamese American press and discussed even in the mainstream press. This development is particularly remarkable given that the community is often presented in the news media as having one voice, that of the anticommunist extremists. The Our Voice open letter showed that there are many silent or silenced community members. The following passage from the letter is particularly cogent:

We, a large number of the Vietnamese Americans living in San Jose and the vicinity, in light of the dispute regarding the naming of the one-mile stretch of businesses on Story Road in the City of San Jose, find it necessary to voice our opinion, [and] hereby declare, WHEREAS: the group that supports the name "Little Saigon," no matter how vocal it has been, does not constitute the majority and is not representative of the Vietnamese Americans living in San Jose and the vicinity. . . . [T]he acts of verbally abusing our City officials and threatening their recall, the weekly demonstrations before the City Hall, and the intimidation and labeling others as "Viet Cong" to fight for the name "Little Saigon" are childish and unacceptable in our civilized society. (Our Voice 2008)

At about the time the letter was to be translated into English for mainstream media distribution, I was approached by members of Our Voice for consultation.

They sought ways to articulate the thinking of what they considered the large silent majority in the Vietnamese American community. I assisted them with their revised letter and began writing speeches on behalf of Our Voice members.

Our Voice came to prominence at the March 4, 2008, city council meeting, at which the council had planned to take up the issue of naming again. Representing Our Voice was a carefully selected group of Vietnamese Americans meant to showcase the diversity of the community and present alternative views of Vietnamese Americans regarding the naming issue. The group included a young board of education member, Buu Thai; a young small-business owner, Vincent Mai; a middle-aged businessman, Henry Le; a respected community leader, Dan The Hoang; and me, the representative scholar. The themes of our speeches were unified support for Madison Nguyen and her decision on the business district name, the rejection of acts of violence and threats from Little Saigon protestors, and a call for peace and compromise within the Vietnamese American community. We were allowed approximately five minutes each to speak before the council.

Our Voice members presented their open letter signed by eight hundred members of the Vietnamese American community. Proponents of Little Saigon presented their own stack of signatures, claiming that they had four thousand names in all. Assuming signatures from both sides were legitimate, it should be made clear that the four thousand signatories of the "Little Saigon" petition did so without any fear of recrimination for their choice. Those who signed the Our Voice petition, however, knew they would likely be attacked and otherwise harassed by anticommunist groups. Dan The Hoang, for instance, received death threats the day of the council meeting and consequently had a plainclothes officer escort him to the meeting. As the petition was published, Ly Tong and others announced that the FBI should investigate all those who signed the Our Voice petition for communist affiliation. As discussed previously, Mayor Chuck Reed and Madison Nguyen followed up with speeches highlighting their own stories of the red-baiting and harassment that they, their staff, and their families faced in the midst of the Little Saigon controversy.

Artist Chau Huynh and Vice-Mayor Madison Nguyen directly stirred the imagination of those in the Vietnamese American community, as seen so clearly with the *Art Speaks* exhibit described in Chapter 4. Cocurator Lan Duong attributed to both women the impetus for organizing the fifty-artist exhibit. Duong (2009) said, "I admire Madison for having taken [her] stance. [My] general impression when I first heard about it [was that] I thought she was brave. She was right in going forward with the motions." Madison Nguyen, Our Voice, and organizers of *Art Speaks* have courageously faced verbal attacks, protests, and political and ethnic pressures. These Vietnamese Americans are newly visible parts of the so-called silent majority in the community. They and others like them enable us to imagine a diverse Vietnamese American population.

Conclusion

On March 3, 2009, the night of council member Madison Nguyen's no-recall victory, hundreds of supporters gathered to watch the big screen while the final results came in. Madison said to people nearby that her relatives in Viet Nam were glued to their computer terminals to watch live updates of the results (M. Nguyen 2009b). When it was clear that the recall effort had failed and that Madison was victorious, I heard her say softly, "This was a victory for all of us" (M. Nguyen 2009b). That short phrase expresses an intense moment in an important juncture in Vietnamese American history. The crowd of supporters included older European American women, young progressive Democrats, and older Vietnamese Republicans. They all joined in jubilation, and their energy was electrifying. The support of many of these people contradicted popular notions of how ethnic politics should operate. Some supported her primarily because they admired her courage in coping with the tumultuous controversy around her, while others supported her because of her general good record and liberal politics.

The victory must have come as a huge relief for Madison as well. She had stood up to a powerful coalition of Vietnamese Americans who maintained the belief that a strong anticommunist stance mandates dictating the limits of acceptable community behavior. Madison was targeted partly to notify the Vietnamese government that its exiled population could still present a strong anticommunist front. Her victory thus showed that ethnic Vietnamese politicians can confront the forces of anticommunism and survive politically. The government of Viet Nam must have realized this, too: the following day, major newspapers in Viet Nam reported an outpouring of pride in response to Madison's win.

More than just keeping her seat by defeating the recall efforts, Madison single-handedly changed Vietnamese American politics. She won a resounding reelection bid in November 2010 and was appointed to the vice-mayor position by San Jose Mayor Chuck Reed. Conversely, anticommunist Vietnamese American Republicans across the country lost their bids, including the very controversial California assemblyman Van Tran, who was aiming for the U.S. Congress. Facilitating a slew of anticommunist activities, Tran was instrumental in shutting down the *Art Speaks* exhibit. Considered the political godfather of Orange County, he had amassed enough power to get other Vietnamese Americans elected in previous elections, but they too failed in the 2010 elections.

The recall campaign that arose out of the Little Saigon controversy was like many incidents that preceded it. At its core it was about control of overseas Vietnamese identity, an identity influenced by the Viet Nam and U.S. governments as well as staunch anticommunist community members. Political actions are undergirded by ideologies, but in these incidents political actions were about obtaining power or increasing standing within the community. "Symbolizing the past" is crucial in this process of community identity making (A. P. Cohen 1985). It evolved to "treat myth as an expression of the way in which people cognitively map past, present, and future" (99). A history of war and loss and the displacement of hundreds of thousands is not a myth. Many in the diaspora experienced these realities firsthand, yet our shared history may be manipulated to legitimize certain ideas when anticommunism goes unopposed as the core of Vietnamese American cultural and political community identity.

It is an act of fiction when *some* members of the community tout anticommunist beliefs as the only acceptable ideology for *all* members of the community. In reality, acts of desperation are due to fear rather than the resurgence of power. As Anthony P. Cohen explains, communities act out "because their members feel themselves to be under so severe a threat from some extrinsic source that if they do not speak out now they may be silenced forever" (1985, 109). Whereas Cohen conceives the community threat as exogenous, I argue that the perceived threat often comes from within. That is, the oppressive forces that community members experience come from others within the community. The tension arises when individuals cannot openly or safely reveal their thoughts on the differences.

Such differences are based on generation and gender and on fundamental ideas grounded in Confucianism as opposed to the individualism and creativity familiar to those growing up in the United States. Beyond the major sources of influence, Madison had to confront Vietnamese cultural norms to survive as a mainstream U.S. politician. This balancing act required deference to a patriarchal order and limiting her sense of self, including her sexual self. It also meant coping with memories of the war and a lost generation of exiles who desire political power in the United States and Viet Nam but have not achieved it.

The notion that a single ideology can represent a community denies the thirty-five years of history of the Vietnamese diaspora. It also fails to account for differing levels of assimilation and ignores the 1.5, second, and third generations who grew up in and were born in the United States. For these populations, it makes sense that Vietnamese American perspectives differ in major and minor ways. Fundamental conflicts arise when subgroups work to preserve a myth of unity and sameness in a community that is actually and inherently diverse. A community is as complex as its members, and claiming ownership not only perpetuates myth of a Vietnamese American monolithic identity; it also causes stagnation and sorrow.

6

Vietnamese Diaspora Revisited

On September 3, 2009, Phương Hồ, a twenty-year-old Vietnamese international student studying math at San Jose State University, California, was brutally beaten by four San Jose police officers. Apparently, one of Phương's roommates, Jeremy Suftin, had slopped soap onto Phương's steak. Phương reacted by taking up a knife and saying, "In Vietnam, I would kill you over that." His roommates laughed at the incident, but Suftin took it seriously and called the police. Witnesses reported that when the police arrived, Phương was unarmed and nonviolent. Police, however, claimed that he was uncooperative and resisting arrest. Fortuitously, our digital era allowed one of Phương's roommates to record the arrest on his mobile phone. The video showed police officers hitting Phương ten times with a metal baton and then tasering him. Some of the strikes took place after Phương was already subdued and on the floor, and he pleaded for mercy during most of this time[1] (Webby 2009).

San Jose City Council members, including Vice Mayor Madison Nguyen, expressed concern over the excessive forced used on Phương Hồ. Vietnamese community members were also outraged by the incident, and groups mobilized demanding justice. However, when they learned Phương was a Vietnamese national, some distanced themselves from the incident. They feared that supporting his cause would label them as communist (M. Nguyen 2009b). News of the Phương Hồ beating appeared in all major newspapers in Viet Nam, reporting the facts without commentary. The Vietnamese Foreign Ministry, however, had strong words in its official statement: "[The] Vietnamese public reacts with resentment to the news. Use of violence and abuse of power by the police is unacceptable conduct that deserves serious punishment. The Ministry of Foreign Affairs has instructed the Vietnamese Consulate General in San Francisco to look into the incident and take necessary steps to provide consular protection for Mr. Ho Phuong" (Nga 2009).

This event reveals the complex interconnectedness of the United States, Viet Nam, and staunch anticommunist Vietnamese in diaspora. In our global age the beating was instantaneously documented with a mobile phone, and news of the event quickly became international. The altercation between the San Jose police officers and the Vietnamese student followed a pattern of cultural and linguistic misunderstanding compounded with racism that has resulted in the wrongful deaths of several Vietnamese Americans in San Jose. As immigrants, refugees, or more generally, persons of color, people find that they must negotiate their places in U.S. society while confronting embedded barriers against assimilation. Phương Hồ was one of a growing number of Vietnamese international students attending U.S. universities. Official Vietnamese representatives in the United States are compelled to speak in support of their citizens in such cases. Yet since normalizing relations with the United States, Vietnamese officials have been careful not to criticize the United States and jeopardize diplomatic and financial ties. This is one of the many ways the history of United States–Vietnam relations comes into play in the lives of Vietnamese overseas. Finally, this event brings into the conversation anticommunist Vietnamese Americans. Ethnic community members initially organized to aid Phương Hồ, but because he was a citizen of the Socialist Republic of Viet Nam affiliation with him was perceived by many people as social and political suicide, so most members of the diaspora distanced themselves from the situation.

The Phương Hồ controversy shows that Vietnamese American lives are transnational and that this diasporic group is directly affected by and affects events in Viet Nam. This ocean-spanning mutual influence is possible because people in Viet Nam and in diaspora have *always* found imaginative ways to (re)connect, even when international policies and ethnic community pressures have discouraged it. Their reconnections dispel popular notions of Vietnamese Americans as merely nation-bound refugees. Their transnational acts, accelerated by globalization, have involved forming virtual communities via the Internet, organizing social movements, sharing music across oceans, creating art, developing new media outlets, finding political representation, and even carefully dissenting within this ethnic community. The participants are often mindful of existing obstacles to these connections, particularly the U.S. and Vietnamese societies and governments and anticommunist Vietnamese Americans. Considering these factors enables a more complex analysis of the diasporic experience while offering a framework for examining many other transnational phenomena.

More than thirty-five years after the Viet Nam War, my study is the first book-length project to expose, among other things, the staunch anticommunist element within the Vietnamese American community. Their reign of terror has included assassination, arson, threats, physical violence, vandalism, and protest—all more akin to developments in the Cuban American community than to those of any other Asian American group. Fear of retaliation forces Vietnamese Americans into a silent majority; correspondingly, scholars are either unaware of the history of red-baiting or, with much angst, avoid its exploration to escape reprisal. My investigation not only documents carefully selected and consequential historical moments for Vietnamese Americans; it also unmasks the hidden causes of these events and the motivations of the actors involved, including intraethnic strife based on characteristics such as time of arrival in the United States, gender, and class. Similarly, my research on the other side of the Pacific, the years that I spent living in Viet Nam for my fieldwork, uncovered how transnational connections go undetected by Vietnamese government officials, who may be unable to stop these flows of exchange even when the officials deploy extreme measures such as incarceration. The significant personal and professional risks that I accepted in conducting research at these politically heated sites was worthwhile because the transnational struggles of the Vietnamese diaspora are a reality and the voices of the people involved need an audience.

Indelible images of Vietnamese refugees fleeing in the aftermath of the war and the climate of the overseas ethnic anticommunist stronghold continue to lead ethnic and mainstream media to depict Vietnamese Americans as a united group with similar political beliefs; the media thus homogenize a population that is actually quite diverse. The controversy around Vice-Mayor Madison Nguyen, who has her own dramatic refugee story, further exposed this diversity. By not choosing the name that a vocal minority coalition favored for representing Vietnamese Americans—Little Saigon—Madison found herself embroiled in a recall campaign. As a popularly elected official with ethnically diverse constituents, she bravely opposed members of her ethnic community by not letting their anticommunist agenda or personal vendettas based on Confucian cultural norms dictate her actions. Her victory over the recall attempt and subsequent reelection had effects felt well beyond the local population of San Jose; these outcomes permanently shifted the dynamics of Vietnamese American politics in diaspora.

Even artworks that in some cases only mildly challenge hegemonic political currents have broken through ossifying suppression in Viet Nam and in diaspora. Attacks on Chau Huynh and the *Nguoi Viet Daily* newspaper, in which her art was displayed, vividly exemplify cultural control, as discussed in Chapter 4. But Chau Huynh and journalists at *Nguoi Viet Daily* found ways to defend their respective art and writing. Their struggles inspired others in the community to speak up. The Vietnamese American Arts and Letters Association's *F.O.B. II: Art Speaks* exhibit—a direct reaction to the oppressive nature of portions of the Vietnamese American community that brought about attacks against Chau Huynh and Madison Nguyen—and the protests against it reveal how the fight to highlight alternative voices runs into the wall of conformity and discipline constructed by powerful anticommunist groups working to keep at bay Vietnamese cultural influences and perceived communist cultural productions. The multigeneration group of fifty Vietnamese and overseas Vietnamese artists involved in the *F.O.B. II: Art Speaks* exhibit ignored threats from the old guard, with its strong anticommunist views. Mobilized by ideas of freedom of speech and artistic license, younger Vietnamese Americans (and some Vietnamese) boldly created art in defiance of censorship by the community and the state. In the same vein Hao-Nhien Vu, managing editor of *Nguoi Viet Daily* who was dismissed over the Chau Huynh controversy, defiantly turned to blogging to report ethnic events unencumbered by censorship. His subsequent rehire at *Nguoi Viet Daily* provides another example of the changing political tides that have begun to allow individuals and groups to diverge from anticommunist dogma while escaping community ostracism.

Perhaps most amazing is that so many of these struggles against the stifling status quo—a status quo buttressed by the Vietnamese and American governments and anticommunists in diaspora—go undetected. As Chapter 3 notes, newsgroups like Vietnam Forum formed online, and once-isolated individuals were able to connect and form virtual communities. Most remarkable about Vietnam Forum is that it existed for years in the midst of strong anticommunist pressures from the real world of the overseas community and alongside political crackdowns in Viet Nam, where the government feared that freedom of communication and information would threaten its authority. However, these primary sources of influence were not able to fatally damage the virtual community, so it continued to provide relatively safe and open spaces for discussion of the most controversial topics imaginable in the minds of people living in Viet Nam and its diaspora.

One could argue that while the exiled community attempted to form its own pseudostate to govern a people in diaspora, Vietnam Forum formed a virtual space to house leaders who through their postings nudged Viet Nam toward reform. Similarly, as much as Viet Nam's government attempted to contain, control, and monitor the Internet, it could not keep its people from connecting with the outside world. As illustrated in Chapter 2, this "transnationalism from below" (Smith and Guarnizo 1999) was likewise apparent when people in the music industry collaborated across oceans to create new, hybrid contemporary popular music and thriving black market businesses. Participants took strengths from both sides of the ocean, such as artistic talent in Viet Nam and technology from overseas, to enhance music production. Transnational opportunities of exchange continue today as singers in the United States and Viet Nam revitalize their careers with new generations of fans overseas.

Vietnamese Americans have proved to be a resilient population. Their historical trials—struggles for independence, in particular against the Chinese and the French; multiple waves of migration from North Viet Nam; oppression under a communist regime; long periods in refugee camps; and efforts to create a home in the often racially intolerant United States while enduring intraethnic oppression and working to (re)connect with Viet Nam—have been remarkable. Many in the diaspora have vigorously tackled these daunting hurdles to create hope for the future of Vietnamese Americans. The actors redirecting the future of the diaspora and the home country are many: the numerous music makers, producers, and consumers who have contributed to the successful creation of hybrid music enjoyed by Vietnamese in Viet Nam and in diaspora; the founders of Vietnam Forum, Hoanh Dinh Tran, and Tin Le, who aided in the development of information communication technology in Viet Nam and formed influential virtual communities; Chau Huynh, who stands behind her politically charged art works; Hao-Nhien Vu, who used new media outlets to report the news; Madison Nguyen, who persevered against the political grain; the Vietnamese American Arts and Letters Association, which promoted controversial art; and Our Voice, which provided support for alternative political and artistic views.

Other forms of transnational connection beyond the scope of my research also involve Vietnamese maneuvering around hegemonic forces in the community to express their ideas and carry out work they deem important. Some Vietnamese American moviemakers, finding the U.S. film industry difficult to break into, offer their training and expertise for creating commercial films in Viet Nam. Their work requires careful strategizing to pass Vietnamese cultural censors but nevertheless serves as a first step to making films for global audiences. Also, humanitarian projects in Viet Nam set up by overseas Vietnamese not only help people in need in the home country but also allow those in diaspora to have direct influence there. To collect funds in the United States, nonprofits carefully ensure that helping Vietnamese citizens does not carry hints of propping up the communist regime. These are further examples of the successful transnational linkages taking place daily and spontaneously, signaling the chance for even more connections in the future.

But even as we usher in the age of globalization and allow for a multitude of transnational practices, many historical injustices—often remnants of the Cold War—remain unresolved. This reality, which demands further study, is not exclusive to Vietnamese Americans. Hmong connections to the United States, for instance, include their involvement in the CIA-led secret war against North Viet Nam. Although the United States finally resettled some of the fighters and their families, it refused to acknowledge their military contribution to the Viet Nam War and never gave them veterans' rights and benefits. This is one example of the continuing struggle by Asian Americans to empower themselves and find their place in the United States while coping with decisions made by their home and host countries in previous decades. Relations are tense among Asian American groups as well. Historical imperialist and colonialist activities of Japan in most of Asia, China in Viet Nam and Tibet, and Viet Nam in Cambodia, for example, have led to extreme mistrust among these ethnic groups, which continues in diaspora. Diverse relationships with home and host countries, with other Asian Americans, and even within particular ethnic groups beg for more research into the various factors constituting diasporic relations.

I could arrive at my conclusions only after decades of ethnographic and political investigation that involved observing, living, and critiquing the many changes in Viet Nam and in diaspora. Culture does not change overnight.

Dramatic events often bring forth major shifts in an individual life, but societies preserve old ways, slowly adapting to new ideas and formulating hybrid culture. My long-term approach has revealed how diasporic identities form through seemingly innocuous or commonplace events and through intraethnic forces, stirring us to rethink ideas around transnational connections, nation building, and community making.

At its core this study is about relationships and shared experiences that have been sometimes exuberant and at other times heartbreaking. This book serves partly as a testament to my struggles as a scholar working in rough political waters while desperately seeking balance. My research and writing has been critical of the forces that shape the (in)actions of people in Viet Nam and its diaspora. Some people in my community find my work offensive and dangerous to their beliefs. Yet Vietnamese in Viet Nam and in diaspora have been conforming to, reacting against, and resisting the conditions of their lives for decades. Government restrictions and community pressures have inadvertently forged strong transnational connections among Vietnamese in diaspora and in Viet Nam. Besides documenting these conditions, I have also lived them, or more poignantly, I have lived through this research and it has lived through me. I and many others in my community have refused to allow our lives to be fully determined by nation-state mandates or ethnic-community pressures. *Transnationalizing Viet Nam* showcases our lived experiences.

Notes

CHAPTER 1

1. In 2002 Vietnam Forum (VNForum) had close to four hundred subscribing addresses. Some addresses relayed VNForum messages to local networks at U.S. universities and other institutions. Including the members of those local networks, approximately three thousand read postings to the list.

2. The lawyer is Hoanh Tran, founder of the virtual community VNForum. This event look place in 2002, during one of my interviews with him over the years.

3. Ho Chi Minh City is the official name for the city formerly known as Sai Gon, but because most people in Viet Nam and abroad use the name Sai Gon, I refer to the city principally by that name (with only an occasional reference to Ho Chi Minh City).

4. This book cannot represent the experiences of all Vietnamese with transnational connections; nor can it document the many who have not maintained close relations with their home country.

5. For a discussion of transnational flows of culture as seen through popular music produced in Viet Nam and the United States, see Chapter 2 herein.

6. For example, see *Crossroads: An Interdisciplinary Journal of Southeast Asian Studies* 19 (2), guest-edited by Nathalie Nguyen, in which articles specifically addressed Vietnamese diasporic issues.

7. For an in-depth discussion of Viet Nam/United States/Vietnamese American relations up to 1994, see Valverde 1994. Hiroko Furuya and Christian Collet (2009) also offer a summary of relations between Viet Nam and Vietnamese Americans up to 2008.

8. There are also hundreds of texts written in Vietnamese by Vietnamese Americans, including many memoirs of former South Vietnamese officials or former internees of re-education camps. Many wrote about their refugee experiences and flight from Viet Nam. There is also no end to their fiction, poetry, and other literature. However, for this book, I primarily discuss works written in English about Vietnamese American experiences.

Note that in 1975 and shortly thereafter early monographs and reports of the Vietnamese refugee experience and resettlement process emerged. I call these works *transit-resettlement* writings. The initial entry of Vietnamese into the United States provoked a corresponding variety of governmental and nongovernmental reporting of the refugee situation: their transit, adjustment issues, medical needs, and financial dependency. Development and humanitarian workers and academicians spearheaded this set of writings. This group includes writers such as Le-Thi-Que, A. Terry Rambo, and Gary D. Murfin (1976); Nguyen Long and Harry H. Kendall (1981); and Robert G. Wright (1981). Their writings included issues such as motivations for leaving Viet Nam when Sai Gon fell, transit from Guam's holding station to one of five refugee camps located in the United States, and early resettlement programs, including sponsorship and the "scatter method," a policy of resettling Vietnamese refugees and immigrants in various locations across the nation so as to not economically burden one community. In addition to non–Vietnamese American citizens, the Vietnamese Americans involved in these research projects included those who lived in the United States before the 1975 fall of Sai Gon, U.S.-employed Vietnamese civil servants, Vietnamese American university students, and Vietnamese spouses of American citizens.

9. Interestingly, writings by those outside Viet Nam have mainly dealt with Vietnamese living in developed, Western countries such as the United States, France, and Australia. There are only a few historical writings on the pre-1975 diasporic populations or studies on the post-1975 Vietnamese who work and live in Southeast Asian and eastern European countries. Trần Trọng Đăng Đàn is one of the few scholars from Viet Nam who have researched the *Viet Kieu* (Vietnamese expatriates or overseas Vietnamese returning to Viet Nam for any length of time) presence globally. He has repeatedly lamented the dearth of writings on Vietnamese in eastern European countries (T.D.D. Trần 1996).

10. Vietnamese Americans were portrayed as hardworking and successful. Darrel Montero (1979) attributed the success of first-wave Vietnamese Americans to certain characteristics: they were a relatively young and highly educated population who had previously held white-collar jobs in Viet Nam. Nathan Caplan, John K. Whitmore, and Marcella H. Choy (1989) and Paul Rutledge (1992) also focused on Vietnamese American upward mobility; however, they attributed the success of this group to Confucian and Buddhist values.

11. Because of the length limitations and focus of this book, my discussion on the evolution of Vietnamese American scholarship is incomplete, leaving out many other themes that contribute to the rich and growing field. I hope others will take on the valuable project of documenting Vietnamese American scholarship. Also, though I am familiar with the writings of the larger Vietnamese diaspora in places like Australia, France, eastern Europe, and Southeast Asia, that body of work was too vast to bring up here.

12. Many of those who left Viet Nam had fought alongside American forces or served in the South Vietnamese government. This first group comprised mostly "impelled or anticipatory" refugees. Egon Kunz (1973) explains these are political refugees whose status might be determined by examining their personal history.

13. Under this act the federal government reimbursed state governments for the cash assistance and medical and social services the refugees received. Grants were given to public or nonprofit private agencies to provide the refugees with English instruction, employment counseling, and mental health services.

14. Ethnic Chinese represented a large number of those who left in the second wave. This exodus was mostly precipitated by the country's internal conflict and attempts by the Vietnamese government to expel ethnic Chinese, including citizens of Viet Nam. Ethnic Chinese faced discrimination from the communist regime, which began a policy to rid Viet Nam of bourgeois elements immediately after the war. Ethnic cultural discrimination took overt form in 1976 with the closing of Chinese newspapers in the South.

By early 1977 the communist government required ethnic Chinese in the country to register for Vietnamese citizenship or risk losing their jobs, house registration, and food rations (Chan 1991). Growing tensions between China and Viet Nam in the late 1970s fueled the idea of Chinese Vietnamese as a fifth column. Viet Nam even asked China to take back this population; China agreed rhetorically but made no plans to do so (Kumin 1988).

15. *First asylum* is where refugees first arrive when they flee their home country. Here they wait to find out what country will grant permanent residence.

16. Intraethnic tensions were not exclusive to the Vietnamese American population. Ethnic Chinese Vietnamese had experienced historical bigotry. Chinese youth, in particular, did not want to appear different and were often offended when their Vietnamese American peers overtly brought out ethnic differences. Some felt alienated enough to adopt an exclusive Chinese American identity in spite of their ties to Viet Nam.

17. There would be a limit to the refugee-immigration process and the "generosity" of host countries. Compassion fatigue hit in 1988 when Hong Kong stopped automatically giving all asylum seekers refugee status, and other countries subsequently adopted the same stance. Consequently, the Comprehensive Plan of Action (CPA) took effect in 1989 to screen refugees more discriminately and to encourage (if not force) nonrefugees to repatriate. All transit camps closed by 1998. Under the Resettlement Opportunities for Vietnamese Returnees (ROVR) program, eligible returnees to Viet Nam were re-interviewed for possible U.S. resettlement. Some 7,525 Vietnamese were admitted to the United States through ROVR between September 1998 and September 1999. The program was to end by December 2000, but as is characteristic of most immigration programs, additional time was needed to process all people eligible for immigration to the United States (U.S. Committee for Refugees and Immigrants 2000).

18. Numerous reports and anecdotal stories discuss the difficulties the internees face once in the United States. In some instances, they come to the United States only to find that their wives have remarried and their children are no longer responsive to them. These internees, most in midlife, find it difficult to find employment and assimilate to the United States.

19. Much of the leadership within the anticommunist groups remains in the hands of the 75ers, who may or may not have served in the military but certainly did not stay in Viet Nam after the war to face imprisonment or worse.

20. Ideas of racial and ethnic tolerance, freedom and democracy are manifestations of the nation-building project set out by the United States. However, how much these ideas hold true is highly debatable given the U.S. history of civil rights abuses, occupation of native and Mexican lands, genocide of natives, and neoimperialist agendas in South America, North America, Pacific Islands, and Asia.

21. Showing allegiance to the Republic of Viet Nam (RVN) anthem and flag remains a staple in most community-based events organized by first-generation Vietnamese Americans. Hiroko Furuya and Christian Collet surveyed Vietnamese Americans on their attitudes about the RVN flag and found that 50 percent younger than thirty-five, 74 percent of those sixty-five and older, 69 percent of any age from the Humanitarian Operation Program, and 66 percent of any age of the boat people favored the RVN flag (Collet and Lien 2009).

22. They have had the support of prominent politicians and met with President George W. Bush and Speaker of the House Nancy Pelosi. The Vietnamese government views Viet Tan as a threat and its members terrorists. Reports from Viet Nam show that Viet Tan members were arrested in 2007, 2008, and 2010, with only a few releases of

prisoners (Associated Press 2007; "O.C. Vietnam Democracy Activist Meets with President Bush" 2007; Việt Tân 2009).

23. This analysis makes sense for Japanese Americans who were a part of the wave of immigration in the early 1900s, when Japan was already an international force and therefore could negotiate with the United States for the welfare of the Japanese living and settling there. Maintaining Japanese culture during this period was a source of pride and was protected and fostered by home country politics. World War II changed this situation when Japanese Americans became suspected of belonging to a fifth column. They were systematically interned, resulting in major losses of property and liberty. By the time of their eventual release around the end of the war, not a single case of espionage or misbehavior had been established. This period ushered in a generation of ethnic Americans who lived with shame and fear. This generation taught the next to reject Japanese culture and assimilate as completely as possible. Not until the third generation, sansei, reached adulthood and strove to bring to light the injustices committed against Japanese Americans did it become communally condoned to reach out to things culturally Japanese (Takaki 1989).

24. Globalization also creates a division of labor in which immigrants are frequently relegated to labor-intensive, menial work. See Guidry, Kennedy, and Zald 2000.

25. In order of power and importance, these institutions and social mechanisms fall into the following categories: regulatory frameworks like the World Trade Organization, national and financial institutions like the World Bank, and legal-rational entities like transnational corporations. Robert Cohen (1997) asserts that these transnational corporations now maintain global colonies of highly trained professionals who run factories that employ locals. New immigrants can have market representation at both ends of the spectrum and anywhere in between.

26. Though *dich vu* (service centers) and small shops offer remittance services less often, some Vietnamese Americans still use their services. My observations and interviews revealed that gift packages remain popular although the contents have changed substantially over the years. In past years packages generally included products that could be easily sold on the black market. Now, the gifts are more for consumption and enjoyment rather than necessity. Inversely, Viet Kieu who have returned to the United States request certain items that can be purchased only in Viet Nam. The family member or friend in Viet Nam purchases the item and sends it by mail, entrusts it to someone traveling to the United States, or waits for the person to come (back) to Viet Nam to pick it up.

27. A 1999 study conducted in Ho Chi Minh City showed that 20 percent of the men and 30 percent of the women who had emigrated since 1989 sent remittances to their families. This money amounted to 7–10 percent of the senders' incomes. Jonathan Haughton (1999) found two primary motivations for remittances: (1) a desire for extended family to receive a proper education and meet other needs and (2) a sense of duty to support parents, relatives, and spouses.

28. Though I cannot, for their safety, list the names of those I had conversations with, dialogue between Vietnamese officials and Vietnamese community leaders has taken place often enough to establish a pattern and is therefore worthy of mention.

29. While recognizing the existence of varying forms of transnationalism, Michael Smith and Luis Guarnizo (1999) still critique those who tend to generalize or celebrate transnational practices as successful actions against nation-states. "One sign of this convergence is the tendency to conceive of transnationalism as something to celebrate, as an expression of a subversive popular resistance 'from below.' Cultural hybridity, multipositional identities, border crossing by marginal 'others,' and transnational business

practices by migrant entrepreneurs are depicted as conscious and successful efforts by or-
dinary people to escape control and domination 'from above' by capital and the state" (5).

30. The idea of Viet Nam as a history, as a nation, and as a homeland resonates for
many Vietnamese Americans. Their history, like that of many other countries, is embed-
ded in nation building. The Viet Kieu–Viet Nam connection exists in Viet Nam as well.
Until 1999 the Vietnamese government considered Viet Kieu to be Vietnamese nationals.
The Committee for Viet Kieu (*Ban Việt Kiều*) changed its name to the Committee for
Vietnamese Living Overseas (*Ủy Ban Người Việt Nam ở Nước Ngoài*) and placed it under
the Ministry of Foreign Affairs. The implication was that Viet Kieu are citizens of Viet
Nam who happen to reside elsewhere. Under pressure from overseas Vietnamese, the
committee updated citizenship policies so that Viet Kieu would lose Vietnamese citizenship upon accepting any other citizenship. This issue is still hotly debated. Although the
new law relinquishes sovereignty over the overseas population, relieving them of any
national ties, it also means that up to 1999 they did not qualify for special citizen rights
like land ownership and subsidized pricing for natives. In 2000 vast changes occurred in
equalizing prices in Viet Nam for Viet Kieu; however, land and citizenship laws for Viet
Kieu are both contested and confusing in 2010.

31. U.S. involvement in Viet Nam, though indirect at first, started long before the
Viet Nam War. For example, before the French defeat at Dien Bien Phu, the United States,
in 1950 under President Truman, granted $15 million in military aid to the French in
what was then called Indochina. By 1954 this amount reached $2.5 billion, paying nearly
80 percent of the cost of continuing the war (Duiker 1989; Karnow 1983, 137).

32. In later years, the argument was extended to boat people as testifying to the
failure of early communist economic planning and the disastrous results of political
punitive programs.

33. When I began my research in Viet Nam in 1993, I was told by the U.S. representative office there that I should not be conducting investigations into Viet Kieu relations
because the topic was too politically explosive. They added that the U.S. government
would not be able to protect or help me if I got into trouble while I was in Viet Nam.

CHAPTER 2

1. Musicians and performers often hold low social status in Vietnamese society. This
was true in the feudal period and continues into modern day. Though there are some
exceptions, it remains true that, no matter how prestigious the audience, the performer
offers a service.

2. The anticolonial, resistance theme of these songs remains popular with Vietnamese in diaspora because the nationalist movement of the first Indochina war is seen
as patriotic and anticolonial as opposed to purely communist.

3. *Chanson* is the French word for "song"—usually secular, such as a satirical cabaret
song of the twentieth century.

4. Other major singers include Phương Dung, Thanh Thủy, and Lê Thu.

5. Christophe was a hugely popular singer from France in the 1960s and 1970s. His
internationally known songs such as *Aline* (1965) continue to be sung by Vietnamese
expatriates worldwide.

6. Vietnamese popular music has several informal categories. Though the categories
are widely used by music makers and consumers alike, there is no consensus on their
definitions. They include (1) *nhạc sang*: music created by trained composers and singers,
which tends to sound like jazz, (2) *nhạc sến*: easy-listening songs with simplistic lyrics

and soft melodies, (3) *nhạc quê hương* and *nhạc bình dân*: songs with a folk or country appeal, (4) *nhạc trẻ*: pop songs mostly targeted to youth, and (5) *nhạc quậy* and *nhạc* rock: fast-paced rock-inspired music.

7. For additional information about the "culture in a bubble" phenomenon, see the discussion of the Vietnamese national dress in Valverde 2006, which notes that even fashion styles from the Viet Nam War era remained popular long after the first refugee arrivals in 1975.

8. Translated by Phi Tran.

9. Boy George was popular among Vietnamese in the 1980s. The "Boy George move" refers to a dancing style in which the dancer bends her knees slightly as she sways from side to side.

10. The Toyota Celica was popular among Vietnamese American youth in the 1980s because it was an affordable, sporty-looking car. "Fish sauce accent" refers to the heavy Vietnamese accent of recent arrivals to the United States from Viet Nam. Fish sauce, or *nước mắm*, is a ubiquitous seasoning used in most Vietnamese cooking. Studio 54 was an exclusive New York nightclub in the 1970s. It was popular among the famous and unfamous alike, who loved its excessiveness.

11. "Linebacker shoulder pads" refers to the clothing style of padded shoulders that was fashionable in the 1980s.

12. The Cotton Club blossomed during the Harlem Renaissance in the 1920s and 1930s and in its heyday showcased some of the best African American talent. Clientele were well-to-do African Americans and even Anglo-Americans. Zoot suits include baggy pants and oversized jackets with broad, padded shoulders. They were worn by youth for swing dancing in the 1930s and 1940s. In the 1980s the zoot suit had a fashion comeback.

13. In the summer of 2010, PBN announced that its 100th video would be its last because of piracy problems (Kornhaber 2010). However, in fall 2010 it released its 101st video, and that number grew to 104 in 2012.

14. Even before karaoke bars came into being, popular music videos were often seen in Vietnamese American restaurants. This eventually led to karaoke machines in restaurants and bars and homes. Deborah Wong and M. Elliot describe this: "The preferred venue for Vietnamese karaoke is restaurants, which are, in [our] view, public extensions of the home" (Wong and Elliot 1994, 157).

15. *Bác Hồ* refers to Hồ Chí Minh, the eminent leader of Viet Nam for the majority of the first and second Indochina wars. *Bác Hồ* as used here means anything communist. *Đấu tranh*, or "struggle," is a socialist Vietnamese political ideology in which the people themselves are seen as the agents of both political and armed struggle against an enemy (see Pike 1986).

16. *Nhạc vàng* refers to the popular Vietnamese songs of South Viet Nam before 1975 that became illegal to listen to after reunification. It includes the works of Nhat Truong and Pham Duy. "You're My Heart, You're My Soul" refers to the 1984 international megahit from the Euro-pop duo Modern Talking. This type of popular music was considered new wave by the overseas Vietnamese in the United States. It also appealed to youth in North Viet Nam, and they obtained cassette recordings of it.

17. Vietnamese living in Viet Nam, especially those coming from North Viet Nam after 1975 and belonging to the Communist Party, tend to refer to April 30, 1975, as the day of *giải phóng*, or liberation, for South Viet Nam and reunification of Viet Nam. The vast majority of Vietnamese who fled or emigrated from Viet Nam after 1975 refer to April 30, 1975, as the day they lost their country of South Viet Nam—*ngày mất nước*. "*Việt Cộng* singers" refers to singers from the North with communist affiliation.

18. Trần Thu Hà eventually married a Vietnamese American from Northern California. They have homes in the Bay Area, Ha Noi, and Sai Gon. Thu Phương defected to the United States in 2001 while on tour there.

19. Taylor estimated fifty Vietnamese singers by counting the names of those coming from Viet Nam in show advertisements for his competitors' and his productions.

20. In 1994 Thanh Lan was the first Vietnamese singer who publicly performed in the United States, but her shows had protestors (Lin 1994). More on Thanh Lan appears in Chapter 1 herein.

21. By 2012 the number of PBN popular music videos is 104 and counting.

22. For more on the Front, also known as National United Front for the Liberation of Vietnam (NUFLVN), and other anticommunist organizations, see Chapters 1 and 3 herein.

23. Though performing in the United States was not an option for entertainers from Viet Nam until 2000, they were able to perform in other countries such as Germany and Australia years before that.

24. For example, that collaborations between Vietnamese and Vietnamese Americans created the so-called Vietnamese music invasion was disclosed to me by a musician who works in the popular music industry in Southern California. One of the earliest and most influential artists of this invasion sold her music to an overseas music producer for remastering and distribution in the United States and Viet Nam. In fact, more than one overseas music house owns copyrights to Vietnamese-produced popular music. Such collaborations have occurred since at least 1995 and possibly earlier, but they are not made public because the popular music producers do not want to be accused of being communist (field notes 1995).

25. Translated by Phi Tran.

26. Translated by Eric Henry.

27. Nguyễn Du (1765–1820) is considered the premier poet of Viet Nam.

CHAPTER 3

1. *Virtual communities* are Internet-based social networks in which participants share common interests, ideas, and goals that evolve over time and can turn into personal relationships. In *The Virtual Community: Homesteading on the Electronic Frontier*, Howard Rheingold defines *virtual community* as "social aggregations that emerge from the Net when enough people carry on those public discussions long enough with sufficient human feeling, to form webs of personal relationships in cyberspace" (1993, 5). My understanding of the term *virtual community* is a combination of the two definitions.

2. By "handler" I mean persons working for the Vietnamese government or following orders from it who took special interest in my whereabouts at all times and on occasion had the power to detain me or withhold permission for me to travel within the country.

3. The Internet originated as a reaction to the threat of Russian scientific superiority with the first Sputnik in 1957. If the Soviets attacked, how could the military communicate if all systems were down? Starting in 1958 the U.S. Department of Defense collaborated with university laboratories to create a communications network that became the Internet we know day (Abbate 1999; Castells 2001).

4. Members of Vietnam Forum use "VNForum" to identify themselves. It is the correct name and spelling, not abbreviated.

5. Usenet newsgroups are Internet bulletin boards on which participants post their thoughts and ideas for others in the group to read. There are thousands of specialized

Usenet forums and groups with central hosts to store and transfer messages. It is a many-to-many system of communication, whereas e-mail is primarily one-to-one or one-to-few communication.

6. *Blog* is an online shared journal that generally discusses daily events, facilitates social networking, discusses hobbies, or informs on a particular subject.

7. The use of "parolees" relates to the emergency Indochina Migration and Refugee Act of 1975. Signed by President Gerald Ford, this bill granted Vietnamese refugees special status to enter the country and established a domestic resettlement program. With Senator Edward Kennedy's (D-MA) sponsorship, it was amended in 1977 to extend financial assistance and allow permanent residence.

8. Orange County in Southern California has the largest population of Vietnamese outside Viet Nam.

9. Anna Lee Saxenian's (1999) research on Silicon Valley immigrant-entrepreneurs shows that two-thirds of all scientists and engineers in Silicon Valley's high-tech industry were foreign born. Of this group, 13 percent are Vietnamese Americans.

10. A large proportion of Viet Nam scholars were located at the ANU because Viet Nam studies were neglected in the United States as an aftereffect of the war.

11. Tran later became the country representative in Viet Nam for Nike Inc.

12. By "e-mail list" I mean a group of subscribers who make postings to a single e-mail address that are then forwarded automatically to all subscribers' e-mail addresses.

13. *Flame wars* occur when *flaming*, sending deliberately hostile and insulting messages to a discussion board on the Internet, escalates.

14. Moderated forums have a person (moderator) who checks postings for flaming and other offensive writings and discards them or otherwise censors them. "Unmoderated" forums' postings go unchecked.

15. An ISP connects customers to the Internet using a data transmission technology appropriate for delivering Internet Protocol connections, such as dial-up service, a digital subscriber line, a cable modem, or a dedicated high-speed link.

16. UUCP refers to a suite of computer programs and protocols that allow remote execution of commands and transfer of files, e-mail, and newsgroup postings between computers.

17. In January 1950, Commonwealth foreign ministers met in Colombo, Ceylon, and created a program in which aid would flow from Western developed countries to developing countries in southern Asia and Southeast Asia. As one of the members, Australia sought to strengthen relations with Asia by promoting economic and political stability. The most memorable component of the program included sponsoring thousands of Asian students to study in Australian tertiary-education institutions. Many of these students remained in Australia and became leaders of their ethnic communities.

18. An *Internet e-mail bomb* is the term for huge volumes of e-mails sent to an e-mail address's inbox in an attempt to disable it by filling it or by overwhelming the server where the e-mail address is hosted.

19. I made every effort to present examples of conversations or threads from the virtual communities I studied. However, rapid changes in technology over the past decade-plus left archives of posts stored in obsolete drive media (floppy discs, super discs, zip drives, CDs, hard drives, etc.). More current posts archived on various machines with limited functionality were also sometimes difficult or impossible to retrieve.

20. The "silent majority" in this case refers to a group of Vietnamese Americans with diverse opinions regarding subjects within the Vietnamese American community and in Viet Nam. For example, they have complex views on communism that are not

represented in media or in academia. See Jenny Dang's (2000) "Ho Chi Minh Haters: Oakland Art Exhibit Rekindles Anti-Communist Movement."

21. The number of ghost investors, or those who invest under third-party names, would if known raise this number substantially.

22. The e-mails were remarkable to me, however. A few months after the first Nike posting by Thuyen, I was scanning through postings on the online Ethnic Studies Graduate Student List when I saw a call-to-action letter from Thuyen Nguyen. It was the same one that he had posted to VNForum and that had become a hot topic of discussion there. A member of an international labor Internet group had forwarded Thuyen's anti-Nike letter to my Ethnic Studies Graduate Student List. I knew then that I was witnessing history on my computer screen. The virtual community I belonged to had expanded its reach to other virtual communities that were operating globally.

23. Vietnamese blogging began innocuously enough through Yahoo! services. Yahoo!'s dominance in providing Internet services such as e-mail accounts and social media websites means it is a recognizable and trusted brand name for a generation of Vietnamese growing up in the age of globalization (H.-N. Vu 2009a). When Yahoo! introduced a personal communication portal, Yahoo! 360°, in Viet Nam on June 24, 2005, Vietnamese naturally gravitated toward it. With this new social network, users were able to create personal profiles, share photos, and most important, maintain blogs. In some cases friendly personal postings shared with selected networks of friends evolved into bolder opinions about society that were open for public viewing. By opting to make posts more open and even public, this new group of bloggers attracted many more like-minded individuals inside and outside the country.

24. Hao-Nhien Vu (2009a), overseas Vietnamese journalist and well-known blogger at *Bolsavik*, was one of the first observers of these early Vietnamese bloggers. Nguyễn Hoàng Hải, best known as "Điếu Cày," blogged on Yahoo! 360° about issues of national concern such as corruption, worker exploitation, police brutality, and Chinese encroachment of the Spratly and Paracels territories. Hao-Nhien read Nguyễn Hoàng Hải's blog and, intrigued, began leaving comments. From there the two political bloggers built a friendship and eventually met during one of Hao-Nhien's trips to Viet Nam. Nguyễn Hoàng Hải was arrested in April 2008 and given a two-and-a-half-year sentence. The grounds for arrest were tax fraud allegations, but by most accounts the arrest and conviction were punishment for his political activities on the blog and for leading a protest against China when the Olympic torch was carried through Ho Chi Minh City.

25. YouTube and Facebook are social networking websites. YouTube users upload video clips such as movie clips, TV clips, music videos, and amateur content, which can include video blogging and short original videos. Facebook users create profiles, which they customize with videos, photos, and personal information, that friends browse and where they leave messages.

26. I became a member of VNForum in its early stages.

CHAPTER 4

1. Because most publications show only one of the three pedicure basins in Chau Huynh's installation, I use the singular *Pedicure Basin*.

2. Vietnamese brides began immigrating to the United States starting in the 1990s. Sometimes, non-Vietnamese men marry these Vietnamese women. More often it is Vietnamese men. Finding wives in Viet Nam is so common that nearly every Vietnamese American knows someone who has returned to Viet Nam to find a spouse. The numer-

ous matchmaking and dating services available on the Internet and in the Vietnamese diasporic communities further facilitate such unions.

3. For an engaging discussing of transnational marriages between overseas Vietnamese men and their Vietnamese brides, see Hung Thai's (2008) *For Better or for Worse.*

4. The Republic of Viet Nam (RVN) is the former South Viet Nam, which started below the seventeenth parallel. The United States allied with the RVN during the second Indochina war, but the RVN fell to communism on April 30, 1975. The Socialist Republic of Viet Nam (SRV) refers to communist-controlled Viet Nam when the South and North reunified in 1976, following the end of the second Indochina war. The RVN flag consists of a yellow background with three red stripes. The SRV flag has a red background with a yellow, five-point star in the center.

5. Trách nhiệm bảo vệ và tôn trọng Quốc Kỳ là nhiệm vụ của tất cả mọi công dân VNCH, xin những ai sử dụng Quốc Kỳ phải thận trọng, không nên bạ đâu cắm đó, cắm xong rồi bỏ mặc nó cho tả tơi rách nát trước gió như chúng ta thường thấy ở trước cửa một vài cơ sở thương mại.

6. Nếu người vn tranh đấu cho quyền tự do dân chủ thì tấm hình hay cái bồn rữa chân không phải là mục tiêu chống đối, nó nói lên cái tự do tư tưởng của một "cá nhân" mà chúng ta hay pháp luật của một nước văn minh như mỹ hoàn toàn tôn trọng và được bảo vệ tuyệt đối. khi nào cái tư tưởng "cá nhân" này ép buộc cho mọi người phải noi theo như chủ nghĩa cs hay xhcn thì chúng ta có quyền chống đối.

7. Annoyed by the anticommunist protest and unable to stop it through legal means, local businesses (mostly non-Vietnamese) near the *Viet Weekly*'s offices countered with their own protest, which included freedom of speech banners and loud rock 'n' roll music (Bharath 2008c).

8. When *Nguoi Viet Daily* got a restraining order on the protest leader Doan Trong during the Chau controversy in 2008, Doan played on the rivalry of competing ethnic newspapers by convincing *Viet Weekly* to write his side of the story. Subsequently, Doan's group of protestors left the *Viet Weekly* site and put all their efforts into protesting at the Nguoi Viet headquarters (Huynh 2008b).

9. Anh Do, *Orange County Register* columnist and daughter of Yen Do, took over as editor in chief of *Nguoi Viet Daily* in February 2008.

CHAPTER 5

1. I often refer to Vice-Mayor Madison Nguyen as Madison. Again, the purpose is to avoid confusion, since Nguyen, her surname, is most commonly used within the Vietnamese community, whereas Madison is most commonly used within the Vietnamese American community.

2. Here I play on the popular saying "Viet Nam is more than a war" to imply that it is also a country. This phrase has been used in myriad ways by people ranging from tourism professionals to scholars.

3. At Madison Nguyen's victory party, I spoke casually to attendees about their feelings.

4. Vietnamese nationals who study or work abroad and then remain in the host country make up a relatively new type of Vietnamese emigrant. Unlike the Vietnamese labor migrants in eastern Europe, this group is generally from well-to-do families with some government connections. Many from this category have studied abroad since their teenage years or earlier. They obtain advanced degrees abroad and find employment in their host country. Some have government approval to stay abroad to further their train-

ing and to eventually return to Viet Nam. Others do not and stay, despite Vietnamese policies fining these "runaway" students, because they believe they have better opportunities in the host country. Some become illegal aliens, while others find spouses to obtain legal residence (see "New Rules" 2000). For those looking to label all coming from Viet Nam as nationalist patriots of the old regime, international students are not easily categorized. As with transnational brides, distinctions are made on a case-by-case and situation-by-situation basis. Close observation of these groups and their acceptance or rejection in the ethnic community could help us understand leading trends in Viet Nam–Vietnamese diaspora relations.

5. Several television news stations invited Madison and Terry's wedding guests to appear to verify that the wedding did not have communists present. Terry Tran even appeared on a show to dispel the rumors of communist ties ("Terry on TV (1 of 2)" 2008; "Terry on TV (2 of 2)" 2008; "Vietnamese TV Discusses Madison's Wedding Part 1 of 2" 2008; "Vietnamese TV Discusses Madison's Wedding Part 2 of 2" 2008).

6. The 1.5 generation comprises immigrants who were born outside the United States but brought up mainly there. The cut-off age of immigration to qualify is usually around eleven years old.

7. Not his real name.

8. I grew up in the district that became Vice-Mayor Madison Nguyen's, in a time before the formation of Vietnamese American ethnic enclaves in San Jose, and I never heard of or experienced the idea that the name Little Saigon meant anything more than residential and shopping centers in Orange County in the area dubbed Little Saigon. I first learned of the purported significance of the name to Vietnamese American San Jose residents when the protests against Madison's business-district naming effort hit the mainstream press in 2007.

9. Tết refers to the Vietnamese New Year following the lunar calendar. Many in the Vietnamese community continue practicing the rituals associated with Tết, including offering gifts or tributes to respected elders.

10. Ly Tong is best known for allegedly hijacking planes and flying them over Viet Nam and Cuba to drop pro-democracy, anticommunism propaganda leaflets. Tong is a controversial figure: some Vietnamese Americans consider him to be a hero, while others see him as an opportunist. Some believe that he starved himself during his hunger strike (his own reports noted that he drank energy shakes), whereas others believe that it was a hoax. Tong is discussed later in this chapter.

11. This agreement was seen as a temporary fix, and the district residents and merchants were to later decide the permanent name for the business district with city support. However, as of 2012, no official name designation from the city has taken place. Instead, private funding through the Little Saigon Foundation paid for the eighteen Little Saigon banners and their maintenance ("City of San Jose Memorandum" 2008; Madison Nguyen, pers. comm., May 8, 2012).

12. As with most protests, nothing is as it seems. Janet Nguyen's actions might have been motivated by political disputes originating before the Little Saigon brouhaha and might even have had little to do with Madison but more to do with her supporters.

13. To protect my respondents, I do not go into greater detail regarding communications between the Vietnamese government and members of the diasporic community.

14. The authors of the letter were Viet Thanh Nguyen, associate professor of English and Asian American studies at the University of Southern California; Hien Duc Do, of San Jose State University; Hung Thai, of the University of California, Santa Barbara; Jeffrey Brody, of California State University, Fullerton; Van Bich Thi Tran, of the Social

Science Research Council in New York; Nguyen-vo Thu-huong, of the University of California, Los Angeles; Yen Le Espiritu, of the University of California, San Diego; Phuong Nguyen, of the University of Southern California; and Dan Duffy, of the University of North Carolina.

CHAPTER 6

1. The Phương Hồ case follows other police brutality cases in San Jose. On May 10, 2009, San Jose police shot and killed Daniel Pham, a mentally ill and violent twenty-seven-year-old. On July 13, 2003, Cau Thi Bich Tran, a twenty-five-year-old mother of two, was wrongfully shot by a San Jose police officer. Madison Nguyen garnered international attention when she mobilized the Vietnamese American community to help Cau Thi Bich's family obtain a settlement from the San Jose Police Department.

References

Abbate, Janet. 1999. *Inventing the Internet.* Cambridge, MA: MIT Press.

Agence France-Presse. 2004. "US City Rolls Out Unwelcome Mat for Vietnam Officials." Agence France-Presse, May 24.

Aguilar-San Juan, Karin. 2000. "Creating Ethnic Places: Vietnamese American Community-Building in Orange County and Boston." Ph.D. diss., Brown University.

———. 2009. *Little Saigons: Staying Vietnamese in America.* Minneapolis: University of Minnesota Press.

Anderson, Benedict. 1983. *Imagined Communities: Reflections on the Origin and Spread of Nationalism.* New York: Verso.

Anderson, Wanni, and Robert G. Lee, eds. 2005. *Displacements and Diasporas.* New Jersey: Rutgers University Press.

Anonymous. 2000. Interview by author with music industry insider. Orange County, CA. June 20.

Anonymous. 2008. *VietWeekly* Forum. March 6.

Appadurai, Arjun. 1991. "Global Ethnoscapes: Notes and Queries for a Transnational Anthropology." In *Recapturing Anthropology: Working in the Present*, edited by Richard G. Fox, 191–210. Santa Fe: School of American Research Press.

Associated Press. 1989. "Vietnamese Author Who Advocated Ties with Hanoi Is Shot." *New York Times*, August 22. Available at http://www.nytimes.com/1989/08/22/us/vietnamese-author-who-advocated-ties-with-hanoi-is-shot.html.

———. 1999a. "Nike Criticized for Vietnam Letter." Associated Press, January 30.

———. 1999b. "Nike Says Labor Protesters Have Vietnam Political Agenda." *Boycott Nike*, January 20. Available at http://www.viet.net/web/nike/public_html/ap12199.html.

———. 2007. "Vietnam Releases Hawaii-Based Activist." *Honolulu Advertiser*, December 11. Available at http://the.honoluluadvertiser.com/article/2007/Dec/11/br/br8751360249.html.

Baily, John. 1994. "The Role of Music in the Creation of an Afghan National Identity." In *Ethnicity, Identity and Music: The Musical Construction of Place*, edited by Martin Stokes, 29–44. Providence, RI: Berg.

Barr, Cameron W. 1997. "Vietnam's New War: 'Social Evils.'" *Christian Science Monitor*, September 24.

Basch, Linda, Nina Glick Schiller, and Cristina Szanton Blanc. 1994. *Nations Unbound: Transnational Projects, Postcolonial Predicaments and Deterritorialized Nation-States*. New York: Gordon and Breach.

Beevi, Mariam. 1997. "The Passing of Literary Traditions: The Figure of the Woman from Vietnamese Nationalism to Vietnamese American Transnationalism." *Amerasia Journal* 23 (2): 27–53.

Bharath, Deepa. 2008a. Interview by author with journalist. *Orange County Register*, May 15.

———. 2008b. "Little Saigon Editor Says She Will Continue to Fight Protesters." *Orange County Register*, March 27.

———. 2008c. "Merchants Plan Protest against Anti-communist Demonstrators." *Orange County Register*, April 11.

———. 2009a. "Little Saigon Protesters Agree to Stop." *Orange County Register*, May 28. Available at http://www.ocregister.com/articles/newspaper-126758-viet-jury.html.

———. 2009b. "Vietnamese Artists' Exhibit Shut Down by Threat of Protests." *Orange County Register*, January 1.

Bharath, Deepa, and Frank Mickadeit. 2008. "Little Saigon Newspaper Gets Injunction against Protesters." *Orange County Register*, April 8, 2008. Available at http://www.ocregister.com/news/newspaper-126270-protesters-injunction.html.

Biers, Dan, and Margot Cohen. 2000. "Return of the Prodigal Sons." *Far Eastern Economic Review*, September 21.

Birchall, Jonathan. 1999. "Nike Slams Vietnam Labour Critics." *BBC News*, January 21.

Bissell, Trim. 1999. "Analysis of New Developments." *Campaign for Labor Rights Newsletter*, January 26. Available at http://groups.yahoo.com/group/konformist/message/171.

Blum, Stephen, Philip V. Bohlman, and Daniel M. Neuman, eds. 1991. *Ethnomusicology and Modern Music History*. Urbana: University of Illinois Press.

Boot, Max. 2009. "The Incurable Vietnam Syndrome: Distorting Our Foreign Policy for Three Decades and Counting." *Weekly Standard* 15 (5). Available at http://www.weeklystandard.com/Content/Public/Articles/000/000/017/059wcvib.asp?pg=1.

Brody, Jeffrey. 1994. "Attack on Editor of Vietnamese Newspaper Is an Attack on Free Speech." *Los Angeles Times*, October 19.

———. 2003. *Yen Do and the Story of* Nguoi Viet Daily News *with Jeffrey Brody*. Self-published.

Bui, Timothy. 2001. *Green Dragon*. Columbia Pictures.

Bui, Tony. 1999. *Three Seasons*. October Films.

Caplan, Nathan, John K. Whitmore, and Marcella H. Choy. 1989. *The Boat People and Achievement in America: A Study of Economic and Educational Success*. Ann Arbor: University of Michigan Press.

Carruthers, Ashley. 2001. "National Identity, Diasporic Anxiety, and Music Video Culture in Vietnam." In *House of Glass: Culture, Modernity, and the State in Southeast Asia*, edited by Yao Souchou, 119–149. Pasir Panjang, Singapore: Institute of Southeast Asian Studies.

———. 2002. "The Accumulation of National Belonging in Transnational Fields: Ways of Being at Home in Vietnam." *Identities: Global Studies in Culture and Power* 9 (4): 423–444.

Castells, Manuel. 1996. *The Rise of the Network Society*. The Information Age: Economy, Society and Culture, vol. 1. Cambridge, MA: Blackwell.

———. 2001. *The Internet Galaxy: Reflections on the Internet, Business, and Society.* Oxford: Oxford University Press.

Central Intelligence Agency. 2012. "Vietnam." *The World Factbook.* Available at https://www.cia.gov/library/publications/the-world-factbook/geos/vm.html.

Chan, Sucheng. 1991. *Asian Americans: An Interpretive History.* Boston: Twayne Publishers.

———. 2006. *The Vietnamese American 1.5 Generation: Stories of War, Revolution, Flight, and New Beginnings.* Philadelphia: Temple University Press.

Chang, Richard. 2009. "Protesters Shut Down 'F.O.B. II' Exhibition." Arts Blog. *Orange County Register,* February 1. Available at http://artsblog.ocregister.com/2009/01/16/protesters-shut-down-fob-ii-exhibition/6432/.

Chin, Andrew. 2002. "The KKK and Vietnamese Fishermen." Available at http://www.unclaw.com/chin/scholarship/fishermen.htm.

"City of San Jose Memorandum." 2008. San Jose City Council. March 25.

Clifford, J. 1994. "Diasporas." *Cultural Anthropology* 9 (3): 302–338.

Coburn, Judith. 1983. "Terrorism in Saigon Town, U.S.A." *Mother Jones,* February–March, 15–22, 42–43.

Cohen, A. P. 1985. *The Symbolic Construction of Community.* New York: Routledge.

Cohen, Robin. 1997. *Global Diasporas: An Introduction.* Seattle, WA: University of Seattle Press.

Collet, Christian. 2000. "The Determinants of Vietnamese American Political Participation (Findings from the January 2000 *Orange County Register* Poll)." Paper presented at the 2000 Annual Meeting of the Association of Asian American Studies. Scottsdale, AZ, May 24–28.

Collet, Christian, and Pei-te Lien, eds. 2009. *The Transnational Politics of Asian Americans.* Philadelphia: Temple University Press.

Đặng, Hồ Phát. 1999. Interview by author with director of Committee for Overseas Vietnamese [Ủy Ban Người Việt Nam Ở Nước Ngoài]. Ha Noi, Viet Nam. October 25.

Dang, Janet. 2000. "Vietnamese American Reaction Divided." *Asia Week,* February 24.

Dang, Thuy Vo. 2005. "The Cultural Work of Anti-communism in the San Diego Vietnamese American Community." *Amerasia Journal* 31 (2): 65–86.

Daniels, Tommy. 2000. "The Jackson-Vanik Amendment." Available at http://isc.temple.edu/hist249/jackson.htm.

Denning, Steve. 2000a. Internet correspondence. May 12.

———. 2000b. Interview by author with archivist, librarian, and human rights activist. Berkeley, CA. April 4.

Dinh, Thai. 2011. Interview by author with assistant publisher of *Nguoi Viet Daily.* Orange County, CA. October 27.

"Dissident 'Attacks' Vietnamese Singer Dam Vinh Hung." 2010. BBC News, July 20. Available at http://www.bbc.co.uk/news/world-asia-pacific-10699376.

Do, Barry Hung. 2008. Interview by author with spokesperson for San Jose Voters for Democracy, a group supporting Madison Nguyen's recall and use of the Little Saigon name. San Jose, CA. June 2.

Do, Quynh Trang. 2000. Interview by author with computer expert. San Jose, CA. May 23.

Do, Thien Chi. 2001. Interview by author with Vietnamese American musician and writer. Oakland, CA. August 15.

Đoàn, Anh. 2000. Interview by author with computer expert, a Vietnamese national living in the United States. Seattle, WA. December 2.

Doan, Van Toai, and D. Chanoff. 1986. *The Vietnamese Gulag.* New York: Simon and Schuster.

Dorn, Geoff. 2008. Interview by author with gallery owner and curator of the Hồ Chí Minh exhibit. Seattle, WA. February 8.

Du, James. 2009. Interview by author with Vietnamese American protester. South Pasadena, CA. January 5.

Dubin, Zan. 1997. "Speaking Their Peace—Laguna Exhibit Features Artists Whose Works Capture a Gentler Vietnam." *Los Angeles Times*, January 18.

Dubin, Zan, and Rick Vanderknyff. 1995. "From Isolation to Mainstream: After an Embryonic 20 Years, the Influence of Vietnamese Artists, Musicians and Writers in Orange County Is Exploding." *Los Angeles Times*, March 12.

Duiker, W. J. 1989. "Vietnam since the Fall of Saigon." International Studies, Southeast Asia Series. Athens: Ohio University Press.

———. 2000. *Ho Chi Minh: A Life*. New York: Hyperion.

Duong, Lan. 2003. "Desire and Design: Technological Display in the Vietnamese American Café and Karaoke Bar." *Amerasia Journal* 29 (1): 97–115.

———. 2005. "Manufacturing Authenticity: The Feminine Ideal in Tony Bui's *Three Seasons*." *Amerasia Journal* 31 (2): 1–19.

———. 2009. Interview by author with assistant professor at the University of California, Riverside, and curator for *Art Speaks* exhibit. Santa Ana, CA. January 6 and 11.

Duong, Lan, and Tram Le. 2009. "Living without Fear." Unpublished press release in the author's possession.

Dzung, Viet. 2005. Interview by author with Vietnamese American singer and anticommunist activist. San Jose, CA. March 15.

Eastland, Sen. James O. 1975. Congressional Record Proceeding and Debates of the 94th Congress, First Session. Washington, DC. May 5.

Eisenbruch, M. 1991. "From Post-traumatic Stress Disorder to Cultural Bereavement: Diagnosis of Southeast Asian Refugees." *Social Science and Medicine Journal* 33 (6): 673–680.

Espiritu, Yen Le. 2005. "30 Years AfterWARd: Vietnamese Americans and U.S. Empire." *Amerasia Journal* 31 (2): xiii–xxiii.

———. 2006a. "Toward a Critical Refugee Study: The Vietnamese Refugee Subject US Scholarship." *Journal of Vietnamese Studies* 1 (1–2): 410–433.

———. 2006b. "The 'We-Win-Even-When-We-Lose' Syndrome: U.S. Press Coverage of the Twenty-Fifth Anniversary of the 'Fall of Saigon.'" *American Quarterly* 58 (2): 329–352.

Fan, Maureen, and Jessie Mangaliman. 2000. "McCain Apologizes for Using Slur: GOP Candidate Renounces 'Bigoted' Language." *San Jose Mercury News*, February 24.

Feldman, Charles. 1999, "CNN's Charles Feldman Shows the Protests and Talks with the Shop Owner." CNN. January 21.

Field notes. 1992. "Sisters and Paris by Night." December 26.

———. 1993a. "Communication Technology in Viet Nam."

———. 1993b. "Popular Music." December 2.

———. 1995. "Music." November 25.

———. 1996a. "Cô Hạnh and Chú Tuấn." August 18.

———. 1996b. "Trip to Center for Southeast Asian Studies." February 2.

———. 2000. "Ho Chi Minh Exhibit." March 19.

———. 2001. "Popular Music Concerts." November 2.

———. 2002. "Tran Dinh Hoanh." February 24.

———. 2008a. "Chau Huynh." June 2.

———. 2008b. "Madison Nguyen No-Recall Press Conference." March 20.

———. 2008c. "March 4, 2008, San Jose Council Meeting." March 4.

———. 2009. "James Du." January 22.

"Five Years, Only 100 Viet Kieu Have Houses in Vietnam." 2007. VietNamNet Bridge, September 3.

Flaccus, Gillian. 2006. "Closer U.S.-Vietnam Ties Help Music Flourish on Both Continents." Associated Press. April 11.

Foucault, Michel. 1977. *Discipline and Punish: The Birth of the Prison*. New York: Vintage Books.

Freeman, James. 1989. *Hearts of Sorrow: Vietnamese-American Lives*. Stanford, CA: Stanford University Press.

———. 1995. *Changing Identities: Vietnamese Americans, 1975–1995*. Boston: Allyn and Bacon.

Furuya, Hiroko, and Christian Collet. 2009. "Contested Nation: Vietnam and the Emergence of Saigon Nationalism in the United States." In *The Transnational Politics of Asian Americans*, edited by Christian Collet and Pei-te Lien, 56–76. Philadelphia: Temple University Press.

Gerke, Frank, and Bui Tuyen. 1999. "Popular Music in Vietnam." *Popmusik*, December 17.

Gibbs, Jason. 1997. "Reform and Tradition in Early Vietnamese Popular Song." *Nhạc Việt: The Journal of Vietnamese Music* 6:5–33.

———. 1998. "Nhạc Tiền Chiến: The Origins of Vietnamese Popular Song." *Things Asian*, July 1. Available at http://www.thingsasian.com/goto_article/article.801.html.

———. 2004. "The West's Songs, Our Songs: The Introduction and Adaptation of Western Popular Song in Vietnam before 1940." *Asian Music* 35 (1): 57–83.

Gilroy, Paul. 1991. *The Black Atlantic: Modernity and Double Consciousness*. Cambridge, MA: Harvard University Press.

Gold, Steven J. 1992. *Refugee Communities: A Comparative Field Study*. London: Sage.

Grant, Jeremy. 1996. "Vietnam Phone Deals Near—Four Foreign Companies Set to Win Contracts." *Financial Times*, February 29.

Guidry, John A., Michael D. Kennedy, and Mayter N. Zald, eds. 2000. *Globalizations and Social Movements: Culture Power and the Transnational Public Sphere*. Ann Arbor: University of Michigan Press.

Hải, Thanh. 2010. Interview by author with executive director of Bạn Yêu Nhạc. Sai Gon, Viet Nam. November 19.

Haldane, David. 2004. "To Vietnamese Communists, from Garden Grove: Stay Away." *Los Angeles Times*, May 12.

Hansen, Arthur A. 1983. *Demon Dogs: Cultural Deviance and Community Control in the Japanese-American Evacuation*. Tempe, Arizona: Western Conference of the Association for Asian Studies.

Harvey, David. 1990. *The Condition of Postmodernity: An Enquiry into the Origins of Cultural Change*. Cambridge, MA: Blackwell.

Haughton, Jonathan. 1999. "Money Transfer." *Vietnam Business Journal* 7 (1). Available at http://www.viet-nam.org/Com-News/moneytransfer.html.

Hayslip, Le Ly, and Jay Wurts. 1990. *When Heaven and Earth Changed Places*. New York: Plume.

Henry, Eric. 2005. "Phạm Duy and Modern Vietnamese History." *Southeast Review of Asian Studies* 27. Available at http://www.uky.edu/Centers/Asia/SECAAS/Seras/2005/Henry.htm.

Hirsch, Marianne. 2008. "The Generation of Postmemory." *Poetics Today* 29 (1): 103–128.

Ho, Truc. 2001. Interview by author with director of Asia Music Corporation and Asia Entertainment (Trung tâm Asia), a Vietnamese American music production house. Orange County, CA. December 10.

Hoang, Dan The. 2009. Interview by author with member of Viet Tan. San Jose, CA. January 2.

Hoang, Mai Minh. 1996. Interview by author with Vietnamese American journalist. Ha Noi, Viet Nam. April 12.

Hookway, James. 2009. "Web Censoring Widens across Southeast Asia." *Wall Street Journal*, September 14.

Huckshorn, Kristin. 1998. "Hanoi, Eager for Link with World, Still Suspicious of Internet." *San Jose Mercury News*, May 31.

Human Rights Watch. 1992. "World Report 1992: Vietnam." Available at http://www.unhcr.org/refworld/docid/467fca54c.html.

Hurle, Rob. 2002. Interview by author with Internet expert and leading ICT expansionist in Viet Nam. Ha Noi, Viet Nam. September 10.

———. 2004. Interview by author. Canberra, Australia. May 28.

Huynh, Chau. 2008a. Interview by author with artist. Davis, CA. February 21 and May 23.

———. 2008b. "Mẹ Chồng Tôi" [My Husband's Mother]. *Nguoi Viet Daily*, February 7.

Internet World Stats. 2010. "Vietnam: Internet Usage Stats and Marketing Report." Available at http://www.internetworldstats.com/asia/vn.htm.

James, David. 1989. "The Vietnam War and American Music." *Social Text*, no. 23: 122–143.

Jayadev, Raj. 1999. "Electronics Assembly for Poverty Wages: Behind Silicon Valley's Instant Millionaires." *Labor Notes*, October 3. Available at http://labornotes.org/node/1801.

Jung, Carolyn. 1994. "Vietnamese Pop Singer Officially Files for Asylum." *San Jose Mercury News*, February 4.

Karnow, Stanley. 1983. *Vietnam: A History*. New York: Viking Press.

Kibria, Nazli. 1993. *Family Tightrope: The Changing Lives of Vietnamese Americans*. Princeton, NJ: Princeton University Press.

Kleinknecht, William. 1999. "Journalists at Risk." *American Journalism Review*, December. Available at http://www.ajr.org/article.asp?id=766.

Kollock, Peter, and Marc A. Smith. 1999. "Communities in Cyberspace." In *Communities in Cyberspace*, edited by Marc A. Smith and Peter Kollock, 3–28. New York: Routledge.

Kornhaber, Spencer. 2010. "We'll Always Have 'Paris by Night.'" *SF Weekly*, June 23. Available at http://www.sfweekly.com/2010-06-23/news/we-ll-always-have-paris-by-night/.

Kubek, Anthony. 1992. "The 'Opening' of China: President Nixon's 1972 Journey." *American Asian Review* 10 (4): 1–22.

Kumin, Judith. 1988. "Orderly Departure from Vietnam: A Humanitarian Alternative?" Ph.D. diss., Fletcher School of Law and Diplomacy, Tufts University.

Kunz, E. F. 1973. "The Refugee in Flight: Kinetic Models and Forms of Displacement." *International Migration Review* 7 (2): 125–146.

Ky, Ngo. 2009. Interview by author with professional anticommunist protestor. Orange County, CA. January 17.

Lai, To Van. 2000. Interview by author with founder of Paris by Night. Orange County, CA. June 16.

Lam, Thanh. 2001. Interview by author with Vietnamese pop singer. San Francisco, CA. February 9.

Landzelius, K. 2006. *Native on the Net: Indigenous and Diasporic Peoples in the Virtual Age*. New York: Routledge.

Le, Christine. 2008. "Stitching Together Memories, Stories: UC Berkeley Alumna, Artist Chau Thuy Huynh." *Xoài Vàng* [The Golden Mango] 3 (3): 2. Available at http://www.calvsa.com/wordpress/wp-content/uploads/2008/Pages%20COLOR.pdf.

Lê, T.D.T. 2003. *The Gangster We Are All Looking For.* New York: Alfred A. Knopf.

Lê, Thương. 1970. "Nhạc Tiền Chiến: Lời thuật của Nhạc sĩ Lê Thương." amnhac.fm. Available at http://amnhac.fm/index.php/bai/55-tan-nhac/4370-nhac-tien-chien--loi-thuat-cua-nhac-si-le-thuong.

Le, Tin. 1998. Interview by author with engineer and founder of VietNet and Vietnam Forum. San Jose, CA. June 23.

———. 2000. Interview by author. San Jose, CA. May 9.

———. 2009. Interview by author. San Jose, CA. January 13.

Le, Ysa. 2011. Interview by author with executive director of Vietnamese American Arts and Letters Association (VAALA). Orange County, CA. November 11.

Lehner, Jennifer. 2004. "City Rejects Envoy's Drive-by." *Washington Times*, May 14.

Leshkowich, Ann Marie. 2003. "The *Ao Dai* Goes Global: How International Influences and Female Entrepreneurs Have Shaped Vietnam's 'National Costume.'" In *Re-Orienting Fashion: The Globalisation of Asian Dress*, edited by Sandra Niessen, Ann Marie Leshkowich, and Carla Jones, 79–116. New York: Berg.

"A Lesson for Carter." 1977. *Nhân Dân*, January 26.

Le-Thi-Que, A. Terry Rambo, and Gary D. Murfin. 1976. "Why They Fled: Refugee Movement during the Spring 1975 Communist Offensive in South Vietnam." *Asian Survey* 16 (9): 855–863.

Lieu, Nhi T. 1998. "Cultural Contestations and Transnational Circulation: Inside the Migratory Path of 'Paris by Night' Videos." Paper presented at Asian Americans and Popular Culture Conference. New York City, November 13.

Lin, Sam Chu. 1994. "Vietnamese Singer Lan Seeks Political Asylum." *AsianWeek*, February 4.

Linh, Xuan. 2008. "Watchdog to Regulate Blogs in Vietnam." VietNamNet Bridge, October 3. Available at http://www.lookatvietnam.com/2008/10/watchdog-to-regulate-blogs-in-vietnam.html.

Long, Lynellyn D. 2004. "Viet Kieu on a Fast Track Back?" In *Coming Home? Refugees, Migrants, and Those Who Stayed Behind*, edited by Lynellyn D. Long and Ellen Oxfeld, 65–89. Philadelphia: University of Pennsylvania Press.

Lowe, Lisa. 1991. "Heterogeneity, Hybridity, Multiplicity: Marking Asian American Differences." *Diaspora* 1 (1): 24–44.

Luke, Timothy. W. 2002. *Museum Politics: Power Plays at the Exhibition.* Minneapolis: University of Minnesota Press.

Lull, James, and Roger Wallis. 1992. "The Beat of West Vietnam." In *Popular Music and Communication*, 2nd ed., edited by James Lull, 207–236. Newbury Park, CA: Sage.

MacQueen, K. M., E. McLellan, D. S. Metzger, S. Kegeles, R. P. Strauss, R. Scotti, L. Blanchard, and R. T. Trotter. 2001. "What Is Community? An Evidence-Based Definition for Participatory Public Health." *American Public Health Association* 91 (12): 1929–1938.

Maira, Sunaina. 2002. *Desis in the House: Indian American Youth Culture in New York City.* Philadelphia: Temple University Press.

Mannur, A., and J. E. Braziel. 2003. *Theorizing Diaspora.* Malden, MA: Blackwell.

Marosi, Richard. 2000. "Vietnam's Musical Invasion." *Los Angeles Times*, August 8.

McKeown, Adam. 1999. "Conceptualizing Chinese Diasporas, 1842 to 1949." *Journal of Asian Studies* 58 (2): 306–337.

McLaughlin, Ken. 1990. "Vietnam Resistance Faces Generation Gap, Militant Anti-Communist Haven't Captured Hearts of the Young." *San Jose Mercury News*, October 29.

———. 1993. "Vietnamese Émigrés Return Guests: Hanoi Reaches Out for Investment Help to Aid Troubled Economy." *San Jose Mercury News*, February 10.

Mele, Christophe. 1999. "Cyberspace and Disadvantaged Communities: The Internet as a Tool for Collective Action." In *Communities in Cyberspace*, edited by Marc A. Smith and Peter Kollock, 289–308. New York: Routledge.

Mickadeit, Frank. 2008. "Tony Lam's Case Chills Politicians." *Orange County Register*, April 18.

Molina, Joshua. 2008. "2,000 Celebrate 'Little Saigon' Victory at San Jose City Hall." *San Jose Mercury News*, May 18.

Montero, Darrel. 1979. *Vietnamese Americans: Patterns of Resettlement and Socioeconomic Adaptation in the United States*. Boulder, Colorado: Westview Press.

Moxley, Scott. 2008. "When Gunner Jay Lindberg Killed Thien Minh Ly, Was It Actually a Hate Crime?" *OC Weekly*, July 16.

Mui, Ylan Q. 2001. "Culture on Rewind: Vietnamese Video Series Links a Far-Flung People to Their Past." *Washington Post*, July 12.

Nakanishi, Don Toshiaki. 1975. *In Search of a New Paradigm: Minorities in the Context of International Politics*. Denver, CO: University of Denver Center for International Race Relations.

Nelson, Vern. 2011. "The Lowdown on Mark W. Bucher, 3rd Supe Candidate." *Orange Juice Blog*, November 17. Available at http://www.orangejuiceblog.com/2011/11/the-lowdown-on-mark-w-bucher-3rd-supe-candidate/.

Newman, Hoa. 2000. Interview by author with former teacher at the Defense Language Institute Foreign Language Center in Monterey. El Cerrito, CA. April 7.

"New Rules Ensure VN Students Abroad Return or Repay Fees." 2000. *Vietnam Economic Times*, August 11.

Nga, Nguyễn Phương. 2009. "Vietnam Public Resents S.J. Police Violent Manhandling of Vietnamese Student." Ministry of Foreign Affairs. October 27. Available at http://www.mofa.gov.vn/en/tt_baochi/pbnfn/ns091028170107.

Ngo, Hieu Van. 2008. Interview by author with Vietnam Human Rights Network activist. Westminster, CA. February 17.

Nguyen, Doan Trong. 2008. Interview by author with *Nguoi Viet Daily* anticommunist activist and leader of *Nguoi Viet Daily* protest. Westminster, CA. May 26.

Nguyen, Kien. 2001. *The Unwanted: A Memoir*. New York: Little Brown.

Nguyen, Long, and Harry H. Kendall. 1981. *After Saigon Fell: Daily Life under the Vietnamese Communists*. Berkeley: Institute of East Asian Studies, University of California.

Nguyen, Madison. 2008. Interview by author with city council member. San Jose, CA. March 4 and December 5.

———. 2009a. "Council Speech." Unpublished. March 4. San Jose, CA.

———. 2009b. Interview by author. San Jose, CA. January 12, March 3, April 5, and November 2.

Nguyen, Ngoc Bich. 2010. "Pham Duy, Vietnam's Music Man." Available at http://www.phamduy2010.com/writings/music_man.php.

Nguyen, Nho. 2008. "Flag for My Daughter." Unpublished speech. November 22. San Jose, CA.

Nguyen, Phu. 2000. Interview by author with Vietnamese American musician. Orange County, CA. April 15.

Nguyen, Qui Duc. 1994. *Where the Ashes Are: The Odyssey of a Vietnamese Family.* Boston: Addison-Wesley.

———. 2009. Interview by author with journalist, writer, and curator. Ha Noi, Viet Nam. October 18.

Nguyen, Thanh. 2000. Interview by author with founder and owner of Kim Loi Music Productions. San Jose, CA. December 9.

———. 2001. Interview by author. San Jose, CA. July 27, August 9, and August 14.

Nguyễn, Thanh Đức. 2001. Interview by author with Vietnamese journalist for *Báo Tuổi Trẻ* (Youth Newspapers) and cultural critic. Sai Gon, Viet Nam. January 31.

Nguyen, Thanh Sky. 2000. Interview by author with Vietnamese American musician. Orange County, CA. May 12.

Nguyen, Thuyen. 1997. "Nike Is Trying to Control Damages as an Internal Document about Labor Problems in Vietnam Was Leaked to the Press." Vietnam Labor Watch, November 7. Available at http://www.viet.net/web/nike/public_html/pr9.htm.

———. 2000. Interview by author with Vietnamese American labor activist and leader of No-Nike campaign. New York. November 3.

Nguyen, Viet Thanh. 2006. "Seeing Double: The Films of R. Hong-an Truong." *Postmodern Culture* 17 (1). Available at http://muse.jhu.edu/journals/postmodern_culture/toc/pmc17.1.html.

Nguyen, Viet Thanh, Hien Duc Do, Hung Thai, Jeffrey Brody, Van Bich Thi Tran, Nguyen-vo Thu-huong, Yen Le Espiritu, Phuong Nguyen, Dan Duffy. 2004. "A Destructive Obsession: Vietnamese-Americans Are Held Hostage by Fanatic Anti-communist Faction." *Orange County Register*, June 6.

Nhat, Tien, Duong Phuc, and Vu Thanh Thuy. 1981. *Pirates on the Gulf of Siam: Report from the Vietnamese Boat People Living in the Refugee Camp in Songkhla-Thailand.* San Diego, CA: Boat People S.O.S. Committee.

Nhu, T. T. 1997. Editorial. *San Jose Mercury News*, April 27.

"Nike." 1996. VNForum Archive, September 15.

"Nike Shoe Factory Expose." 1996. *48 Hours.* CBS News, New York. October 27.

Ninh, Hải. 2005. "Overseas Vietnamese Musician Pham Duy Returns Home." *Báo Thanh Niên*, April 27.

"O.C. Vietnam Democracy Activist Meets with President Bush." 2007. *Orange County Register*, May 29.

Okamura, Jonathan Y. 2003. "Asian American Studies in the Age of Transnationalism: Diaspora, Race, Community." *Amerasia Journal* 29 (2): 171–194.

Ong, Nhu-Ngoc T., and David S. Meyer. 2008. "Protest and Political Incorporation: Vietnamese American Protests, 1975–2001." *Journal of Vietnamese Studies* 3 (1): 78–107.

OpenNet Initiative. 2007. "Internet Filtering in Vietnam in 2005–2006: A Country Study." Available at http://opennet.net/studies/vietnam.

Ortiz, Erik. 2007. "Community Rallies against Magazine's Message: Charging *Viet Weekly* of Its Pro-communist Stance, Vietnamese-Americans Protest against Garden Grove Publication." *Orange County Register*, July 22.

Our Voice. 2008. "Open Letter." February 12. Available at http://www.ourvoiceforum.com/aboutus/openletter.html.

"Overseas Vietnamese." 2009–2010. Wikipedia. Available at http://en.wikipedia.org/wiki/Overseas_Vietnamese (accessed December 19, 2010).

"Overseas Vietnamese Are Integral Part and Resource of the Vietnamese Community: President." 2009. *Nhân Dân*, January 20.

Parreñas, Rhacel, and Lok Siu, eds. 2007. *Asian Diasporas: New Formations, New Conceptions.* Stanford, CA: Stanford University Press.

Peck, M. Scott. 1998. *The Different Drum: Community Making and Peace.* New York: Touchstone.

Pelaud, Isabelle Thuy. 2005. "Entering Linh Dinh's Fake House: Literature of Displacement." *Amerasia Journal* 31 (2): 37–49.

Pham, Andrew X. 1999. *Catfish and Mandala: A Two-Wheeled Voyage through the Landscape and Memory of Vietnam.* New York: Farrar, Straus, and Giroux.

Pham, Dan. 2008. Interview by author with Vietnamese American supporter of Little Saigon name. San Jose, CA. January 18.

Pham, De [pseudonym]. 2000. Interview by author with cofounder of Vietnamese Students Abroad e-mail list. Seattle, WA. October 9.

Pham, Linh. 2005. Interview by author with Vietnamese American music enthusiast. San Jose, CA. April 2.

Philato. 2008. "Nghệ Thuật . . . Chuồn Chồ" [Art . . . Alert]. Đoàn Thanh Niên Việt Hôn (Youth Group Heart of Viet Nam). Available at http://www.vietsoul.com/home/forum/viewtopic.php?topic=7787&forum=36&0.

Phong, Dang. 2000. "The Vietnamese Diaspora: Returning and Integrating into Vietnam." *Revue Euopéenne des Migrations Internationales* 16 (1): 183–205.

Phuong, Elvis. 2002. Interview by author with popular Vietnamese American male singer. Sai Gon, Viet Nam. June 2.

Pike, Douglas. 1986. *PAVN People's Army of Vietnam.* Novato: Presidio Press.

"Portrait of Vietnamese Americans by Census 2010." 2011. Eye Dr DeLengocky, September 8. Available at http://www.eyedrd.org/2011/09/portrait-of-vietnamese-americans-by-census-2010.html.

Ramos, Abe de. 2006. "Don't Miss Saigon: Doing Business in Vietnam Is Better Than Ever, but Still Not for the Faint-Hearted." *CFO Asia.* May.

Recall Madison Nguyen Committee. 2010. *Sự Thật Đã Được Phơi Bày [The Truth Was Exposed].* DVD.

Reed, Thuy. 2004. "'No-Communist Zone' Has No Place in America: A Hard-Core Few in Orange County's Little Saigon Need a Civics Lesson." *Los Angeles Times,* May 29.

Reid, Anthony, ed. 2003. *Southeast Asian Studies: Pacific Perspective.* Tempe: Southeast Asian Studies Monograph Series of Arizona State University and the Asian Pacific Monograph Series of the UCLA Asia Institute.

"Resolution No 36-NQ/TW, March 26, 2004 by the Politbureau of on the Overseas Vietnamese Affairs." 2005. *Quê Hương,* February 2. Available at http://quehuongon line.vn/VietNam/Home/Van-ban-phap-luat/2005/02/1DEC0452/.

Reuters. 1999. "U.S. Merchant Wins Ho Poster Case, Is Assaulted." Reuters, February 11.

Reyes, Adelaida. 1999. *Songs of the Caged, Songs of the Free: Music and the Vietnamese Refugee Experience.* Philadelphia: Temple University Press.

Rheingold, Howard. 1993. *The Virtual Community: Homesteading on the Electronic Frontier.* New York: Addison-Wesley.

Ribeiro, Gustavo Lins. 1998. "Cybercultural Politics: Political Activism at a Distance in a Transnational World." In *Cultures of Politics, Politics of Cultures: Re-visioning Latin American Social Movements,* edited by Sonja E. Alvarez, Evelina Dagnino, and Arturo Escobar, 325–352. Oxford: Westview Press.

Rutledge, Paul. 1992. *The Vietnamese Experience in America.* Indianapolis: Indiana University Press.

Saxenian, Anna Lee. 1999. *Silicon Valley's New Immigrant Entrepreneurs.* San Francisco: San Francisco Public Policy Institute of California.

Schiller, Nina Glick, Linda Basch, and Cristina Szanton Blanc. 1995. "From Immigrant to Transmigrant: Theorizing Transnational Migration." *Anthropological Quarterly* 68 (1): 48–63.

"School Candidate Can Add Actual Malice Claim." 2009. *Courthouse News Service*, March 3. Available at http://www.courthousenews.com/2009/03/03/School_Candidate_Can_Add_Actual_Malice_Claim.htm.

Schou, Nick. 2008. "The Anti-Commie Protests against *Viet Weekly* and *Nguoi Viet* Limp along in Little Saigon." *OC Weekly*, May 22.

Sherbert, Erin. 2009. "Territorial Dispute." *Metroactive*, February 25. http://www.metro active.com/metro/02.25.09/news-0908.html.

Sherman, Ann Elliott. 1996. "Viet Lux: An Art Wave." *Metro*, June 6–12.

Shimbun, Yomiuri. 1993. "NEC Gets Vietnam Order for Telecom Equipment." *Daily Yomiuri*, July 31.

"Shop Owner in Ho Chi Minh Poster Protest Nears Eviction." 1999. CNN, March 12.

Smith, Michael Peter, and Luis Eduardo Guarnizo, eds. 1999. *Transnationalism from Below*. New Brunswick, NJ: Transaction.

Smith, Michael Peter, and Bernadette Tarallo. 1995. "Who Are the 'Good Guys'? The Social Construction of the Vietnamese 'Other.'" In *The Bubbling Cauldron: Race, Ethnicity, and the Urban Crisis*, edited by Michael Peter Smith and Joe R. Feagin, 50–76. Minneapolis: University of Minnesota Press.

Soh, Chung-Hee Sarah. 1993. "Sexual Equality, Male Superiority, and Korean Women in Politics: Changing Gender Relations in a 'Patriarchal Democracy.'" *Sex Roles* 28 (1–2): 73–90.

Sowell, Thomas. 1981. *Ethnic America: A History*. New York: Basic Books.

Stokes, Martin. 1994. *Ethnicity, Identity and Music: The Musical Construction of Place*. Providence, RI: Berg.

Takaki, Ronald. 1989. *Strangers from a Different Shore: A History of Asian Americans*. Boston: Little Brown.

Tan, Sumiko. 1994. "Vietnam Rolls Out Red Carpet for Returning Sons, Daughters." *Strait Times*, March 27.

Taylor, Clarence Dung. 2007. Interview by author with Vietnamese American owner of D&D, a Vietnamese musician talent booking agency. San Jose, CA. October 10.

Taylor, Philip. 2000. "Music as a 'Neocolonial Poison' in Post-war Southern Vietnam." *Crossroads* 14 (1): 99–131.

———. 2001. *Fragments of the Present: Searching for Modernity in Vietnam's South*. Honolulu: University of Hawaii Press.

"Terry on TV (1 of 2)." 2008. Available at http://www.youtube.com/watch?v=Iz77zsNQjRI.

"Terry on TV (2 of 2)." 2008. Available at http://www.youtube.com/watch?v=2T8LhQ_kCnA.

Tessler, Ray, Daniel Yi, and Henry Weinstein. 1999. "With Communist Flag Down, Free Speech Questions Fly." *Los Angeles Times*, January 23.

Thai, Hung Cam. 2008. *For Better or for Worse: Vietnamese International Marriages in the New Global Economy*. Piscataway, NJ: Rutgers University Press.

Thanh, Thủy. 2001. Interview by author with Vietnamese music producer. Sai Gon, Viet Nam. February 9.

Thuận, Nguyễn Việt. 2002. Interview by author with vice-director of Ho Chi Minh's Committee for Vietnamese Residing Abroad (Ban Việt Kiều). Sai Gon, Viet Nam. September 30.

Timberlake, Ian. 2010. "Vietnam Steps Up China-Style Internet Control." Agence France-Presse. July 1.

Titon, Jeff Todd. 1984. *Worlds of Music: An Introduction to the Music of the World's Peoples.* New York: Schirmer Books.

Trần, Bá Thái. 2009. Interview by author via e-mail with founder of NetNam, the first Internet service provider in Viet Nam. February 28.

Trần, Chân. 1997. Letter. *Vietnam Insight*, August 12.

Trần, Diệu Hạnh. 1993. Interview by author with Vietnamese music enthusiast. Sai Gon, Viet Nam. April 5.

Tran, Doan [pseudonym]. 1996. Interview by author with Vietnamese American businessman living in Sai Gon. Sai Gon, Viet Nam. June 19.

Tran, Duy. 2000. Interview by author with Vietnamese American sound engineer and musician. Oakland, CA. April 8.

Tran, Ham. 2006. *Journey from the Fall*. ImaginAsian Pictures.

Tran, Hoanh. 1999. Posting. Vietnam Forum. April 5.

———. 2000. Interview by author with Vietnamese American lawyer and founder and administrator of the Vietnam Forum e-mail list and *Đọt Chuối Non* blog. Richmond, VA. March 4.

———. 2002. Interview by author. Richmond, VA. February 21.

———. 2005. Interview by author. Richmond, VA. September 20.

———. 2008a. Interview by author. Richmond, VA. November 2.

———. 2008b. Interview by author. Oakland, CA. December 2.

———. 2010a. Interview by author. Oakland, CA. October 2.

———. 2010b. "Nhà thơ Hữu Loan qua đời." *Đọt Chuối Non*, March 18. Available at http://dotchuoinon.com/2010/03/18/nha-thơ-hữu-loan-qua-dời/.

Tran, Hoanh, and Tin Le. 1992. "Vietnam Forum Code of Conduct." E-mail for VNForum members, in author's possession.

Tran, Mai. 1999. "Owner with Communist Display Evicted." *Orange County Register*, January 21.

Tran, Mai, and Stuart Silverstein. 2006. "Obituary: Yen Do, 65; Publisher of First, Largest U.S. Vietnamese Paper." *Los Angeles Times*, August 18.

Tran, My-Thuan. 2009. "Vietnamese Americans Take Action against Redbaiting." *Los Angeles Times*, April 6.

———. 2010. "A Son's Loyalties Tested." *Los Angeles Times*, September 20.

Tran, Phi. 2010. Interview by author with music enthusiast. Oakland, CA. October 2.

Trần, Thu Hà. 2002. Interview by author with popular Vietnamese singer. Berkeley, CA. October 30.

Trần, Trọng Đăng Đàn. 1996. *Người Việt Nam ở Nước Ngoài* [Overseas Vietnamese]. Ha Noi: Nhà Xuất Bản Chính Trị Quốc Gia [National Government Publications].

Trần, Tuấn. 1993. Interview by author with video store manager. Sai Gon, Viet Nam. July 17.

Tran, Tuyen Ngoc. 2007. "Behind the Smoke and Mirrors: The Vietnamese in California, 1975–1994." Ph.D. diss., University of California, Berkeley.

Trường, Lam. 2001. Interview by author with Vietnamese pop singer. Boston, MA. August 7.

T. S. 2000. "Brain Drain." VNForum Archive, October 29.

Tsang, Daniel C. 2003. "Sanitized for Your Consumption: Saigon, USA White-Washes Local History." *OC Weekly*, May 8.

Tuan, Ngoc. 2001. Interview by author with Vietnamese American singer. Orange County, CA. July 10.

U.S. Bureau of the Census. 1993a. "1990 Census of Population and Housing: Summary Tape File 3A." Available at http://www.census.gov/mp/www/cat/decennial_census_1990/1990_census_of_population_and_housing_summary_tape_file_3a.html.

———. 1993b. "We the Americans: Asians." Available at http://www.census.gov/apsd/wepeople/we-3.pdf.

———. 2002. "U.S. Summary: 2000: Census 2000 Profile." Available at http://www.census.gov/prod/2002pubs/c2kprof00-us.pdf.

———. 2010a. "Trade in Goods with Vietnam." Available at http://www.census.gov/foreign-trade/balance/c5520.html.

———. 2010b. "The Vietnamese Population in the United States: 2010." Available at http://www.vasummit2011.org/docs/research/The%20Vietnamese%20Population%202010_July%202.2011.pdf.

U.S. Committee for Refugees and Immigrants. 2000. "U.S. Committee for Refugees World Refugee Survey 2000: Vietnam." Available at http://www.unhcr.org/refworld/docid/3ae6a8c80.html.

Valverde, Kieu-Linh Caroline. 1992. "From Dust to Gold: The Amerasian Experience." In *Racially Mixed People in America*, edited by P. P. Maria Root, 144–161. Newbury Park, CA: Sage.

———. 1994. "The Foundation and Future of Vietnamese American Politics in the Bay Area." Master's thesis. San Francisco: San Francisco State University, Ethnic Studies Department.

———. 2002. "Making Transnational Viet Nam: Vietnamese American Community—Viet Nam Linkages through Money, Music, and Modems." Ph.D. diss., University of California, Berkeley.

———. 2003. "Making Vietnamese Music Transnational: Sounds of Home, Resistance and Change." *Amerasia Journal* 29 (1): 29–50.

———. 2008. "Nguyen Takes Stand against Tyranny." *San Jose Mercury News*, February 7.

"Về Họa Sĩ Trần Thủy Châu." 2008. *Người Việt*, Westminster, CA. February 1.

"Viet Kieu Citizenship." 1997. VNForum Archive, July 1.

Vietnam Business News. 2010. "US Becomes Largest Investor in Vietnam." *Business Times* (Ho Chi Minh City), April 12.

"Vietnamese TV Discusses Madison's Wedding Part 1 of 2." 2008. Available at http://www.youtube.com/watch?v=WwL9KZsxczE.

"Vietnamese TV Discusses Madison's Wedding Part 2 of 2." 2008. Available at http://www.youtube.com/watch?v=p2Feo4iOT2Q.

Viet Nam News Agency. 2000. "'Artful' Peddlers of Social Evils Still Dodging the Law." *Việt Nam News* (Ho Chi Minh City), August 30.

———. 2008. "Revised Nationality Law Lives Up to Overseas Vietnamese's Expectations." *Communist Party of Vietnam Online Newspaper*, November 14. Available at http://www.cpv.org.vn/cpv/Modules/News_English/News_Detail_E.aspx?CN_ID=257384&CO_ID=30184.

———. 2011. "More Cash Pours in from Overseas Vietnamese." *Việt Nam News*, February 1. Available at http://vietnamnews.vnagency.com.vn/Economy/Business/208161/more-cash-pours-in-from-overseas-vietnamese.html.

"Vietnam Seeks to Silence Its China Critics." 2009. *Asia Sentinel*, September 21. Available at http://www.asiasentinel.com/index.php?option=com_content&task=view&id=2064&Itemid=18.

"Việt Nam Tăng Cường An Ninh Mạng" [Vietnam to Strengthen Network Security]. 2009. *Người Việt*, September 18.

Việt Tân. 2009. "Mission." Available at http://www.charity-charities.org/France-charities/Paris-1586921.html.

———. 2010. Home page. Available at http://www.viettan.org.

VietUnity. 2004. "Statement in Opposition of 'No-Communist Zone' Resolutions." May 21. Available at http://groups.yahoo.com/group/change-links/message/40143.

Võ, Linda. 2003. "Vietnamese American Trajectories: Dimensions of Diaspora." *Amerasia Journal* 29 (1): ix–xviii.

———. 2007. "Whose School District Is This? Vietnamese American and Coalitional Politics in Orange County, California." *AAPI Nexus* 5 (2): 1–32.

———. 2009. "Transforming an Ethnic Community: Little Saigon, Orange County." In *Asian America: Forming New Communities, Expanding Boundaries*, edited by Huping Ling, 87–103. Piscataway, NJ: Rutgers University Press.

Vu, Hao-Nhien. 2008a. "Another Campaign for Long Pham." *The Bolsavik*, April 14. Available at http://bolsavik.com/2008/04/another-campaign-for-long-pham/.

———. 2008b. Interview by author with managing editor of *Người Việt Daily* and blogger at Bolsavik.com. Los Angeles. April 17.

———. 2009a. Interview by author. Orange County, CA. September 18 and 19.

———. 2009b. Interview by author. Irvine, CA. October 3.

———. 2009c. "Ly Tong Spray Painted FOB II's Art Works." *The Bolsavik*. Available at http://bolsavik.com/2009/01/ly-tong-spray-painted-fob-iis-art-works/.

———. 2011. Interview by author via e-mail. October 20.

Vu, John. 2008a. "Lost in Translation: The Little Saigon Conflict." Voters 4 Democracy. Available at http://www.sjvoters4democracy.com/e/lostintranslation.htm.

———. 2008b. "Vietnamese Americans Thirst for Blood over a Name." *New America Media*, January 27.

Wang, Ling-Chi L. 1995. "The Structure of Dual Domination: Toward a Paradigm for the Study of the Chinese Diaspora in the U.S." *Amerasia Journal* 21 (1–2): 149–170.

Webby, Sean. 2009. "San Jose Police Officers Caught on Video Using Baton, Taser Gun on Suspect." *San Jose Mercury News*, October 24. Available at http://www.mercurynews.com/bay-area-news/ci_13635707?source=rss.

Wellman, B. 2002. "Designing the Internet for a Networked Society." *Communications of the ACM* 45 (5): 91–96.

Winn, Robert C., and Lindsey Jang. 2004. *Saigon, U.S.A.* DVD.

Wong, D., and M. Elliot. 1994. "'I Want the Microphone': Mass Mediation and Agency in Asian-American Popular Music." *TDR: The Drama Review* 38 (3): 152–167.

Wong, Sau-Ling C. 1995. "Denationalization Reconsidered: Asian American Cultural Criticism at a Theoretical Crossroads." *Amerasia Journal* 21 (1–2): 1–27.

Woolfolk, John. 2009. "Madison Nguyen Has Fundraising Edge in San Jose Recall Battle." *San Jose Mercury News*, February 19.

Wright, Robert G. 1981. "Voluntary Agencies and the Resettlement of Refugees." *International Migration Review* 15 (1–2): 157–174.

WTO. 2006. "General Council Approves Viet Nam's Membership." November 7. Available at http://www.wto.org/english/news_e/prcs06_e/pr455_e.htm.

Zhou, M., and C. L. Bankston III. 1998. *Growing Up American: How Vietnamese Children Adapt to Life in the United States*. New York: Russell Sage Foundation Press.

Index

Kieu-Linh Caroline Valverde is Associate Professor of Asian American Studies at the University of California, Davis.

www.ingramcontent.com/pod-product-compliance
Lightning Source LLC
Chambersburg PA
CBHW030839270326
41928CB00007B/1127